SEMIOTICS OF MISOGYNY THROUGH THE HUMOR OF CHEKHOV AND MAUGHAM

Anna Makolkin

The Edwin Mellen Press
Lewiston/Queenston/Lampeter

Library of Congress Cataloging-in-Publication Data

Makolkin, Anna, 1955-
 Semiotics of Misogyny Through the Humor of Chekhov and Maugham / Anna Makolkin.
  p. cm.
 Includes bibliographical references and index.
 ISBN 0-7734-9570-3
  1. Semiotics and literature. 2. Women in literature. 3. Misogyny in literature. 4. Chekhov, Anton Pavlovich, 1860-1904--Political and social views. 5. Maugham, W. Somerset (William Somerset), 1874-1965--Political and social view. I. Title.
PN98.S46M34   1992
809.3' 9352042--dc20   92-18419
                                                                     CIP

A CIP catalog record for this book is available
from The British Library.

Copyright   ©1992 Anna Makolkin.

All rights reserved. For more information contact

The Edwin Mellen Press   The Edwin Mellen Press
P.O. Box 450   Box 67
Lewiston, NY 14092   Queenston, Ontario
USA   CANADA L0S 1L0

The Edwin Mellen Press, Ltd.
Lampeter, Dyfed, Wales
UNITED KINGDOM SA48 7DY

Printed in the United States of America

To Maria, Nick, and Paul

Look at 0.9 clothing stores, is there anything for men's consumption? It is women who demand and support all luxuries in life. Count all the factories, most of them are engaged in production of useless decorations, carriages, furniture, toys for women. Millions of people, generations of slaves die in this servitude [producing at the factories those things] only to satisfy women's whims. 0.9 of human kind is kept in this captivity of hard labor and servitude by women-slave-owners.

Leo Tolstoy, Kreutzer Sonata

TABLE OF CONTENTS

Preface - acknowledgements   i

Note on Translation and Transliteration   ix

Chapter One

Eco, Chekhov and Maugham and Their Perception of Women

1.1	Umberto Eco's Women as Signs	1
1.2	Maugham and Chekhov as Producers of Identical Signs	5
1.3	Maugham's Idiosyncrasy and Chekhov's Manifesto: Misogyny Uncovered	12

Chapter Two

Women, Nature and Zoosemiotics of the Literary Text

2.1	Women as Zoological Signs	19
2.2	Women as "Id" Signs	34
2.3	Women as Gastropornosigns	47
2.4	Woman as a Predator	53

Chapter Three

Women as Signs of Economic Exchange

3.1	Women as Buyers	65
3.2	Women as a Sign of Fluctuating Value	78
3.3	Marriage and Men	88
3.4	Marriage and Women	95

Chapter Four

Women, Their Semiotic Value

4.1	Women as Symbols of Inferiority	103
4.2	Pink Stocking as an Icon of a Female	117
4.3	Maugham's Soothing Sign – Woman as an Archetype	124

Chapter Five

Women as Signs of Otherness

    5.1   Jews and Females – Signs of Equal Value   133
    5.2   Woman as a Sign of Otherness – Maugham's Russian Woman   152
    5.3   Taking the Mask off a Character-Desire   156

Chapter Six

Women, Slavery and an Interim Sign

    6.1   Women – Dynamic Signs   167
    6.2   Women as Alarming Signals   178
    6.3   Blue Stocking Anxiety   186
    6.4   Origins of "Blue Stockings"   190
    6.5   Anxiety, Tension and Sign-o-phobia   198

Notes   207

Bibliography   227

Index   235

Preface

What we now call culture and civilization may be viewed as a multilayered, multivoiced, polysemantic text of varying cognitive, aesthetic and semantic complexity, a text which is read selectively by various readers of varying competence, taste and perspective. Some aspects of this text may be attractive only to a certain, very limited circle of readers. For instance, opera, ballet, cinema or painting could be of interest only to a certain more limited audience around the world, or this part of the Cultural Text is read by fewer readers.

Nonetheless, there are some layers in the Cultural Text that are shared by all readers, irrespective of their cultural expertise and exposure. These are the earliest human observations which are recorded in folklore, proverbs, sayings and common mythology of the most basic kind. They reflect the earliest encounter of Man with Nature and represent the basic explanations of the world. (Veselovsky, 1940: 494). Confronting the world man has always had numerous unanswered questions that were traditionally separated from clearly understood phenomena. Language reflects this pathway of discovery; for instance something as "clear as day" as opposed to something as "dark as night". If achievements of modern astronomy, biochemistry, physics or mathematics are accessible to a limited number of readers, interpreters, and consumers of Culture, a fairytale is understood by all.

If the dichotomy of the Dionysean and Apollonean myths preoccupies a narrow circle of humanists, it looks quite obscure to modern computer scientists or nuclear physicists. However, myths about female inferiority are shared and understood by all. "Long hair--no brain" summarizes the collective historical perception of women by men captured by standard expressions in the universal cultural text. Myth about female instability, unpredictability, mysterious evil nature, and mental inferiority is the basic expression, the most familiar "idiom" in the universal cultural text. In all times, among all nations, in all languages one may unmistakenly find this myth tinged with fear, anxiety and hatred of the Other. Otherness of women is the most ancient, if not one of the first, human observations as primary and eternal as Moon, Sun, Water, Earth. One of the earliest discoveries of difference and distinction is Male and Female, while prejudice towards women is, perhaps, one of the most ancient **semiotic loyalties** established in the process of conquering Nature and creating what is now called "Culture" or civilization.

The cultural text is permeated with prejudice towards women and in many instances with open misogyny. The Western version of the cultural text nurtures the myth of its civilized superiority over other parts of the global cultural universe. After all, our Western women enjoy more liberties than their African, Asian, Oriental, Pacific and other representatives of the "weaker sex" on the planet. We are appalled at the incidence of reported violence against women and treat them as individual cases of behavioral pathology rather than manifestation of the expected cultural programming. From legends, myths, songs, fairytales, to elaborate novels, plays and discourse in general, the Cultural Text is oversaturated with female images which validate the most ancient motif-the idea of female inferiority.

World literature constitutes the most sophisticated layer of the Cultural text at large or its cultural model. It is through the world classics that humanity seeks its values, forms attitudes, and transmits a universal experience permeated with subtle forms of misogyny. The producers of Culture have traditionally viewed women as a sign of Nature rather that of Culture, Nature that was feared and required man's control by men. If gender bias in earlier literary texts may be justified by a general allegedly low cultural level or a low level of progress, the post-feminist cultural contributions which continue to perpetuate the ancient stereotype are more intriguing examples for analyzing misogyny.

The present study limits its textual boundaries by genre and cultural tradition and focuses upon the semiotics of misogyny in Chekhov's and Maugham's short stories.

Both writers, physicians by training, came to literature after exposure to medicine. Their literary works create semiotic universes that most vividly display the traditional dichotomy between Nature and Culture, Woman and Man, Body and Mind.

Chekhov (1860-1904) and Maugham (1874-1965) lived and wrote at a time when women's presence in culture was becoming more visible. It is precisely why their fictional worlds with their enormous resistance to abandoning the traditional myth about women may be regarded as symbolic responses to the changing culture.

The first chapter begins, though, neither with Chekhov nor with Maugham, but with Umberto Eco and his concept of women as signs (Eco: 1979). This seemingly unrelated introduction has two main functions: to re-introduce the old popular myth through the modern cultural discourse; and to recall the traditional opposition between nature and culture as the cultural justification of the stereotype. Eco's women-signs are a product of the traditional culture that masks its own cultural products, transforming them into signs which stand for something other than what they actually represent. Eco's semiotic statement paves the way to the fictional worlds of the two writers. In so much it is related to them. The three producers of their own signs, Eco with his semiotic theory and Chekhov and Maugham with their fictional symbolic universes, display the same cultural programming: the same uneasiness in the presence of women and the inability to part with the ancient myth.

The second chapter demonstrates how, affected by the super sign--culture, Chekhov and Maugham reinforce its main postulate regarding women. Their women parade there as **gastro and pornosigns** or **zoosigns**. The semiotic universe of the two writers reaffirms the ancient myth about female sinfulness, inferiority and generally primitive level of development. In this chapter, women are represented as sex-food signs and natural evil.

The third chapter leads the readers into a special part of Chekhov's and Maugham's fictional universes where women shrewdly engineer marriage. Their libido-driven women force "poor men" to enter the feared union in exchange for other signs, money. Thus, female participation in this special part of the cultural text is allegedly dictated by Nature as well. This desired **semiotic matrix** controls the fictional universe and its imposed fictional plot, that is men's fear of marriage and forced "collaboration" in the unpleasant union.

The fourth chapter reiterates the **semiotic constant,** the motif of female inferiority and function of women as **singular signs.** It demonstrates the impact of the **semiotic imperative,** the ancient mythical axioms about women as lower species, upon the fictional universe in the distant, removed cultural layer. On the other hand, it displays the **semiotic intention** of the author-producer of signs who is a very conservative reader of the Cultural text, ready to repeat the mythic profanity in order to establish the mythical order.

The chapter recreates nostalgia over the ancient division of societal roles according to gender and is a hymn to the woman of the past, symbolically named a "pink stocking." This Chekhovian creation is a response to the protoicon **Blue Stocking** which already is an established allusion to a woman-anomaly, a representative and producer of culture. **Pink Stocking** is a pleasurable sign as opposed to the unsympathetic **Blue Stocking.** The two writers display their semiotic loyalty to the icon of the past, to the mythical perception of women as consumers of culture and not its producers.

The fifth chapter introduces another category, ethnicity, to emphasize Otherness of gender, Maugham's Russian woman and Chekhovian Susanna, a Jewess, are exaggerated characters-signs, hypertrophied icons of Otherness which introduce some carnivalesque images and, at times, produce laughter. They bring in the semiotic paradox: the Other is other than itself, but rather something else. Maugham's Russian woman is a pseudofemale, a woman-man in disguise; Chekhov's Susanna is a challenge to the ignorant prejudiced crowd that produces myth and stereotype. In general, the two characters both undermine and support the ethnic fiction. One encounters myth-fusion when the misogynist myth is preserved and the ethnic stereotype is simultaneously displayed and destroyed with the help of the familiar woman-sign.

The last chapter documents the anxiety of males during the rising feminism and gradual changes in the societal functional hierarchy. Maugham speaks through his humorously created new women-signs. He is basically loyal to his original semiotic intention, **woman as a sign of danger**. However, the traditional woman-hunter, a sex-driven predator who was previously intimidated by her own biological strength, and is now a new woman-cultural lioness, in charge of culture and cultural production. The sign of the first degree of danger has been transformed into an even more dangerous creature, the woman-writer, a sign of second degree of danger, the woman-sign, a part of nature was less dangerous than the woman who is a part of culture.

Chekhov who died earlier and did not witness the intense competition between the sexes is less alarmed. His new women are still subordinate to men, despite their active participation in society. He never reached Maugham's level of misogyny.

Both writers anticipated some basic changes in the traditional order of things. They foresaw conflict, but regrettably reinforced the primordial mythical past which still continues to haunt modern culture. The comic fear in the fictional universes of the two writers is a disguised real frustration of the old power. The purpose of this semiotic enterprise is to disclose the regrettably simplistic interpretation of the Other and the potential for violence that the seemingly innocent fictional signs carry. It also challenges the pervasiveness of the dangerous myth that even involves the contemporary interpreters of culture, myth and song.

The title of this book was originally planned to be "Women, Signs and Prejudice." While the work was still in progress, a horrendous tragedy which would have been appropriate for a fantastic tale occurred: fourteen women were killed on the University campus in Montreal just because they were women. The crime is still unresolved; the killer who has been described as a normal individual without any previous criminal record nor any drug or alcohol history remains a psychological enigma. Canadian society, university communities across the country, the public at large and media were shocked. For a while, the topic of feminism, women's rights, women's studies programs and the relationship between the sexes polarized our entire society. Daily debates were going on in classrooms, libraries, on the air; it was the topic of discussion in private homes and public places. Right after the tragic incident one noticed some uneasiness in daily encounters between men and women in public and at work. Some men would be emphatically polite to women, some would avoid eye contact while some would be unusually rude and hostile.

In this atmosphere, my analysis of the fantastic universes of Maugham and Chekhov and the semiosis of stereotype became much more relevant. The motif of killing a woman either for her stupidity or her overly loving nature, a dominant feature in the fictional universe under scrutiny, appeared much less unreal. What seemed as a mere stereotyped mode of imagining the "Other," now could be openly presented as misogyny, sincere hatred of the "Other," and, thus, a new title, "Semiotics of Misogyny", became quite justifiable. This new title seems to reflect the focus of the examined fictional world, and simultaneously to be a symptom of the general societal malaise, which we now dare to name, analyze and attempt to eradicate.

The fact that such a killing as the one in Montreal École Politechnique, could occur in 1989 signifies the fragility, vulnerability and embryonic stage of the new, changing attitudes and images of women. The old perceptions based on legitimized inequality, male domination and rule by violence are still far more viable than the new signs of changing reality. What sustains the old meaning and what is the semiotic mechanism of the meaning production--these are the basic questions asked in this study.

When I shared my plans with an older male colleague, his first question was: "Was Chekhov a homosexual?" He automatically dismissed that misogyny could be a part of the general, but not of the marginal world where women are excluded completely. I could not answer his question and honestly was not curious about Chekhov's sexual orientation. What was more important to me that both, men-writers, a Russian and an Englishman, were originally trained as doctors, respectable and powerful members of their respective societies, shared the same worldview that was indicative of something other than their sexual preferences. It was a sign of the sign, meaning produced by other meanings and agreed concepts. The fictional worlds produced by those two different writers contained some semiotic invariants which are present in culture at large. They represented signs behind the semiotic macrocosm of the shared cultural universe.

These two random sign-producers indicated other sources of their signs, common perception of the Other. It was important, in my mind, to demonstrate where the two seemingly different cultural traditions meet: on the unpleasant misogynist ground where women are the same signs regardless of their language, origin, class, age, faith and culture.

With all respect to the numerous feminists who have pointed out how "language behavior and unconscious assumptions" may downgrade women, I do not join the familiar feminist rebellion. I do not wish to be isolated, labelled, and gettoized into a special train of feminist, i.e., different thought. As a semiotically inclined thinker, I am firmly convinced that the basic mechanism of sign production is the same, regardless of what is produced-whether an atomic bomb, a peace project, a myth, a stereotype or a scholarly treatise-and who is the producer.

Thus, the purpose of the work is to challenge Eco's concept of women as signs, not in the feminist but in a traditional sense, from a semiotic perspective. I intend to show that Eco's semiotic vision and Chekhov-Maugham's misogynist world are all signs of the same "Other", the deeply ingrained desire to win, to prevail, as much as of the sophisticatedly masked fear of competition, that anxiety of intellectual impotence. I refuse to accept the idea that because I am a woman therefore I think differently. *Cogito ergo sum* - I think, therefore, I am-means to me much more. It does not matter to me that it was said by Descartes who was not a woman, but what matters is that I am able to apply the known traditional tools and to rediscover the sign.

This book was written during 1989-90, a fortunate year when I had the honour and privilege to become one of the four Northrop Frye Fellows at the newly opened Centre for Humanities at Victoria College, University of Toronto. This gave me a wonderful opportunity to audit Northrop Frye's lectures and to be inspired by his marvellous intellect as well as by his theory of archetypes related to my own research.

I would like to thank all my colleagues, members of the Toronto Semiotic circle, who's intellectual input helped me to shape my ideas over the years. Special thanks to Paul Perron, Paul Bouissac, Aida Gruff, Marcel Danezi whose most recent support I enjoyed during the time of writing.

Ms. Lorraine Gillis deserves enormous gratitude for transforming the manuscript into a typescript – the modern version of a presentable manuscript. Miss Alfreda Hall edited the final draft bringing her years of professional experience to improving its expression many, many thanks to her.

The idea of writing this book belongs to my daughter Maria who labelled her mother a "semiotician" before she actually realized it.

Lastly, my husband deserves thanks for enduring my infatuation with semiotics and participation in Culture.

Note on Transliteration
and
Translations

Very few cases of transliteration followed accepted types. Transliteration of Russian words was done according to J. Thomas Shaw's system II (Shaw, 1967). Transliterations by other authors have preserved other versions.

Some titles of Chekhov's stories provide both translation from Russian and transliteration, those were done by the author. Most examples from Chekhov's stories were rendered in English by the author unless indicated otherwise.

CHAPTER ONE

Eco, Chekhov and Maugham and Their Perception of Women

> The text is a sign composed of signs composed of signs composed of signs...
> Wojciech Kalaga. *The Literary sign: A Triadic Model.*

1.1 Umberto Eco's Women as signs

> Semiotics is in principle the discipline studying everything which can be used in order to lie.
> Umberto Eco. *A Theory of Semiotics.*

In his introduction to *A Theory of Semiotics* Eco returns to the familiar opposition between Nature and Culture, or to the two types of signs.[1] He proposes to view culture as a semiotic phenomenon and a byproduct of semiosis where tools, commodities and surprisingly women play a significant role. By tools, Eco means communicative or semiotic tools, such as "names-observable sign-vehicles." Then he proceeds to commodities or their use in the process when the economic exchange takes place. By exchange, Eco implies "exchange of signals names or sign-vehicles and physical goods such as women. If his first category-"tools"- is introduced with the help of Peirce, Barthes and Robinson Crusoe, the second is referred to in the context of *Das Kapital*.[2] If women appear as goods or objects in the economic exchange, it is not clear why Eco chooses to introduce women afterwards as independent semiotic categories. Nonetheless, his section on page 26 of the work contains only twelve lines which claims to explain fully the significance of women in culture. According to Eco, women, commodities who participate in Marx's economic exchange, in fact realize a "symbolic process" where they are "physical objects to be used through physiological operations, as in case of food and other goods."(26) Let us semiotically follow the trend of Eco's thought. In the known opposition between nature and culture, Eco gives preference to the latter; his system of distribution of signs, semiotic forces and sign producers may perhaps be represented like this:

II	Culture	verbal signs = tools beliefs tools
I	Nature	physical objects = commodities animals women

Albeit a part of the traditional semiosis, included in the intricate Culture-Nature exchange, Eco's women are clearly a part of the more primitive semiotic layer. Nonetheless, they are present. Their presence is more visible when they come in close contact with men through marriage. Marriage becomes a semiotic act when the lower semiotic stratum-Nature-is connected with the higher semiotic stratum-Culture, or when the given signs affect the production of other signs created by men. Eco writes:[3]

> The woman, the moment she becomes "wife", is no longer merely a physical body: she is a sign which connotes a system of social obligation.

The semiotic message to be derived from this statement may be:

Nature	Marriage	Culture
Woman	Woman	Man

A woman in Eco's system acquires the role of a tool through marriage whereby natural signs can become a part of Culture and a woman's presence is more visible. Her status within the order of natural signs changes. If physical objects, or animals could coexist with man in a separate universe, or be ignored despite their presence, a woman married to a man loses her former kinship with natural objects. Marriage imparts visibility to a woman-sign and not only that, but she begins to influence cultural conventions. Otherwise our sense of order would have been different, as Eco suggests. Through marriage, a woman is no longer a physical body, but some kind of a tool which controls male sexuality and affects a sense of morality, another cultural manifestation. To those who may question this new woman's role Eco provides the following explanation:[4]

> However, if the woman were merely the physical body with which the husband enters into sexual relations in order to produce sons, it could not then be explained why every man does not copulate with every woman.

For the purposes of analysis, let us first examine the conditional clause of his statement. Obviously, Eco does not see women solely as physical or biological entities. Had they been such, they would have been used by men with greater freedom. What strikes one here is the notion that women give birth only to sons. This mythical concept assists Eco in denying women their connection with objective reality beyond control of man. Since they produce sons only, they do not multiply or appear naturally, but mythically and the semiotic graph of Eco's denial may be illustrated as:

Women	Men
biological beings	social beings - husbands
producers of males	producers of humans

In Eco's mythical universe females are not produced at all, since his mythical women are producers of sons only, but males as representatives of Culture are given a special mythical origin:

Men	Women
born by married women	?
copulate with some women	

Through marriage, men come into contact with women, but the mythical reason of this liaison seems to be solely for the sake of preserving producers of Culture. Men, these producers of Culture, are regrettably denied copulation on demand with every woman because women are no longer solely physical bodies, but **tools of Culture**, and Eco asks:[5]

> Why is man obliged by certain conventions to choose one (or more) according to custom following very precise and infusible rules of choice? Because it is only a woman's symbolic value which puts her in opposition, within the system, to other women.

In addition, women happen to possess symbolic value, much like commodities which possess market value, and since symbols are products of Culture, women as wives are signs within the system of Cultural signs. Here, Eco distinguishes two stages in the transformation of a woman from a Nature-sign to a Culture-sign:

> prior to marriage
> after marriage

According to the semiotician, before a legalized *coitus*, woman is merely a physical object, present in nature, while after the legalized copulation she is a sign. Eco presents the formula of this sign production:

> woman - non-wife + physical object = Nature
> woman - wife = commodity, tool = Culture

Simultaneously, Eco does not hide his attitude toward his semiotic creation. He is quite annoyed that women are not identical in their symbolic value and cannot be merely used for the reproductive purposes of male progeny and be excluded from free trade exchange among males. His emotional "why is man obliged" may be the Freudian desperate cry of a confused intellectual on the eve of another civilized catastrophe, or, perhaps, a semiotic performance of another staged lie. After all, it is his belief that:[6]

> semiotics is in principle the discipline studying everything which can be used in order to lie.

This "lie," however, is not an individual utterance or a particular fiction; it derives from other "lies," false stereotypes and dangerous assumptions which have been and still are perpetuated. The Eco's system is only a small fraction of a larger system, a symbol of what Culture so far has been.

Eco's concept of women as signs with predetermined cultural functions merely reflects the universal cultural reality, the semiotic text at large. His mythical genesis of women as "producers of sons," restricting male sexual freedom, is nothing more than a metaphor for the universal, unanimous gender anxiety. It is another "lie" to avoid the real causes of societal conflict over sex and gender, invented on the basis of ancient archetypes. Eco's women as signs stand for their entire biased representation in Culture, and are clearly verbalized symptoms of chronic cultural malaise. It indirectly recognizes that misogyny is much more pervasive in Culture than we like to admit. A semiotic mediation of a true "lie" is the best evidence of the numerous other lies in other texts. Culture is after all a multitude of texts and to "read is always to read in relation to other texts, in relation to the codes that are the products of those texts" that constitute Culture (Culler, 1981:21).[7] What Eco admits to be a re-examination of Lévy-Strauss's anthropology is also an echo of other texts, or other textual motifs which have been migrant permanent cultural archetypes, freely moving from one cultural tradition to another, and whose origin needed not be explained either. Clearly sexist semiotic genesis provided by Umberto Eco is also a sign in itself, "something there," given and existing in Culture. The best illustration of this semiotic presence might be a comparative analysis of Eco's representation of women as signs, according to his theory of semiotics, and Chekhov's and Maugham's depiction of women combined in their respective fictional worlds. The Italian literary critic, and Russian and English writers independently from each other arrive at astonishing but similar conclusions regarding women and their role in Culture. This striking resemblance may be semiotically explained as the manifestation of similar semiotic composition at its basic epistomological and cognitive level, namely, the signs composed of some similar signs.

1.2 Maugham and Chekhov as Producers of Identical Signs

Somerset Maugham was perhaps not aware of Umberto Eco, but he was familiar with Chekhov and a rather elaborate expression of this familiarity one may find in Maugham's preface to the 1953 edition of his short stories.[8] There he conducts an emotional polemic with the imaginary critic and tries to establish his role as a writer, anticipating possible critical analysis of his work in the future. Maugham attempts to provide guidance by referring to an anonymous critic who allegedly had already correctly defined Maugham's style and established his mentor:[9]

> An intelligent critic, who combines wide reading and a sensitive taste with knowledge of the world rare among those who follow his calling, has found in my stories the influence of Guy de Maupassant. That is not strange. When I was a boy he was considered the best story writer in France and I read his works with avidity.

Maugham, as any self-assured writer, could foresee the possibility of a future posthumous debate over the place of his writing among other writers, and the origins of his craft and he tries to direct this future possible discourse in the desired mode. First, he places himself next to Maupassant, "an author who is unlikely to be surpassed," despite another literary luminary, Anton Chekhov.

Maugham then makes an unexpected transition from the French to the Russian master of short story:[10]

> If his excellence is not at the moment so apparent it is because what he wrote must now stand comparison with the very different, more subtle and moving work of Chekhov

Maugham is slightly annoyed in this preface, Chekhov's popularity bothers him since "it is impossible not to like what he wrote. Not to like him is to declare yourself a Philistine," says Maugham (IX)

Recognizing Chekhov's power as a creator of short stories, he nonetheless finds them to be, not the "representation of action" but rather stories without plot. He argues with the imaginary critic:[11]

> If a short story is a piece of prose dealing with more or less imaginary persons no one wrote better short stories than Chekhov. If, however, as some think, it should be the representation of an action, complete in itself and of a certain limited length, he leaves something to be desired.

He stresses that Maupassant, to whom he himself is so close, was the master of drama in a short story while Chekhov was too concerned with the ordinary, the mundane side of reality where nothing actually happened. If Chekhov was concerned with the depiction of dull reality, Maugham feels he was not artistic enough, since "the imitation of life is not a reasonable aim of art" as he puts it (XI: 1953). One may surmise from Maugham's statements that he upholds a different view. To him, a writer is not a mere imitator of life, but a sarcastic critic who is permitted to exaggerate, to change colours and shift the focus. Where Chekhov "sighs sadly," Maugham would prefer "pot the red, bring off a loosing hazard or make a canon" (XI: 53). Nevertheless, he admits that "Chekhov is extremely readable," the art which he shares with Maupassant:[12]

> Both of them were professional writers who turned out stories
> at more or less regular intervals to earn their living.

Maugham reminds us that Maupassant and Chekhov were not always inspired, for writing became a daily chore for them and, routinely performing, they also had to "please their readers" and publishers and editors. Being an obvious admirer of Chekhov's creativity and brevity and being unable always to follow in his footsteps, Maugham hypothesizes that, perhaps,[13]

> Chekhov's great merit concision is due to the fact that the
> newspapers for which he habitually wrote could only give him a
> certain amount of space.

To defend his own verbosity, the pupil gently enlightens the readers about the possible creative circumstances of his mentor, which presumably forced him to be miraculously concise. However, this does not last long, for eventually Maugham allows himself to explain Chekhov's success in a very peculiar fashion. He explains Chekhov's clear vision of reality by a strange "fact" and an amazing variety:[14]

> The Russians are a semi-barbarous people and they seem to
> have retained the power of seeing things naturally, as though
> they existed in a vacuum; while we in the West, with our

> complicated culture behind us, see things with the associations they have gathered during long centuries of civilization. They almost seem to see the thing in itself.

Consequently, a master of a laconic short story, a miraculous teller appears as a representative of a semi-barbaric people. While he, Maugham, is to be seen as a symbol of a sophisticated superior culture who cannot be confined to fewer words, because he is more civilized and more complex, Chekhov's gift is presented as a national quality of a "semi-barbarous people." Nonetheless, this representative of a "barbaric nation," a natural prodigy, is still praised for his ability to re-create life, present original characters and uncover human subconsciousness, with the least of linguistic material and effort:[15]

> It is their (characters') souls that you seem to see. The subconscious seems to come to the surface and they communicate with one another directly without the impediment of speech.

Maugham, the manipulator of benign patriotism, gives way to Maugham, an admirer of an artistic talent. Towards the end of his short exposé, he, in fact, no longer wishes to discredit Chekhov's art but ranks him even higher than Maupassant. Where he finds "brutal vitality" in the French author, he discovers subtlety in the Russian master of short stories. The Chekhovian fictional universe is likened to Dante's Hell, and the ultimate panegyric may be detected in the following:[16]

> I do not know that anyone but Chekhov has so poignantly been able to represent spirit communing with spirit. It is this that makes one feel that Maupassant in comparison is obvious and vulgar.

Let us recall the beginning of Maugham's discourse. First, he introduces his own stories written during 1919-31, then he talks about Maupassant as his mentor whose glory is wrongly overshadowed by another master Chekhov, and finally he not only comes to terms with Chekhov's fame, but turns it into an important symbol:

Maugham the master star	Maupassant the mentor star	vis-a-vis	Chekhov the rival star
Maugham =	old culture		Chekhov = new culture
Maupassant =	civilized		Chekhov = barbaric

Maugham leaves the heroic territory of the old civilization, his old *alliance francaise* with the West and moves towards the East. He rediscovers *arts nouveau*, the new literary technique, as it appears to him in Chekhov's stories.

This comparison is designed to direct future critics of his own work and set standards of criticism. This long introduction is rather unusual and it reveals Maugham's anxiety concerning possible criticism in the future. His appeal to the critics ends with the proclamation:[17]

> Maupassant and Chekhov are the two authors of short stories whose influence survives to the present day and all of us who cultivate the medium must in the end be judged by the standards they have set.

He obviously informs us that his mentors were both masters and that he would like to be judged by the degree of their influence upon his own work.

Towards the end, Maugham identifies with Chekhov more and more. He likes Chekhov's low opinion of literary critics, whom the latter likened to "horse flies which prevent the horse from ploughing." He also admires Chekhov's definition of the short story itself which "must have neither beginning nor end." This definition appeals to him very much since it enables the author to mediate his "view of universe," to paint a picture which one may "either take or leave."

There is also another feature of the Chekhovian fictional world that attracts Maugham and this is his portrayal of women. This is what he writes about Chekhov's women:[18]

> His women are lachrymose, slatternly and feeble-minded. Though they think it a sin they will commit fornication with anyone who asks them, not because they have passion, not even because they want to, but because it is too much trouble to refuse.

The analysis of his own characterization of women demonstrates how similar were the two fictional worlds of both Maugham and Chekhov where women appear as an inferior race. Maugham, as much as Chekhov, is touched by the "tenderness and passivity of beautiful youthful women." The entire misogynist vision is cleverly hidden behind this seemingly honest opinion about Chekhov's attitude and depiction of women, while, in fact, Maugham's summary of Chekhov's women could have been easily applied to his own fictional world.

The 19th provincial Russia, its boredom, its dilemmas, its national portraits and caricatures surprisingly meet Maugham's cosmopolitan world. Chekhov's characters in Tula, Kaluga, Taganrog, Moscow and Sakhalin are occasionally shockingly similar to Maugham's portraits of women from China, Hawaii, Tahiti, Malaysia, England, and Java. The creatures depicted by Chekhov and Maugham share their boredom, disillusionment, cynicism, despair and confusion in the modern and post-modern world. Their stories are impressionistic paintings of the chaotic, disjointed reality of the same old culture, where women had a special, well-defined inferior place.

Was Maugham, the "English Maupassant," aware of the fact that Chekhov was very much a product of the same culture, influenced by the same French authors as Maugham himself? Stendahl Balzac, Flaubert, Voltaire, Racine and Murger and Daudet were a part of Chekhov's culture and tradition as much as of Maugham's. On the other hand, Tolstoy and Dostoevsky were literary mentors for both authors, and both were influenced by the naturalistic school of writing perfected by Zola and Stendahl. Both lived and wrote in the post-Darwinian world dominated by natural sciences. Both were physicians by training and both shared a definite dislike of women.

Many critics were puzzled by Maugham's attitude to women. Some, like Sven Arnold Jensen, called it "idiosyncrasy," while others, liberated by the post-Freudian discourse, openly classified it as misogyny. Both writers experienced the paradoxical whims of their popularity during and after their lifetime. Richard A. Cordell, Maugham's friend and confidant and a well-known critic, summarized this, perhaps, typical phenomenon of a disparity between the likes and dislikes of readers and critics. He correctly observes that serious critics took "little notice" of Maugham's short stories and paid significant attention to his plays and novels, despite the fact that:[19]

> Somerset Maugham is more widely known as a writer of short stories than a dramatist, novelist, or critic, for through the medium of the magazine, radio, film and television, particularly the popular magazine, his short stories reached hundreds of thousands, perhaps millions who never attend the theater and seldom read a book.

Something similar but of a different sort happened to Chekhov. Despite his major contribution to the short story he gained, particularly, in the English-speaking world, fame and glory as a playwright, the author of "Seagull," "Cherry Orchard," and "Uncle Vania." Despite the fact that Chekhov's predominant literary production is not in the area of drama, which is his less explored genre but in the genre of short story, Western literary critics still classified him as a dramatist. This literary paradox was discovered by students of Chekhov's writings when they had to learn the unusual twist in his literary fate.

While exploring the available critical ground in reference to Chekhov, one may discover another significant feature. Critics have acknowledged Chekhov's enormous talent, sophisticated technique, observant eye, sympathetic heart and the rich philosophical world of his short stories. Nonetheless, Chekhov's world, so generously full of women's characters, and the particular devices and discursive tools that have helped him to create it, had been ignored by various scholars inside and outside Russia. Critics hardly mention women who constitute precisely half of his fictional world.

Boris Eichenbaum spoke about Chekhov's discovery "of a whole broad realm of life" (22), and exposure of the "sickness of Russian life"

(30).[20] Leonid Grossman compared Chekhov with Goethe and labelled him as a "poet who wonderfully harmonized with the naturalist (32).[21] Dmitri Chizhevsky granted Chekhov the title of the innovator in Russian literature who "was creating new paths" (51).[22] Chekhov, the poet, the critic of Russian life, the literary impressionistic painter and philosopher still is presented to the readers as an artist who painted a sexless world, peopled with creatures of indefinite gender and operated solely by abstract ideas. Astonishingly enough, women who inspired the poet, the painter and the philosopher are virtually nonexistent in the ongoing literary analysis of Chekhov's work. Recently, Barbara Heldt does mention Chekhov's women in her book *Terrible Perfection*, but her seemingly standard feminist perspective is very much in line with the expectation of more influential predecessors, and unfortunately supports existing scholarly biases.[23] Consequently, the topics of Chekhov's misogyny remain a gap in literary criticism at large, much as the topic of Chekhov as a short story writer. Thus, the fictional worlds of the short stories of both Maugham and Chekhov have remained somewhat neglected. It was not until 1951 that Maugham, the "English Maupassant" was finally recognized as a short-story writer. Prior to that, his stories were more popular in France where Maugham was born and where they first became popular. Nonetheless, the topic of misogyny, the predominant theme in his work, was only cautiously tackled in literary criticism. One of the reasons for this was Maugham's homosexuality, a taboo topic until the late 60's and 70's.

1.3 Maugham's Idiosyncrasy and Chekhov's Manifesto: Misogyny Uncovered

If Jensen labelled Maugham's attitude to women as "idiosyncrasy" in 1957, Ward was even less coherent in 1937 when he talked about Maugham's preoccupation with sex and adultery of women.[24] His friend and biographer Cordell described Maugham's treatment of women as "unromantical" and admitted that it would be annoying to "millions of his women readers" (81).[25] Cordell, writing in 1961, already uses the word "misogyny," but he does not accuse Maugham of it. He talks about Maugham's experience of "unrequited love" in his youth and the possible influence of a sardonic professor of gynecology who concluded that "no man is quite so cynical as a well bred woman" (82).[26] Nonetheless, Cordell merely asks a careful question touching this sensitive topic. He wonders whether Maugham's peculiar attitude to women "was a reaction of a man of sense against the Victorian idealization of women" and gives no reply. The readers and critics of Maugham had to wait till the liberated and uninhibited 80's to find out about Maugham's misogyny and homosexuality. F. Rafael (1976) and finally Ted Morgan (1980) present Maugham's bisexuality in its open nakedness and seem to accept his misogyny.

Ted Morgan is explicit about Maugham's misogyny, but he mainly approaches it from a single perspective, his subject's sexual orientation, and sees homosexuality as the cause. Nonetheless, being careful with the documentary sources, Morgan allows the readers of his biography to tackle the presented facts differently. For instance, he mentions the infamous remarks of the old professor of gynecology when Maugham was a medical student. A similar attempt to trace Maugham's misogyny to this source was made by Cordell; however, unlike Cordell, Morgan actually quotes this alleged mentor in misogyny:[27]

> "Gentlemen, woman is an animal that micturates once a day, defecates once a week, menstruates once a month, pasturates once a year, and copulates whenever she has the opportunity."

Obviously, these remarks made by a person who was a figure of authority must have been remembered by Maugham and his fellow students. However, can one trace Maugham's homosexuality and dislike of women to this single influence in his life? Morgan obviously rejects Cordell's earlier suggestions. This remark clearly documents the prevalent and pervasive stereotypes in culture at large. This view expressed by Maugham's former professor is a mere summary of the dominant belief and a concise metaphor of the universal cultural archetype. The same professor could have been a Freudian mentor as his later theory of sexuality and human psychology would manifest.

Morgan does not, however, attempt to justify Maugham's pronounced dislike of women, nor does he suggest that the notorious professor of

14 *Semiotics of Misogyny*

gynecology could have shaped Maugham's thinking. The biographer states that:[28]

> Women, going back to his mother, were a disappointment, an unreliable species. They never lived up to one's expectations. He rarely missed a chance to make unpleasant remarks about them.

Morgan claims that Maugham discovered his homosexuality very early and had to hide it in face of several trials of homosexuals (In his time Oscar Wilde was imprisoned and had to leave England). Upholding Victorian morality, Maugham married and fathered a child. Eventually, his homosexuality was accepted in artistic circles, although he insisted that no biography should be written and all correspondence be destroyed. If at the beginning of his biography Morgan attributes Maugham's misogyny to homosexuality, by the end of the discourse he is no longer sure of it.

In the middle of the biography Morgan distinguishes misogyny and homosexuality albeit still treating both as crucial factors of influence in Maugham's expressive writing:[29]

> Maugham the misogynist and Maugham the homosexual created one of the most memorable female characters in twentieth century English fiction.

After this statement, one can no longer attribute writer's dislike of the half of the human race to sexuality alone. Misogyny as a manifestation of a biological condition appears as a sign of culture, rather than of nature.

Similar causes of his own misogyny are established by Maugham himself. According to Morgan, in 1929 a young graduate student from the University of South Carolina, Elizabeth Douglas, raised the question of misogyny in her letter to Maugham. Writing a Master's thesis on his art, she wanted to clarify Maugham's views, Maugham replied in a nine-page letter admitting the negative, unflattering and unsympathetic depiction of women in his work. He also objectively analyzed the causes of this attitude:[30]

> The average woman of my generation . . . had neither the merits of her mother nor of her daughter, she was a serf set

free who did not understand the circumstances of freedom.
She was badly educated, she was no longer domestic, she had
not yet become companionable.

A man of Victorian upbringing, the contemporary of Freud and Tolstoy, Ibsen and Chekhov, Galsworthy and Wilde, the witness of the suffrage movement and socialist revolution, Maugham was intrigued by the prospects of change in women and women's status. He clearly anticipated those changes and was sincerely fearful of the new liberated woman, a sign of a different time and a product of a different tradition. The motif of "an alarming female-a writer," is quite prevalent in his stories. Maugham admits that the woman of the past was indeed the "serf," but he is terrified of the new woman of the future, an educated being with whom he will have to share the material and spiritual world. The woman-serf, albeit hated, is an acceptable norm, a natural sign, while this "alarming female" is a cause of his own anxiety. Perhaps his misogyny, as well as Chekhov's, was a metaphor for a collective universal societal uneasiness over the changing gender roles. The familiar sign, as Eco would later define woman, no longer signifies the familiar, convenient and accepted meaning. It is the fear of the new meaning of the sign which causes the clearly manifested misogyny. This **semeophobia** could be, perhaps, also a sign of something else. Contrary to the traditional connection between homosexuality and misogyny, may it be possible to suggest that it is **semeophobia** or fear of the new woman sign that may explain some cases of sexual inversion or retreat from the disturbing sign? Maugham himself recognized the phenomenon of woman-sign in transition, neither like her mother nor like her daughter.

Leopold Bellak, who analyzed ten of Maugham's stories defined the type of author's personality, and came to a very disturbing conclusion.[31] Based on the thematic analysis of these ten stories, Bellak, a psychiatrist, concludes that Maugham displayed "hostile feelings toward women" and was unaware of his pathological aggression "projecting especially on women" (105). His writings, in Bellak's view, reveal a paranoid perceptual selectivity when the author's emotional pattern is so monotonous and excludes variety. It neurotically fixes his creative attention on one side of reality: the negative

16 *Semiotics of Misogyny*

power of women, and fear of heterosexual relations. He suggested that the author, then in his nineties, undergo psychoanalytic treatment.

Chekhov also lived at a time when women began to rebel against traditional roles. He faced the rise of Russian feminism, was the contemporary of such Russian feminists as Sophia Perovskaya, Sophia Kovalevskaya, Elizabeth Kovalskaya, Catherine Breshkovskaya, Sophia Briullova, Volkova, Lermontova, E'vreyinova, Alexandra Efimenko.[32] Nina Selivanova reports that four hundred women in 1868 signed a petition to the President of the University of St. Petersburg asking for the organization of a series of lectures for women" (154).[33] By 1872 medical courses for women were opened in St. Petersburg (155). Russian women, Chekhov's contemporaries already had access to education both in Russia and abroad, and "proved themselves capable in medicine, law, history, and other sciences" (156). Chekhov's female friends, as reported by most of his biographers, were educated women who were not strangers to feminism. Chekhov and his contemporaries could not have been outside the heated debate around the woman question. In 1883, he expressed his most sincere and controversial position regarding the issue. Writing to his brother Alexander, he exposed his utter contempt for women and announced his policy in the light of Darwinian concepts and naturalistic infatuations:[34]

> I am now investigating, and shall continue to investigate, a certain little question: the woman question.

Already in the opening sentence of his letter, Chekhov denounced women by calling the woman question "little." This not only set the tone of his coming exposé, but summarized his entire opinion. He obviously does not conceal his vexation, being annoyed that so much time and energy is devoted to such an insignificant topic as the "little question." Having provided a proper semantic ground, and semiotic base (little = women), Chekhov proceeded:[35]

> But first of all, do not laugh. I place it on natural ground; and erect "the history of sexual authority." Looking at natural history you will notice (as I did) *fluctuations* of the authority. From cell to insecta the authority is equal to nought or even to a negative entity. Among worms occur females whose muscles

surpass those of males. Insecta provide a mass of material for investigation: they are the birds and amphibia among the invertebrate (if birds below). With rayfish, spiders, and mollusca the authority, with the slightest fluctuation is equal to nought. With fish, too. Pass now to ovipara, and mainly to hatching. Here the male authority is law, its origin; the female sits twice a year for a month, hense loss of muscular energy and atrophy. She sits and the male fights--hence the male is stronger. Should there be no sitting there would be no inequality.

He ends this long letter with a glorious remark:

Man is superior.

Chekhov thought he had managed to convince his brother that man is superior to "little women." He is delighted that presumably nature itself made such a comfortable choice and put *homo sapiens* females in the inferior position.

A true naturalist, Darwinian, zoologist, physician and scientist, Chekhov professes that Nature is always right. "She" is the only female that does not make any errors. It was her clever decision not to grant inequality to the mammals, including *homo sapiens* and they must accept their fate. In a humorous fashion, Chekhov dreams about the possible time when the nine-month production period of a future off-spring would be shortened or would cease to exist. At that time, as Chekhov continues to fantazise, there would be a new kind of post *homo sapiens* who may avoid the present inequality. He does not wish to expand his fantastic ideas about the new type of mammalia. Instead, Chekhov leaves natural history and returns to the history of man and woman. There he states:[36]

Woman is as a rule passive. She brings forth flesh for cannon. Never and nowhere is she superior to man in the political and sociological sense.

And this statement expressed in a private letter to his brother Alexander, becomes Chekhov's manifesto on the woman question, a response to feminism and the "alarming female" of his time. It would become the archetype of his fictional world.

CHAPTER 2

Women, Nature and Zoosemiotics of the Literary Text

> Hen is not a bird.
> Woman is not a human being.
> A Russian proverb.
>
> Nature is the chart of God, mapping
> out all his attributes.
> Tupper.

2.1 Women As Zoological Signs

Dean MacCannell and Juliet F. MacCannell attempt to describe the specifics of the literary sign and pay significant tribute to Sassure. They basically adopt the well-known concept of sound-image unity and do not go much beyond the Sassurian tree-arbour graph:[1]

> The initial formulation of the linguistic sign is as a picture, the so-called phonic substance is a graphic image, and the entire sign, often assumed identical to the word or verbal unit.

This definition does not help the readers to understand the literary semiotic environment and its functioning mechanism. However, it provides new point of epistemological departure: return to the notion of iconicity and significance of visual stimulation in the production of literary meaning. The literary text is thus iconic by definition. The world painted in verbal colours appears before the readers as a recognizable picture of reality.[2] The specific iconic perception of each individual reader may differ, but the basic visual intentions of the discursive painter-author are always understood as "something there" mediated through the basic universals that are drawn from the most familiar experiential universe.

The zoological allusions that frequently occur in literary texts are the "universal symbols which appear in the same form cross-culturally" (Portis Winner, 1986: 181).[3] They are the images of the same natural environment and provide the same pattern of movement from nature to culture, the same primary semiosis, in the direction of the **supersign**, as Portis Winner defines culture. They confirm the expected concrete, universal biological environment and, when introduced into the literary text require the least artistic and the least interpretative effort on the part of the reader to decode them. The zoological allusions are the signs of the **greatest iconic power** immediately recreating the concrete real world around, and simultaneously they are the signs of the highest **semiovalence**: the most intense encoded meaning. They are particularly useful when the human world is downgraded, lowered to the animal kingdom and ridiculed in a literary text.

To convince the readers that women are creatures of the lower order Chekhov and Maugham used precisely such signs that constitute literary zoosemiotics. Zoological allusions are placed side by side with the portraits of women to force upon the readers the desired image, the image of animal species, sub-human rather than human. For instance, in the story *Rain* Mrs. Davidson, the wife of a missionary, is presented in the following way:[4]

> She was dressed in black and wore round her neck a gold chain, from which dangled a small cross. She was a little woman, dull hair very elaborately arranged, and she had prominent blue eyes behind invisible pince-nez. Her face was long, like a sheep's, but she gave no impression of foolishness, rather of extreme alertness; she had the quick movements of a bird.

Maugham's first impulse is to present a female as stupid as a sheep. However, when he remembers that a page earlier he had introduced her as the wife of a missionary, he checks himself. His character is pardoned and generously compared with a bird. Birds being insignificant creatures even among animals still have a mythically higher status due to their ability to fly and cover large distances. Remembering the stereotypical "for the birds" as a sign of foolishness, readers will recognize the allusion as presenting a creature that is not particularly bright.

The signs are merely substituted. "Sheep," a sign of more powerful **zoosemiotic effectiveness** and more **transparent** is replaced by a "bird," another zooicon which assists Maugham in conveying the desired derogatory meaning, albeit not as direct and forceful as in case of "Sheep". On the level of **semiovalence** "Sheep" is a more potent sign, which immediately places a woman into the zoological kingdom of harmless but not very intelligent animals. "Bird" establishes the same relationship between the signifier and the signified although the sign is less **semiovalent** and less culturally violent. The wife of a missionary represented as a "sheep" might have been more offensive to Maugham's readers. Her position as a servant of the servant of God requires some respect for the mythical world while "sheep" might have violated the connection between the archetypal images of Divinity and God's children, destroyed the mythical order and mocked even more the juxtaposition between the sacred and profane. The "bird" sign puts Maugham's character into a slightly different semiotic plane, closer to God and angels, or to the traditional Christian symbolism:

Sky	Angels	Birds	God
Earth	Sheep	Animals	Humans

In another story, the *Happy Couple*, Miss Gray is described as "a sentimental donkey." In a story *The Pool* one finds a woman named Ethel introduced in the following way:[5]

> She wrung out her hair, and as she stood there, unconcerned, she looked more than ever like a wild creature of the water of the woods. He saw now that she was half caste.

Unlike Miss Gray or Mrs. Davidson, this woman is a native of Samoa, and a half-caste who does not even deserve the privileged allusions, such as "bird," "donkey," "sheep." She is utterly alien to the zoological kingdom shared by

22 Semiotics of Misogyny

the two females of the privileged nation. Ethel is almost unreal, "creature of water" or "woods," an unfamiliar animal specie, although lower than the traditional farm animals:

I	divine creatures	Air
II	Mrs. Davidson	birds
III	creatures of the Earth	sheep, donkey,
IV	creatures of the underworld	Miss Gray,
	native woman of Samoa	Ethel water

The native woman of Samoa symbolically represents the most natural woman, female in her most natural state; in the water. Of all the three female characters she signifies nature in its virgin state.

Anne, the heroine from *The Door of Opportunity* is even liked, but she is still compared to a monkey:[6]

> She was like a little monkey, but very sweet little monkey and very human. She had a neat figure that was her best point. That and her eyes. They were very large of a deep brown, liquid and shining; they were full of fun, but they could be tender on occasion with a charming sympathy. She was dark; her frizzy hair was almost black, with large nostrils, and much too big a mouth, but she was alert and vivacious.

Taken out of context, this passage may be mistaken for a description of an animal. Both her appearance and mannerisms, behavior and disposition are on the level of an animal image:

    She -   Alert
             like a monkey
             bright brown eyes
             large nostrils
             frizzy hair
             very human

    She -   an animal?

The visual image is paradoxically similar to the portrait of a monkey. The single signal "very human" is of a polysemantic nature, a **dynamic sign** (Peirce, 1958: 304). It could be taken as a literal description or, when applied to a monkey portrait, may become a sign which clearly indicates two meanings:

Man	She	animal
	very	
	human	
	?	

The images of "brown," "big Mouth," "wide nostrils," "frizzy hair" restore a familiar icon, a monkey, a **universal sign** known to humans since their early childhood. This grotesque physical portrait of a woman is stronger than a traditional simile. At some point the resemblance between the imaginary monkey and the real female of the fictional story is so powerful that the portraits are superimposed one upon the other. The reader may confuse the two unless attentive to the context. This is precisely the intention of device used. The **visual displacement** is employed to convince the reader that the woman was physically ugly indeed without resorting to more visibly didactic statements. Rather than "telling" that Anne was ugly, Maugham actually "shows" it by appealing to the visual senses of the reader and his ability to see the desired world of the author.

When Maugham presents the traditional likeable woman who does not threaten either to destroy a man physically or steal his possessions, she is still compared to an animal. For instance, Marie Louise, an eighteen year old French beauty, is such a woman. She was attractive physically and comfortable to be with:[7]

> She was small, with a pretty little figure, with large grey eyes, a pale skin and soft mouse-coloured hair. She was rather like a little mouse. She was not beautiful, but pretty, in a quaint demure way, there was something appealing about her. She was easy to get on with. She was simple and unaffected. You could not help feeling that she was reliable and would make a good wife.

The traditional cultural stereotype is a silent, invisible, obedient female who may be likened to a mouse. Easy to send away, she is small, fearful of anything beyond her little world of grey inconspicuous habitat. On the other hand, a "mouse" is a symbol of a nuisance, good for domestic pet food, but basically better be avoided. Maugham, the misogynist, cannot help revealing his true self, even when he tries to be tolerant and sympathetic towards women. He chooses not to liken them to cats, a more familiar archetypal allusion. "Cat" alludes to a graceful, peaceful and useful animal who even performs the task of destroying mice, the domestic plague of many a household. Maugham deliberately opts for "grey mice," that need be destroyed by other animals. Basically, he subtly sends a message; "women are creatures who are a domestic nuisance, better be destroyed," like mice.

If critics finally acknowledged Maugham's misogyny, Chekhov's attitude to women, particularly in Russian and Soviet literary criticism, has been misrepresented if not falsified. John Gassner states in his essay "The Duality of Chekhov":[8]

> Chekhov is passionate in both his scorn and his sympathy even when he displays a cool surface of detachment, a surface of naturalistic objectivity. (177-8)

His biographer Ronald Hingley claims that Chekhov's denunciation of negative behavior "shows no bias in favor of either sex when portraying these powerfully drawn negative characters" (85).[9]

Most of his critics avoided the question of women in his writing as well as the possibility of misogyny. For instance, Valentin Kataev in his work *Proza Chekhova* (Chekhov's Prose) indirectly acknowledges the possibility of negative perception of women in Chekhov's writings, but he calls such versions "legendary," referring to the work by Virginia Llewellyn Smith, *Anton Chekhov and the Lady with the Dog*.[10] Mentioning the chapter in Smith's book entitled *Misogyny*, the Soviet researcher fails to pass any independent judgement on the interpretation proposed by Smith. Once Chekhov entered the canon of Russian classics, any negative references to him were traditionally discarded by Soviet pre-Gorbachev literary criticism. Kataev acknowledges the difficulty and duality of Chekhov's world in the story called *Ariadna*, but he does not dare to speculate about the possible misogyny in Chekhov.

Virginia Smith, uninhibited by the restrictions of gender and "general critical line," expresses a quite daring opinion about Chekhov, the man and writer. Having the goal of presenting the true Chekhov and dispelling the myth of a gentle lady-like man, Smith establishes Chekhov's misogyny by connecting the evidence provided by his own literary work and the biographical materials about his personal life. Nonetheless, even this perceptive analysis fails to pay attention to what is much more obvious in Chekhov's fictional world, the zoological signs which serve as the best manifestation of his misogyny.

Every negative description of women in his short stories contains zoological allusions but, woman-goose motif is the running motif of his short stories. A "goose" may be replaced by a "herring," a "horse," a "rabbit," a snake or a "rat". Chekhov is quite consistent. Women who are no longer young and beautiful or those whom he simply dislikes are usually compared with some animal species who rank lower than *mammalia*. The zoological markers which are abundant in Chekhov's texts convey the basic contention about female inferiority. This device is consistently used by Chekhov and is particularly visible in his short stories where his zoological signs are in turn signs of other signs within the **Supersign**-Culture.

Some critics, like A. Chudakov, for instance, maintain that Chekhov's "fictional world has no place for purposeful selection of things, motifs and features of character" (262).[11] The artificial zoological kingdom created by Chekhov within the fictional boundaries of woman's world is the most convincing evidence of a deliberate **motif-selection** and **motif-adjustment** on the author's part. Chekhov's poignant satire is aimed at women and derives from his obvious dislike of women. Misogyny permeates Chekhov's stories, his biting tongue does not spare the beautiful creatures whom he loved or even sometimes worshipped. Mother, from the early story called *Papasha* (Daddy) (1880), is colorfully presented as a "Holland herring." Here she is not alone. She shares the bright label with her "fat and round as a bug husband." They complement one another. Despite the fact that Chekhov describes adultery, his sympathies are not with the wife, this "Holland herring." Moreover, Chekhov is somehow annoyed with her because she "is accustomed to the small weaknesses of her husband" and pretends to overlook the love affair between him and the girl servant. Chekhov sarcastically characterizes her attitude as the standard reaction of "a clever wife" who understands her "civilized husband". It is quite true that both husband and wife do not evoke any pleasant feelings, Chekhov treats both of them with equal disgust. The question arises, "Why does he still detest the wife more?" There is a trace of blaming her for the hypocritical and immoral behavior of her husband. She not only far from being a victim, she is the culprit after all, she is "as thin as a herring."

Critics frequently mentioned that Chekhov's fictional world is rather simple and could have been created by any provincial dweller. Nothing spectacular happens, nothing which is particularly interesting. I. Sukhikh claims that what is said by Chekhov may well have been said by anybody in a small Russian provincial town (157-2).[12] Much like any Taganrog dweller, Chekhov repeats the eternal banality hinting that a wife must be plump and not thin as a "Holland herring." Chekhov appeals to the average reader, whose primitive stereotypical collective thinking is founded on the known trivial myths; and the myth about female weight and faithfulness is just one of such creations. Repeating the familiar triviality, Chekhov adjusts his zoological signs accordingly.

The function of a sign "Holland herring" lies in connecting the authorial own fictional world with the collective stereotype of his readers:

Chekhov	wife	His readers
myth	she	myth:
woman must be	as thin as	woman must be
plump	a Holland herring	plump

Nastasiia L'vovna from the story *Strazha pod Strazhey* (Guard under Observation) (1885) is likened to a pike fish. The story is intended as a sympathetic message to all men-victims of despotic females. The plot is constructed as a description of the sufferings of a judge travelling with his wife who looked like this in Chekhov's story:[13]

> Nastasiia L'vovna was walking behind him with a motley umbrella in her hand; she was a little freckled blond, with a jaw falling forward and bulging eyes – the exact picture of a young pike when it is being dragged by the hook out of the water.

"Pike" is a predatory fish. Nastasiia L'vovna likened to a pike has to symbolize a true despot next to her poor husband who parades as a "poor donkey" under the heavy load of voluminous luggage that the travelling couple carries. "The sweat which runs in streams from the red face of a poor husband" symbolizes the invisible tears of a tortured victim.

The "poor donkey" not only carries all the useless things to the train, but he is not allowed to go for water. Nastasiia L'vovna allows him to get some boiled water only at the fourth railway station. The judge is embarrassed that he has to walk down the platform with a copper kettle in his hand. The readers learn about the judge's martyrdom only after he tells his sad story to his friend whom he happens to meet at the station. His friend suggests that he run away from his wife, and the last phrase of the story is: "Let's meet in Paris."

Chekhov, as we have established by his customary discursive strategy, constructs an opposition of the two universes of unequal "degree of expression" inside the Animal Kingdom:

she	*he*
pike	donkey
fish	mammalia
lower class	higher class

The opposition of the animal orders is quite clear. If one recalls Chekhov's "manifesto on women" one may notice a certain strict correlation. The author does not depart from his own conceptual plane: a woman = lower order-animal-motif is subordinated to the prevalent mythology which is taken for granted and remains undisputed. The textual semiotic world finds its semiotic roots outside the story, going back to Chekhov's letter to his brother Alexander. The chosen ideology dictates the choice of poetic devices. Chekhov's desire to deal with the woman question from a natural history perspective leads him to the very zoological world which he had considered predestined for the half of human kind. His "manifesto" becomes a binding **semiotic contract** which Chekhov has to follow.

M-me Shchukina from the story *Bezzashchitnoe Sushchestvo* (Defenceless Creature) is likened to the house manure bug. The story's title discloses the ironic plot.[14] Following Chekhov's semiotic strategy, it is not the old lady who is a defenceless creature, but the office manager who becomes a victim of her persistent claims. The author employs the standard cliché "woman is a defenceless creature," and defamiliarizes the familiar concept turning it upside down. The applied metaphor is misplaced; and instead of a female, the male protagonist obtains the desired iconicity, which reverses the common designation of a sign. The **zoological sign**-Horse Manure Bug-discloses enormous and unusual power to victimize a male. Instead of the "pike"-icon used elsewhere, it is the "horse manure bug" which bullies the defenceless male in an important societal capacity and function. The semiotic universe is reversed to convey the idea of female despotism:

Office Manager   victim
Male

horse manure bug
M-me Shchukina   harasser

M-me Shchukina's viciousness and devilish power is replaced by a more humble allusion in the story *Volodia bol'shoi i Volodia malen'ky* (Big Volodia and Little Volodia) published in 1893. Sofia L'vovna is the wife of the "big Volodia" who is thirty years older than she, and unhappy in her marriage which everybody describes as *par debit* act. The opposition "little" versus "big" is used to emphasize the age of both males:

big   little
Volodia   Volodia
30 years older   10 years older

The pitiful Sofia regrets her choice and wishes she had married the younger man, "little Volodia." Chekhov describes her as "a little dog who is awaiting for a piece of ham to be thrown to her." The two males may be compared to two masters:

little Volodia		big Volodia
younger man		older man
	Sofia	
	little	
	dog	
	waiting	
	for	
	a piece of ham	

Occasionally, the zoological signs are not directed at the female characters, but to denounce the fall of a male protagonist. For instance, in the story *Kryzhovnik* (Gooseberries) which was published in 1908, Chekhov attempts to portray the physical and moral decline of a man who aged, settled in the village, gained weight and reconciled with the boring life in the country. To reach the intensity and veracity of his description, the author imparts unflattering features to the landlord's dog and servant. Both are likened to a fat pig:[15]

> I am on my way to the house, while a red haired dog, fat and looking like a pig goes towards me. She wants to bark, but too lazy to do it. The kitchen maid comes out of the kitchen, bare feet, fat and also looking like a pig.

To intensify the degradation of the rich land owner who escaped the problems of exciting, but hard urban life, Chekhov places him in the environment of two pigs, two powerful zoological signs. Having done that, Chekhov introduces another signal, the noise which his brother lying in bed is about to produce:[16]

> Entering brother's room see him sitting on his bed, with his knees covered with a blanket; he looked aged, grew fat and flabby, his cheeks, nose and lips move forward in a pig-like way, ready to grunt in the blanket.

Although the male character is also depicted in a rather unflattering fashion using **zoomarkers**, nonetheless, his image has a different cultural meaning, the other sign amidst the rest of the animal icons-the "dog" and the "servant girl" which are merely the natural beings in their natural state. Thus, even within this triad of **zoological signs**, the male is granted a privileged status:

30 *Semiotics of Misogyny*

	brother	
	almost a pig	
animal		animal-female
dog		servant girl
looking like a pig		looking like a pig

This triad of zoological markers may be represented as:

$$Sa$$

$$Sb \qquad\qquad\qquad\qquad\qquad Sc$$

The signs Sb and Sc respectively represent **semiotic helpers** in transforming Sa from a civilized urban man to a village dweller. This transformation denotes the gradual regression of Sa (Civilization) towards Sb Sc (Nature) or the decline of Civilization:

$$Sa = male = Culture$$

$$Sb\ Sc = female = animal = Nature$$

Proximity to Nature and village females is synonymous with the regrettable male downfall. At least, this is how Chekhov happens to represent the distribution of species and the two worlds of Nature and Culture.

Despite the fact that condemnation of a woman is not in the center of this story, female signifies the Chekhovian lower world, the world of primitive animals or primitive nature. In this respect his humorous story *Moi Zhiony* (My Wives) published in 1885 is the most explicit. It is the story written in the form of a man's confessional letter that describes the reasons for killing his seven wives. The author establishes some peculiar relationship between himself and his imaginary readers, manipulating the familiar misogynous mythology, he seeks the admiration of his male audience and resorts to those standard hackneyed stereotypes that are bound to have the approval of the intended male readership. Through the narrator, "Raul'-Blue Beard," he establishes this communication link between himself, a man, and his readers, men. He obviously wins the male audience and captures their attention when he proclaims his sincere dislike of the opposite sex:[17]

> I do not like women. I would have been happy not to deal with them at all, but am I guilty that *homo sum et humani nihil a me alienum puto.*

This disarms any male reader and wins his approving smile, but Chekhov is not yet confident that the cunning introduction really produces the desirable effect. He expands this mythical world further and heightens it with the most fantastic universe where the secret dreams of all misogynists are fulfilled. Making a statement that women deserve to be killed he utters the following:[18]

> As far as I am concerned women are not worthy to be killed with a revolver, their rank is too low for that. Rats and women are customarily poisoned by phosphorus.

In the line of his naturalistic perceptions, woman is again placed in the lowest rank of *mammalia.* In his presumably highly fictional world rats are still named first. At this moment, Chekhov "sees" the delightful expected smile, "hears" the approving laughter of the woman haters and confidently leads them into his seductive fictional world where all women get killed. He starts to describe his wife No. 1:[19]

> She was a small brunette with long curly hair and eyes which were as big as pennies – I was touched by her humbleness and meekness and ability to be permanently silent, a talent which I rank above the artistic talent, when it comes to women.

His first wife is likened to a young horse she is killed because Raul' could not tolerate her burdensome love and devotion. The humorous effect of this section of the story lies in the ultimate killing of a perfect wife, who loved Raul' with the cat's love strength:[20]

> I bet anything you want but meet a single cat that loved her cat lover as much this tiny woman loved me.

Among the rest of the endowments of his first wife was that she "had been as natural as a silly, young lamb" (26).

32 *Semiotics of Misogyny*

> The second wife was the complete opposite to the humble No. 1:[21]
>
> A novel writer would have called her a woman composed solely of nerves, but I was not far from truth, when I called her a body which was composed of equal parts of soda and acid. It was a bottle of sour cabbage soup at the moment of opening.

His second wife, an unknown biological organism whose *perpetuum-mobile* energy allegedly killed her, and she dies without a proper naturalistic allusion. Raul's third wife was killed for having "her own God" and her own moral principles. He finds no place for her either in the world of nature or in his own mythical world. Chekhov does not apply the zoological sign next to the wife No. 4, since she is a totally different sign-she is an item of economic exchange, a merchant's daughter with 200,000 roubles of dowry. Raul's wife No. 5 was a strange being who "swallowed" Mille and Buckle and was hated for her education and her spiritualism, positivism and materialism.

Wife No. 6 fitted into the known zoological order and was exterminated like a rat. She was a typical woman who loved clothing and latest fashions and frivolously spent Raul's money. This last wife was killed by mistake. She was killed instead of his mother-in-law whom Raul usually exterminates applying ammonium, a specialty reserved for killing mothers-in-law. The story has a very interesting semiotic matrix:

The universe of a woman hater
all women = rats
but

I Rats			II Woman
1 cat pony lamb	2 mysterious body soda acid	3 creator of her own God	4 sign of exchange 200,000 roubles
5 educated specie product of Culture	6 typical female	7 destroyer of man's property	8 mother-in-law animal to be exterminated rat

1 woman = animal = cat = pony = lamb = Nature
2 woman = mysterious body = soda/acid = Nature
3 woman = culture = source of mysticism = civilized Nature
4 woman = economy = goods = culture
5 woman = civilized Nature
6 woman = animal = rat = Nature
7 woman = animal = Nature
8 woman = animal = Nature

Despite the fact that all women are classified as beings, very primitively developed, the only one which is treated with relative respect is the merchant's daughter, or wife No. 4. In awe of the economic power that her inheritance of 200,000 roubles represent, Chekhov does not specify how exactly she was treated, neither how she died, nor how much she was hated. In fact, she was not hated as much as the rest, she simply annoyed him with her singing and piano playing. Nonetheless, she is placed in the middle of the hated female companions. Finally, in the fictional world of a woman-hater Raul begins and ends on the same note:

Rats and Women must be exterminated.

He lumps them all into the same category of primitive beings:

1. the meek loving cat
2. the *perpetuum-mobile* acid/soda
3. the dreaming blond with her own God
4. the predatory intellectual who swallowed all philosophers
5. the merchant's daughter with 200,000 roubles
6. the typical narrow-minded frivolous rat
7. the unknown animal
8. a mother-in-law who received the wrong poison

All of them symbolize the worst part of the natural world which subverts and ultimately destroys Man's World of Culture that basically does not need women but simply lets them into their world because of the general typical male generosity of the average *homo sapiens*.

This utterly humorous story is structured on ancient mythical ground bringing in the eternal sexual and social anxiety. Nonetheless, Chekhov does not assume the role of an educator. He does not represent high culture. On the contrary, the 19th century Russian intellectual exploits the myths of the low Culture or Myth of the Crowd. Is it only to win laughter or to hide his own secret feelings? The laughter is too malicious at times to be taken strictly as such. As the Ukrainian popular proverb maintains, indeed, "there must be a little truth in the midst of a lie." But Chekhov, the semiotician, hides behind his own zoosemiotics in a truly Ecovian manner. After all, everything can be used in order to lie" (Eco, 1979:7).[22]

2.2 Women as "Id" Signs

> Women represent the interests of the family and sexual life; the civilization has become more and more men's business. It confronts them with ever harder tasks, compels them to sublimations of instinct which women are not easily able to achieve.
> S. Freud, *Civilization and Its Discontents*.

Maugham's views support Freudian, rather low opinion about women and their desires. When Freud asked a rhetorical question "What do women want," he basically showed his indignation that women may wish to desire more than they obtain. He saw them locked into their alleged primitive nature, traumatized by their sexual desire and incessant bodily demands. All emotional problems that women could have had were, in the Freudian view, of an erotic origin so that regular sexual life controlled by the institution of marriage was their only cure. Chekhov and Maugham shared Freudian views or the traditional cultural stereotypes about women, To exclude women from social semiosis, social text production, and reduce them to the position of **singular signs** society had to find a plausible explanation. The theory of sexual authority elaborated by Chekhov, along with the hypothesis of hysteria in women suggested by Freud, had become myths conveniently supporting the existing gender system and gender division within the societal organisation.

Somerset Maugham, a product of the same patriarchal traditional culture and a part of the same generation that Chekhov and Freud belonged to, whole-heartedly accepted any views which supported his own misogynist mythology. His story *Winter Cruise* is the best documentary evidence of his own, as well as Freudian biased views. Miss Reid is the Freudian archetypal woman driven by her erotic desires who takes his prescription, a huge dosage of sex.

Maugham's heroine is not married; she owns a successful business, a tea-room, and every winter goes on a cruise. Apparently she travels not because she is interested in sight-seeing, but because this is her only opportunity for finding male partners. Maugham presents her to the readers at the point when Miss Reid is so desperate that she even takes a cargo ship *Frederick Weber* with only twelve passenger cabins on board. Somehow, it happens that, after visiting Port au Prince, Miss Reid is the only female passenger on the all-male-crew ship. Her pleasant behaviour somehow changes, and she begins to irritate the crew members. They continue being kind to her and polite, offer her drinks, talk to her and finally, they notice some change in her behaviour: she begins to bombard them with questions. They all get tired of her and their opinion of Miss Reid is now unanimously negative. If at first she appeared to them as a "good mixer," "a good sailor," a "good reader," not "a snob" and a "good companion," now they no longer wish to associate with her. She forces the captain to confess:[23]

> Oh, what a bore that woman is, I shall certainly kill her if she goes on much longer. She's a bore, she's a bore. I shall throw her into the sea.

Their desire to get rid of the formerly pleasant lady is unanimous as now she is a nuisance on board the ship:[24]

> She was a crashing, she was a stupendous, she was an excruciating bore. She talked in a steady monotone, and it was no use to interrupt her because then she started again from the beginning. She had an insatiable thirst for information and no casual remark could be thrown across the table without her asking innumerable questions about it.

Finally, Maugham entrusts a doctor who happens to be on the ship to analyze his heroine's behaviour. The doctor comes to the same conclusion as Freud:

> She's not a bad old soul; all she wants is a lover.

The sailors are shocked that Miss Reid "at her age" may still desire a man. But the doctor enlightens the crew members:[25]

> Especially at their age. The inordinate loquacity, that passion for information, the innumerable questions she asks, her prosiness, the way she goes on and on – it is all a sign of her clamouring virginity. A lover would bring her peace. Those jangled nerves of hers would relax.

36 *Semiotics of Misogyny*

The crew enjoys the doctor's diagnosis and the prescription he gives to Miss Reid. The trouble is how to follow it. The doctor himself declines, since he feels that his "professional duty is to prescribe remedies for the patients, but not to administer them personally" (1351, vol. 3). The captain declines also. He is married, old, fat and asthmatic, while the doctor insists that:[26]

> "Youth in these matters is essential and good looks are advantageous," said the doctor gravely."

Their choice falls on the young radio-operator who is only twenty one and just recently engaged. The captain asks him to come in and announces his decision that he is best suited to satisfy Miss Reid's needs. The radio-operator tries to protest:[27]

> But she's old enough to be my mother.

However, the captain convinces him that it is even a great honour to be chosen for such a role and the sex seance begins. After that she is under the constant collective supervision of the crew members who finally notice a change in her behaviour:[28]

> Miss Reid did not come in until the officers were seated, and when they bade her good morning she did not speak but merely bowed. They looked at her curiously. She ate a good dinner but uttered never a word. Her silence was uncanny.

The crew concludes:[29]

> It has happened, she's a changed woman.

The captain suggests to the doctor that he should ask how his patient feels. The doctor is victorious; his treatment of the woman's "bad nerves" has proven to be helpful indeed:[30]

> Of course, she is feeling quite well. She's eating like a wolf.

To reinforce the positive effect of the "treatment" the doctor orders wine. The crew members play chess and bridge with Miss Reid. She is no longer a bore. She is accepted on the ship again. She is normal and cured from her "hysteria." The rest of the cruise is quite pleasant for all. It is crowned with a Christmas party when Miss Reid gives presents to all of her travel companions. Everybody is happy, order, peace and normal behaviour is restored. Miss Reid undergoes two stages of behaviour, asexual and sexual. In her asexual, celibate stage she also has two images:

I	II
good sailor	bore
good mixer	incessant talker
good companion	jangled nerves

Her sexual, or normal stage brings her happiness, calms down her "jangled nerves" and cures her of her "inordinate loquacity." Erotic demands seem to be primary to Miss Reid. She stands for the archetypal Freudian woman, the central mythical figure of the eternal human myth about woman, the carrier of premordial desires, the embodiment of the inferior half of humanity whose primary goal is Eros-orientated and Body-centered. As a being of a lower organization, a woman in this myth is not a part of culture; she is a part of the animal kingdom where satisfaction of bodily demands is the alpha and omega of their *raison-d'être*.

The doctor on board the ship symbolizes the archetypal figure of authority, the king, judge, guru, shaman or the God of psychoanalysis himself who canonized Eros in modern culture and over-prescribed it to women. Nobody questions his decision when he prescribes sex with a twenty-one year old radio-operator. The unanimous approval of the doctor's remedy is a symbolic representation of the real image of a woman, a sexual maniac driven solely by her erotic impulses.

Men on board the ship are pictured as faithful partners to their absent wives whom they do not dare to betray. Moreover, they seem not to manifest any sexual desire at all. Miss Reid is surrounded by some mythical, asexual males who have to be forced into a relation with a woman. The young radio-operator who is used as a sex therapist for Miss Reid does it unwillingly, upon Captain's order, out of fear to his job. Consequently, the gender system in Maugham's representation is semiotically arranged like this:

38 *Semiotics of Misogyny*

Men	Woman
asexual	sexual
representatives of Culture	representatives of Nature
pure	sinful
societal duty-minded	erotically-minded
work-oriented	pleasure-oriented

Maugham successfully uses the grammatical substitute "she" for ship in semiotic parallel with the name-substitute, pronoun "she" for Miss Reid. The two symbols of feminine gender are used in two different contexts:

She	She
boat	woman
carried phosphates, cement & passengers	carried sinful plans
useful	useless

The boat of feminine gender symbolizes man's daily societal performance which is useful to society. It performs valuable tasks, contributes to the well-being of society, while the other "she" is a useless being driven by lust, seeking constant pleasure. The irony of the situation is that Maugham's Miss Reid is initially presented as a person who travels to obtain information that "would enrich her mind." After she ends her sex therapy on board the ship, the reader discovers the paradox, the mocking irony. She, the boat called *Frederick Weber*, is the carrier of "dirt", a "dirty female" engaged in sexual seances with the radio-operator. This "she", who is actually a man, becomes a metaphor for a male victim who, by the peculiar destiny of his higher organization and due to the unjust distribution of roles in society, is doomed to "carry" or support the primitive, sex-driven female:

Frederick Weber
archetypal man
carrying female on his back
victim of oppression

Thus, the reader may follow the semiosis inside Maugham's text when:

He	She
Culture	Nature
victim	oppressor
He	*She*
She	He

Despite the fact that the ship and man's back may stand for slavery, man is still a sign of Culture. While woman is a sign of "Id," or a being of a lower order, the transformations of signs female into male and vice versa, constitute the semiosis which seems to convey the meaning of the major **woman-sign**. This sign is the image of primitivity. It is not a producer of traditional signs, but the sign of the "Other" which is alien and hostile to men, the industrious toilers, productive members of society. Maugham's "utterance is indeed, a social phenomenon," sign of the other text, the social text where woman has to be silent (Hodge & Kress, 1988: 37).[31] Her role is in physical activity, in movement of her body, but not in the work of her mind. As soon as Miss Reid stops talking after the dosage of prescribed sex she is accepted again as a part of the human universe where she is present, but silent. Copulating is her main function. Is Maugham following in the footsteps of his professor of medicine? Is it a natural expression by a homosexual? Or is it merely a confirmation of the cultural tradition where woman may be seen, but not heard, present, but merely symbolically, an unavoidable trace of connection, but an unpleasant reminder of kinship, resemblance and sameness?

Similarly, Chekhov as a physician and a thinker displayed very much closeness to Freud, despite the fact that biographers have not established whether the great Russian story-writer had been familiar with the Viennese psychoanalyst. He also juxtaposed nature and culture, placing the latter in the male domain. Women were also perceived by Freud as lower biological species who were closer to nature, by their natural instincts, and, thus, sexual instincts were a part of their psychological make-up. According to Chekhov, women were also the carriers of sexual anxiety, since most of their life has been traditionally spent around reproduction and care for their offspring. Their bodily functions constitute the predominant preoccupation of this inferior biological breed and, consequently, women are unable to raise themselves beyond the powerful "id". The primordial in women prevails in Freudian, as much as in Maugham's and Chekhovian worlds.

If Freud entertained a hypothesis that a Man of High Culture may suppress his primordial instinct completely and may concentrate strictly on the mind, so did Chekhov and Maugham. Freudian narcissistic man could presumably survive without women, without sex. Much like Chekhov, Freud was a Darwinian naturalist who relied very heavily on the evolutionary concept. Darwin assisted Freud in his restructuring of the Natural and Cultural universes in terms of gender, sex and power. Using Darwin, Freud placed women in the rank of the evolving species of lower intelligence. Women were creatures of the "Id", according to Freud, and the same concepts were shared by Chekhov and Maugham.

Echoing Freud, Chekhov was very preoccupied with the dichotomy of mind and body, biological and spiritual, physical and intellectual sides of human beings. He regarded the sexual instinct as an atavistic heritage from the past. Chekhov was disturbed by the universality of the biological world and the allegedly humiliating similarities between humans and other representatives of the natural world. His story *Ariadna* is a classical case of this bewilderment. Power of sex and the reminder of biological affinity between *homo sapiens* and other biological creatures disgusts Chekhov. He questions the distance in their evolutionary past and tries to place male *homo sapiens* above the rest of the living organisms:[32]

> Is it true that I, a cultured man, endowed with complex spiritual organization, have to explain my strong attraction to women only by the fact that she has a bodily shape so different from mine? It would have been so terrible! I would like to believe that human genius which had been fighting nature had been fighting physical love as his enemy, and even if he did not manage to conquer it, he still managed to put it in a web of illusions, of brotherhood and love; and for me at least it is not merely a bodily function of an animal organism similar to that of a dog or a frog, but a real love, and my each and every embrace is spiritualized by a pure impulse of my soul and respect towards woman.

Chekhov attempts to place male *homo sapiens* into the highest biological hierarchy, and yet, the reality of being does not permit him to do so. His male characters are not pure mythical souls who live in the world beyond Nature and faulty Culture. They commit immoral acts; they are confused in their impulses; they are caught in between Christian morality, world civilization, Darwinian evolution and nature. Chekhov's men experience lust, the ordinary lust which he regards as a degrading human experience levelling his revered *homo sapiens* to a "dog or a frog." The travellers heading from Odessa to Sevastopol attempt to resolve the complicated problem of woman and man while killing time in their debate on board the ship. They discuss the Western versus the Russian point of view. A Moscow landowner Shamokhin places the Russian view higher, since he believes that Russians still adhere to the traditional Romantic woman-worshipping. In fact, he is convinced that Russians suffer greatly because they cannot accept the fact of women's inferiority. According to Shamokhin:[33]

> Women are deceptive, petty, unfair, cruel – in one word, they not only fail to be superior but are immeasurabley inferior of us men.

It is remarkable that this statement appears in the text of the story much earlier than the discussion about physical love and man versus a dog or a frog. The key signal which the reader receives prior to the canonical dichotomy, nature and culture, is "Woman is inferior to man."

After that, Chekhov spends a significant discursive time trying to convey a message to the reader on the degrading physical side of the relationship with women. It is precisely this biological bond which lowers the status of idealized *homo sapiens*, and Chekhov wonders how a civilized man, after centuries of cultural evolution, still cannot conquer his enemy, physical love, or intercourse with women. Chekhov claims that this aversion towards the physical side of the relationship between a man and a woman had been gradually developed by centuries of civilizing attempts. He calls the physical drive "an atavism" or "a psychiatric disease."

According to Chekhov, relations based on a purely physical ground, are unacceptable to a civilized man. "There must be more to human love than merely physical love," such is Chekhov's message. It is a signal to a thinking civilized man who is trying to establish his own place in the cultural and biological universe. If Ivan Shamokhin is the voice of the mediocre crowd, expressing the standard opinion about women, the narrator's monologue on the essence of human love is the voice of the "cultured people," Western intellectuals at the end of the nineteenth century. These two voices may seem to be the two poles of the complicated (Chekhov's) vision or may be viewed as the logical extension of each other, subordinated to a single semiotic universe in which women are lower than men.

Chekhov's biographer, Virginia Llewellyn-Smith, paid significant attention to the same story *Ariadna*. She also noticed Chekhov's obvious sense "of repugnance for sex" (43).[34] In this respect the critic perceptively uncovers the possible influences of other Russian writers, such as Turgenev or Tolstoy. Tolstoy's sex manifesto proclaimed in his *The Kreutzer Sonata* immortalized the debate on sex, women and civilization which was apparently the ethos of the time. Tolstoy, the moralist, condemned sex on the religious, rather than on the intellectual ground. Tolstoy's woman was only the source of reproduction, and he allowed sex only for procreation. There is no place for sex in Tolstoy's puritanical original ascetic world. This is how Tolstoy resolved the dilemma, to be natural or to be civilized.

Chekhov's biographers and Chekhov himself acknowledged the profound impact of Tolstoy's theory which lasted for about six to seven years (Smith; 1973: 50). Tolstoy's view dominated in the circles of Russian intellectuals at the end of the last century. On the other hand, Tolstoy's religious doctrine did not escape the influence of such works translated from German as Schopenhauer's *Maxims* or Max Nordau's *Entartung*. Critics A. Grishunin, T. Ornatskaya and E. Polotskaya date the Russian translations of these works to 1892 and 1894. Accordingly, that is precisely the time when Chekhov may have been working on the story *Ariadna*.[35]

The main thrust of the arguments coming from German and other Western authors at that time was to reiterate the old stereotypical vision of women and undermine the feminist movement in Russia and in the West. At a time when Russian and Western European women were defending their right to be educated and not to be excluded from societal activities, Schopenhauer, Nordau, teachers of future psychoanalysts and Tolstoy, the preacher, were proposing the old alternative female exclusion from Culture either in the name of Nature, or the Christianity of Rousseau and the improvement of half-humanity.

Chekhov's story *Ariadna* echoed Tolstoy's sex manifesto and was a symbolic response to the on-going debate. He could not reject a very seductive semiotic universe: Woman = Beast. Chekhov constructs it very elaborately. He begins the story with the vivid ironic description of a man bringing pastries and oranges into the ladies' section of the ship, while the men discuss the woman question. Thus, already at the beginning of the narration, women are segregated into the special place, a semiotic section where they are associated with Nature and Food. They are excluded from the debate of the cultured men. The skillful impressionistic verbal painter Chekhov uses the **logo-imagery** for semiotic purposes; he conveys the message that a woman is inferior to man and places her amidst Nature-Food icons:

Ladies	Oranges	Gentlemen
Woman		Man
gluttons		intellectuals
actual food	Food	spiritual food
Body		Mind
beast		*homo-sapiens*
mammals		higher creatures
Natural	Pastries	Civilized

"Oranges" and "pastries" serve as an introduction to the ladies' world, they are the Peircean **sinsigns** leading to the semiotic "Other."[36] What was later semiotically characterized as a phenomenon or a semiotic quality, was graphically introduced by Chekhov in his discursive practice. The **sinsigns** "oranges" and pastries" create a state of **semiotic alertness**, forewarning the reader about the later message, "Women inferior to men" which appears on the next page. Then, within the narrative space of one more page comes the panegyric to Ariadna's beauty which is followed by the notorious narrator's monologue about Physical and Other Love, Man and Dog or a Frog. A beautiful woman appears as a connection between the two dramatically opposed worlds. In fact, it is she who forces the Man=Male to be likened to the representatives of the animal world:

	Ariadna	
He	Nature	He
Biological Male	Dog	Cultural Being
	Frog	
	She	

To intensify the degree of female repulsive affinity with Nature, Chekhov defamiliarizes the familiar, transforming the sacred female function of giving life into an aesthetically revolting process:[37]

> The entire trip I somehow had been imagining Ariadna pregnant, and she was repulsive to me, and all the women I saw in the trains and on the stations somehow appeared pregnant as well and were equally pitiful and disgusting.

Where Tolstoy excused women for being in the world because "they produce sons," Chekhov, the author of a fantastic civilized world, is turning his head away in disgust. The fact that women participate in lengthy childbearing and are for nine months not as elegant and beautiful as he wants them to be, is degrading to Chekhov, a *nouveau homo sapiens*. The ideal being of his fantastic civilization must be the conqueror of Nature. His females should not be engaged in this supposedly humiliating and highly unaesthetic act of child birth. Gestation is seen by Chekhov as an obstacle for civilizing his cultured man. Woman is repulsive to Chekhov because she comes closer to the primitive forms once she is in the family way. Lowering herself in her pitiful state of pregnancy, she lowers the opposite sex as well, for man entering into a relationship with a woman automatically steps into the animal universe of "dogs and frogs."

The image of pregnant Ariadna connects her with all other women pregnant or not, as well as with the entire primitive world of non-culture:

> Ariadna
> Woman
> pregnant
> part of female gender
> part of animal kingdom
> part of lower world
> Nature

The possibility of beautiful Ariadna looking exactly like any other pregnant woman in her presumably pitiful state transforms the original attraction into a feeling of disgust. Ariadna, who before appeared as a fresh, charming, youthful creature, is now described in the most unflattering way:[38]

> As far as her sleeping habits, she used to sleep till 2, 3 o'clock in the afternoon, she took her coffee and breakfast in bed. For dinner she would eat soup, langet, fish, meat, asparagus, fowl, and then, when she would go to bed, I used to serve her roast beef, and she would devour it with a sad and concerned expression on her face then, having awakened at night, she would eat apples and oranges.

Ariadna's gluttony was needed to sooth her appetite; as a metaphor for her bond with Nature. Chekhov exploits the expected familiar myth about women as primitive creatures who are preoccupied solely with their body. The account of Ariadna's daily food consumption is proportionate to the degree of her natural, animalistic state. Ariadna is signaled as an animal and a predatory one. The character who was originally enamoured, not only loses his original feelings, but his love is turned into Lust, Lust into Disgust:[39]

> Little by little I grew cold towards her and began to be ashamed of our relationship.

It is remarkable that while the male discovers his new feelings he undergoes a transformation himself. Having fallen out of love with Ariadna, he begins to "visit museums, read books, stop drinking and start to eat less" (128). The juxtaposition of these two worlds, male and female continues. Having left Ariadna, a woman-beast, he is again part of the civilized world. Ariadna stands for a **woman - sign** = lowly state, pregnancy, birth, primitive animal existence. The other world implies Culture, Museums, Books, Abstinence, Civilized Morality. Chekhov draws two semiotic planes:

Nature	Culture
Animal Existence	Civilized Existence
Loose Morality	High Morals
Physical Freedom	Restraint
Procreation	Non-procreation
Primitive Female	Highly Organized Male

The juxtaposition ends with the final conclusive statement:

> She is already half beast.

As if contradicting himself, Chekhov includes into the category of such half beasts only gorgeous urban women, while the village woman is paradoxically equal to man.

If woman is a natural obstacle on the way to Man's metamorphosis from the man-beast state to the phase of Civilized Man or Cultured Man, as Chekhov describes this ideal man, then the logical result is to eliminate the obstacle, to eliminate women, but how? Chekhov, the radical angry man in the story *My Wives* offers a fantastic but known brutal solution by poisoning and exterminating the beautiful sex like rats. The sophisticated thinker from *Ariadna* is on the way to another fantastic solution—withdrawal from any contact. Finally, Samoilenko in the story *Duel* announces with relief:[40]

> As far as I am concerned, the broads can disappear completely. To hell with them! (380)

Chekhov acts as the omniscient narrator and warns his readers that Samoilenko "had never read Tolstoy" (381). Perhaps, it is Chekhov who insists upon his ignorance of *The Kreutzer Sonata*, since the story *Duel* was published in 1891. He also insists that the conclusion on the woman question are solely his and his own:[41]

> As far as love is concerned, I have to tell you that it is equally unexciting to live with a woman who has read Spencer and is ready to follow you to the end of the world as with any other Anfisa or Akulina.

Chekhov who speaks through Samoilenko puts a sign of equality between an educated and undeveloped woman. Both can be easily dispensed with for a civilized world constructed in Chekhov's fantasy and men can survive without them. He can live in the "world without love," without physical love, without women, that is without Nature. It is the woman who needs sex and physical contact. She is the culprit of Man's downfall from the "civilized Himalaya" to the abyss of sensuality, sinful desires and primordial past. Samiolenko's verdict is better formulated is from the same story *Duel*, by Laevsky who proclaims:[42]

> It is the bedroom that women primarily seek.

The Freudian woman from the *Civilization and Its Discontents* finds its precursor in Chekhov's woman who is constructed from various signals, signs and markers. Chekhov's bedroom euphemistically stands for "sex," "Id" "primitive past," and the "dark subconscious" which controls Man and precludes his complete separation from Nature. As an ingenious solution of this purely Chekhovian trauma of the cultured man, the Russian amateur psychologist proposed some kind of inversion or withdrawal from the Natural World. Unlike Freud, Chekhov proposed to ignore the seductive female, the source of ancient primitive desires. To create the special World of Civilization implied excluding women from their lives, "The devil with them. They may disappear." Chekhov concludes his own evolutionary pathway based on Darwin, Schopenhauer and Nordau.

The conclusion is the logical ending of a Chekhovian semiotic scenario in which women symbolize Nature and men are associated with Culture. To eliminate women means to destroy the connecting bridge between the animal and the *homo sapiens* world. Women whose needs are predominantly physical, natural and primarily associated with sex or bedroom affairs, tend to prevent men from pursuing their civilized activities beyond the bedroom: economic exchange, production of cultural signs and ruling society.

2.3 Women as Gastropornosigns

Similarly, Maugham's female characters are inferior creatures, closer to the animal species than to humans. Women are carriers of "ID," eros-minded and sex-oriented, an inferior part of the human race. Copulation and sex for pleasure is their main preoccupation. Much like animals, they spend their lives searching for food, consuming it, and using thus obtained energy to prolong the incessant erotic feast. Such is the mythic misogynist scenario of the daily life of women. The story "The Three Fat Women of Antibus" is the partial metaphor for this mythical female existence. Unlike other of Maugham's women, these females do not hunt for sex partners, they indulge in food. The story plot revolves around food and food consumption. Three girlfriends, Beatrice Richmann, a widow, Mrs. Sutcliffe, a divorcée, and Miss

Hickson, a spinster, form a symbolic tribal union, they are the three fat women:[43]

> They were great friends Miss Hickson, Mrs. Richmann and Arrow Sutcliffe. It was their fat that had brought them together and bridge that had cemented their alliance.

It is interesting that the three fat women are not of the same weight, Miss Sutcliffe, a spinster, is described as a "slim fat" among the other two. She was never married, a state which is a little unnatural for a female specie. The three overweight females pose a grotesque antithesis to the mythical memory. The **collective cultural memory** has another triad of females in its stock: three Muses, three Graces which signify female spirituality, grace, athletic quality and the worshipping of femininity in general. Maugham's three fat women destroy this familiar cultural archetype and, instead, present women as hogs, who devour food incessantly.

It is curious that they are supervised or treated from this disorder by a doctor whose orders they fail to obey. To prove that women's lives are separate from men's, Maugham pictures his female characters as clannish creatures who do everything together like animals in a group:[44]

> They drank their waters together, had their baths at the same hour, they took their strenuous walks together, pounded about the tennis court with a professional to make them run and ate at the same table their sparse and regulated meals.

The doctor who supervises their unsuccessful attempts to lose weight has also another function in the story. He is the man who tries to civilize these otherwise primitive creatures and divert their interests from food. The distribution of signs in the text may be seen as:

	Culture	
	Doctor	
	Man	
	Above	
Women	Women	Women
	Nature	

He tries to curb their appetite, to tone down their primitive gastro drive and to reshape their bodies, so that these presumably ugly creatures acquire human shape and aesthetic quality. The doctor's role is that of humanizer who is trying to raise these animals to a higher level:

> he = human   man
> they-subhuman woman   Culture
>   Nature

Maugham does not depict these creatures as totally unattractive. They are even pleasant to look at. However, there is something of an animal-like pleasantness about them. Their likeable appearance is not of a human quality. This is how Maugham describes one of them:[45]

> Beatrice Richmann was enormous, she was a handsome woman, with fine eyes, roughed cheeks and pointed lips. She was very well content to be a widow with a handsome fortune. She adored her food. She liked bread and butter, cream potatoes and sweet puddings and for eleven months of the year ate pretty well everything she had a mind to, and for one month went to Carlsbad to reduce. But every year she grew fatter.

The meaning which could be derived from this sign is:

> She = Woman = Pig = Ready to be killed

Eating like a pig, looking like a pig, she has to share the same fate with the animal that looks so much like her.

Miss Hickson, the spinster, is the symbolic male in the tribe, and consumes less food:[46]

> She wore tweeds and heavy boots, and whenever she could went about bareheaded. But she was as strong as an ox and boasted that few men could drive a longer ball than she.

This strange type of female is the leader of the group:[47]

> Though her name was Frances, she preferred to be called Frank. Masterful, but with tact, it was her jovial strength of character that held the three together.

Even within the primitive female tribe Maugham cannot leave to a woman any kind of order. That is why even this female leader is not exactly a female. There is the internal temporary gender reversal in this **woman-sign**:

```
                    she = he
    Frank            ox
    Frances
                   Frank
              pigs       pigs
```

The symbolic leader is an "ox" who is in charge of the two fat "pigs." Occasionally, Frank=Frances assumes the voice of a male narrator, Maugham himself who passes his strict judgement upon the habits of the three fat women:[48]

> "It's so vulgar to attach all this importance to food," Frank boomed, and her voice was deeper than ever. "After all the only thing that counts really is spirit."

However, the metamorphosis is temporary. The rest of the time Frank is another **gastropornosign** amidst the gastropornographic display of flesh and food, gluttony and **gastro-orgasmic** pleasure of eating. The words standing for food, signs of **gastropornography**, arouse appetite.[49] The scene of gluttony is structured like an intense sexual intercourse with the displacement of signs:

```
sexual organs    = digestive system
movements of     = movements of
the body         = food products
male = female intercourse = food
```

The food consumed or penetrating into female bodies is the substitute for the missing male organ. However, butter and croissants, jam and cream, potatoes and meat, *pâté de foie gras*, martinis and drinks perform the same pleasurable function; they enter the female bodies so that they desire more and more:[50]

> They spread the cream on the pâté and they ate it. They devoured great spoonfuls of jam. They crunched the delicious crisp bread voluptuously. What was love to Arrow then? Let the Prince keep his palace in Rome and his castle in the

> Apennines. They did not speak. What they were about was much too serious. They ate with solemn ecstatic fervour.

After this energetic "intercourse" between Food and Females, they still desire more. Maugham ends his gastropornographic scene:[51]

> But Beatrice suddenly thought she would like a meringue.

Much as in a pornographic movie verbal discourse is absent; with the exception of the few bodily sounds there is no word. The erotic fantasy creates the symbolic discourse of the flesh; the moving bodies speak in movements which have replaced words. Similarly, Maugham's fat women do not talk; the food which moves from the plates into their bodies creates a semiotic discourse. The amount of consumed food and total lack of order, disruption of the gastronomic ritual, and finally the insatiable female bodies craving for more food-all this is associated with sexual perversion. However, Maugham reverses the physical organs which participate in the pornographic discourse. Instead of the sexual organs, now it is a stomach which is engaged in similar perverse fantasy. The graphic sign has a different meaning, while the function is similar, namely to recreate the non-verbal picture of the body movements which lead to a taboo state and in turn arouse the readers' indignation. To imitate females engaging in pornographic scenes, these **women-signs** were intended to arouse disgust and hate.

Similarly, Chekhov associates women with bodily functions, food, sex and the primitive in man. Women are treated as a given, "something there," albeit inferior to men. They represent primordial forces, the physical reality and they are still necessary for the physical survival of man. Man needs them as much as he requires food and shelter and normal bodily functions. That is why Chekhovian women are very frequently placed amidst food. Makar Tarasych from the story *V Bane* (In a Bathhouse) complains about the difficulties of marrying off his daughter Dasha. He wonders why men do not marry her despite the 8,000 roubles of her dowry and her very pleasant appearance. The father describes his own daughter as a very seductive creature to whom nobody could fail to be attracted:[52]

> Remember that Dasha was not even twenty then. Such a beauty was she that everyone that was in awe, a real fig! Plumpness, "formalism" of the body and the rest.

Chekhov, idealizing Culture, has to denounce the seductive Nature. He does it through laughter. Instead of using the word "shape," his Makar Tarasych says "formalism of the body." "Form" and "shape" are superimposed upon one another, "form" which may denote a sign of confused and misused culture and "shape" which stands for a physical object. These signs create a humorous effect. The author takes pleasure in describing how men escaped the temptations of this young, voluptuous female, despite the fact that her own father described Dasha as a "fig". Chekhov frequently uses this sign as a connecting link between various associations, here women and gastronomic delight. It is remarkable that Dasha's father acts as a salesman for his own daughter. Knowing as a Man what is pleasurable and desirable in a woman, her father laconically names Dasha "a fig". This **gastronomic sign** embraces the entire gamut of emotions that a female is presumably capable of arousing. She must be as tempting as an elaborate dish, on a delicacy and as indispensable as food. "She" is also a part of Nature that is consumed, for the survival of Man:

she	he
female	male
fig	eater
food	consumer
Nature	Culture
body	mind
Source of the "Id"	"superego"

If Dasha is a "fig" the pharmacist's wife from the story *Zhena Aptekaria* (The Pharmacist's Wife) is a "pineapple." A young woman married to an old pharmacist, Chernomordik, cannot fall asleep. Her husband is so sound asleep that "one cannot wake him up either with injections, cannons or love." She is presented as the victim of her young demanding body, a seductive female tortured by the "id." Young officers who come to buy some soda late at night actually come to tease her. They know she is married to an old and unattractive man who perhaps is asleep late at night. They come to wake her up, to look at the delicious "pineapple." The officers disturb her peace:[53]

> Her heart is beating, her temples feel the pumping of her blood, but why-she wonders to herself . . . Her heart is pounding so heavily, as if those two outside whisperingly decide its destiny.

Chekhov juxtaposes the two desires the sexual and presumably gastronomical. If males see the young pharmacist's wife as " a pineapple", she is sexually aroused. Men just merely watch the pretty "pineapple" in the exotic garden of a pharmacy, while "she" is presented as a female animal in heat. The Chekhovian semiotic strategy is subordinated to the semiotic universe where again female is the source of "id," and primordial instincts. In the Chekhovian fantastic world "she," "female" is the victim of her own body, tortured by the mysterious calls of Nature which she herself cannot decipher. Deprived of sex, the young "pineapple" utters":

How unhappy am I.

and angrily looks at the old sleepy husband.

Chekhov, the cultured man, despises the fact that Man is connected with Nature, but there are some natural processes like eating that cannot be avoided. After all, "pineapples," "marmalade" and "figs" are necessary for a balanced diet for Man who is born to create civilization at the expense of Nature and "Natural Products."

2.4 Woman as a Predator

According to Kalaga (1986:64) the represented world of a literary text may be called a "stateme" which has "the relation between its constituent objects" called the "ground of the sign".[54] Nonetheless, the analysis of the fictional worlds or **statemes** suggests the extratextual connections which seem better to qualify as the "ground of the sign." The ground of Maugham's and Chekhov's signs is in the **Super-sign** or Culture that has already established the semiotic performance for various signs, including women. The supersign dictates the secondary cultural performance for women in all cultural systems with varying degrees of complexity during their restricted role. One of the components of the supersign (Culture) is the concept of the female diabolic nature, the capacity to commit Evil.[55] If, however, society usually puts restrictions on feminine "demonic powers" through legitimized oppression, encouraged dislike and mistrust, the fantastic or fictional world knows no boundaries. The producers of literary signs are freer than traditional contributors to the supersign. Where society restricts punishment of otherness, literary discourse escapes societal censorship so that the **stateme** realizes the suppressed fantasies of the real world.

If women have been traditionally treated with caution, their otherness being defined and legitimized through distinct societal roles, in fictional discourse the Real is permitted to reach grotesque proportions and imaginary women can become desired extremes. The extreme feeling towards the "Other" is hate, called "misogyny" if directed at women. It is precisely this feeling which is freely expressed in the discussed fictional universes and may be defined as the mythical ground of Maugham's and Chekhov's semiotic system. Their gastropornography and **zoosemiotics** applied to the portrayal of women find their ultimate fictional conclusion in women as predators expressed particularly vividly in Maugham. He actually allows his women to kill men physically, while Chekhov dwells only on the metaphorical destruction of males by females.

Maugham's story *The Letter* is the classical example of the utter freedom when the desired becomes possible despite its fantastic irrational character. What is significant is that the meaning developed and prompted by the **supersign** evolves completely within the writer's semiotic system. Whatever the supersign had to suppress, Maugham, the producer of his signs, permits to evolve.

If the woman of the concrete universe is only capable of Evil, Maugham's Mrs. Crosbie actually performs it. She kills her former lover who abandons her for another woman. Being still married to a "stupid" man she initially presents her killing as a defense during rape. When her husband is presented with additional evidence, a letter to her lover, he is put in the position of buying this evidence for $10,000.00 to save his wife from prison. The symbol of Evil is initially introduced as a woman who:[56]

> had elegance, but it was the elegance of good breeding in which there was nothing of the artifice of society.

This "quiet unassuming woman" with engaging manners seems to be incapable of any wrongdoing. After the killing, she presents her rape version as killing in self-defence, and all her friends feel utmost sorrow, finding it "a damned shame that they should have arrested her." She is a heroine in their eyes:[57]

> She did what any decent woman would do in her place. Only, nine women out of ten wouldn't have the pluck, Leslie's the best woman in the world. She wouldn't hurt a fly.

When "the best woman in the world" is arrested her good breeding does not fail her:[58]

> She appeared to bear her ordeal with composure. She read a great deal, took such exercise as was possible, and by favour of the authorities worked at the pillow lace which had always formed the entertainment of her long hours of leisure.

Maugham's Mrs. Crosbie is a typical representative of the traditional civilization where she performs the tasks predetermined by the societal customs and traditions. However, the writer sees her as the utmost danger to men and society. Since this new sign, woman-predator, is not transparent enough and, it requires substantial **decoding**. Having killed a man, she presents her account of the murder in which she appears as a victim of man's sexual desire:[59]

> He lifted her off her feet. She tried to kick him, but he only held her more closely. He was carrying her now. He wasn't speaking anymore, but she knew that his face was pale and his eyes hot with desire. He was no longer a civilized man, but a savage.

56 *Semiotics of Misogyny*

In her version:

he	she
savage	civilized
burning with desire	indifferent to sex
rapist	victim
aggressive	calm

Maugham exposes her lie, and the second version provided at the end of the story reverses the performance of the characters. It turns out that the man who allegedly raped her was her lover for years. They had been seeing each other twice or three times a week while she pretended that she "was tired of him." Eventually, when her lover found another woman (it was only a normal thing for him to do.), she reacted aggressively. What happened indeed was:[60]

> I was frantic. I made him scenes. Sometimes I thought he hated me. Oh, if you knew what agonies I endured. I passed through hell. I knew he didn't want me any more and I wouldn't let him go. Misery! Misery! I loved him. I'd given him everything. He was my life.

Maugham allows his readers to see the falsehood and hypocrisy of this woman-predator. She did not need the man; he filled in the gaps between her husband's trips. But when she discovered that her rival, a Chinese woman, could posses her prey she began to contemplate her crime:[61]

> She was older than I was. Horrible! They all knew in the kampong that she was his mistress, and when I passed her, she looked at me and I knew that she knew I was his mistress too.

Thus, a man falls prey to two females:

Mrs. Crosbie		Chinese Woman
young	man	older
pseudocivilized		pseudoprimitive

The stronger predator destroys her victim not out of passion, for hers is not a crime of passion, but out of her desire to possess. The signs within **the stateme** reverse places:

Stage I	he	she
	savage	civilized
	rapist	victim
Stage II	he	she
	victim	killer
	civilized	savage

The "true" meaning of this sign is elaborately exposed and powerfully refers to the two worlds: the space of supersign and the territory outlined by Maugham's system of signs.

The discourse even acquires some didactic quality, warning the reader how to decode the "true meaning of the sign" or how to discover a predator in the elegant, well-bred lady. Maugham's message to the reader is the "Other", what the sign actually stands for in his fictional universe, rather than what it appears to be in the space of **Supersign**.

To emphasize that Woman is more primitive, Chekhov even depicts her sometimes as the epitome of barbarism and cruelty. Such is Aksiniia from the story *V ovrage* (In the Ravine) published in 1900. She kills a child pouring boiling water on him. The child is a baby boy, Nikifor, who would have inherited the property of his father, Aksiniia's brother-in-law. Aksiniia kills the baby in rage over the property. During the funeral the unpunished killer appears all "dressed in new clothes and powdered face." Having killed the baby, she orders the mother of the child her sister-in-law, Lipa, out of the house and brutally bullies the grieving mother. Chekhov's Aksiniia is the embodiment of the female demonic power, a barbarian in a skirt who ruthlessly runs the brick plant , the village, the family and the estate. This primitive brutal force resorts to the methods of the animal kingdom to protect her territory. The implied name of this diabolic creature is "lioness." It is remarkable that the villagers and the family ignore the event. The mother of the killed child, Lipa, is blamed for the unfortunate death of Nikifor, the possible beneficiary of Tsybukin's property:[62]

> Oh, Lipa-he said,-you have failed to protect the little grandson.

The passive, frightened and grieving Lipa becomes the culprit of the event, while she herself is the victim of the brutal force, woman-lioness, Aksiniia.

58 *Semiotics of Misogyny*

The predatory lioness eventually devours all the rest of the passive creatures in Tsybukin's kingdom. The old father-in-law leaves Lipa, who goes back to her mother; her husband dies in prison; little Nikifor is dead; and brutal Aksinia is in charge of everything:[63]

> In the village they say about Aksiniia that she had taken great power; and it is true, when she in the morning goes to her plant, happy, beautiful and with a naive smile on her face, and when later gives orders in the plants, one feels some great power in her. Everybody at home, in the village and at the plant is afraid of her.

Aksiniia whom everyone fears is likened to an elemental force which is beyond the civilized world, the embodiment of uncontrollable Nature, much like hurricane, earthquake, flood or any other natural disaster. Aksiniia is the signal from another world which has more power than the world created by civilized men. She is the power of the mysterious primordial "id" facing the less capable "ego" or "super-ego." Chekhov concludes the passage concerning woman as a **natural sign** on a surprising note. The mood of fear surrounds this brutal, primitive force and the barbaric creature who may be transformed into a beast. The seductive "pineapple," "fig" or "marmalade" undergoes a very interesting metamorphosis, it gains strength on its way from a pleasurable, seductive creature to a frightening, powerful demonic force. The progression of the sign is as follows:

Natural sign zoological	Low Nature
Gastronomic sign	Higher Nature
sign of the "id"	Uncontrollable Nature
Woman	Omnipotent sign

Chekhov creates the bipolar semiotic universe of Nature and Culture. First, he places the latter above Nature and Women. Then, in the course of his denunciation, he resigns, like any civilized being confronted with a brutal, uncontrollable elemental force. The semiotic progression from a Woman-sign of Nature to a Woman-sign of "id" is marked by the semantic transformation of the expressive attitude on the part of the author, as producer of this sign. The feeling of superiority, disgust and desire to ignore Nature is replaced by the attitude of resignation. Civilization and Chekhov's fantastic sexless world of cultured Man accepts brutal Nature. Knowledge gives way to mystery. The Cultured man cannot fathom the power of Nature, and wishes to create his own structure within itself, outside the barbaric world of women.

Maugham's predator is Miss Thompson from his story "*Rain.*" She also stages rape and explains her killing of a man she seduced as an art of self-defence. The man she killed was a Christian, a married missionary, Mr. Davidson, who naively believed that he could reform a professional prostitute and make her turn away from the path of sin. Their first meeting occurs when Miss Thompson has to stay in Mr. Davidson's mission while waiting for favorable weather and a ship sailing for Apia, because of the pouring tropical rain she needs some temporary shelter. Thus, the unfavorable weather or act of God brings Miss Thompson into Mr. Davidson's life. At the moment of their first meeting:[64]

> She was twenty-seven, perhaps, plump, and in a coarse fashion pretty. She wore a white dress and a large white hat. Her fat calves in white cotton stockings bulged over the tops of long white boots in a glacé kid.

It is remarkable that though most of Maugham's women appear dressed in black silk or black suits, Miss Thompson is dressed in white. The writer exploits the semiotic value of the white color: the archetypal notion of purity, innocence and a reminder about the wedding ritual. White color has become almost an **icon**, in a sense that it is traditional referring to the same theme-a woman, a virgin, a young bride and is "a graphic representation, more or less faithful to the object" (R. Thom, 1985:272).[65] Maugham, who is in process of creating a new symbol or woman predator-sign, sacrifices the familiar icon for the desired meaning. It turns out that this young woman dressed in white is exactly opposite to what "white" traditionally stands for. She is a professional prostitute pending criminal charges and commits another crime while the poor missionary tries to implant in her some morality converting her into Christianity.

Their readings of the Bible apparently end in a trivial manner. The prostitute manages to seduce the dedicated missionary. One day he is found

60 *Semiotics of Misogyny*

dead in her room. The "dreadful object," the body of Davidson, appears brutally mutilated:[66]

> The throat was cut from ear to ear, and in the right hand was still the razor with which the deed was done.

And when curious visitors enter Miss Thompson's room, she shouts:[67]

> You men! You filthy, dirty pigs! You are all the same, all of you, pigs, pigs! Dr. Macphall gasped. He understood.

Richard Cordell sees the story as "a little masterpiece" with its Freudian undertones focussing on the male character, the missionary Mr. Davidson, whom he perceives as the victim of "sexual repression" and "unhealthy ascetics" (Cordell, 1961: 173). Despite the fact that this is obviously the theme of Maugham's story, the critic and biographer fails to see any other features in the story. Limited to the single story Miss Thompson is merely a structure in "Freudian fiction." However, perceived in the light of Maugham's symbolic trend, Miss Thompson is another proof of female demonic power and dangerous presence in Man's world of Culture. She is a predator who kills her weak prey. To her:

> a man = a filthy pig
>
> while she is a heroine

This is the desired icon for which the more traditional "white virgin" is sacrificed. Maugham destroys the familiar icon and, instead, constructs another one which is more suitable for his fictional world:

> white bride ======== dark demon
> pure ============ corrupt
> innocent ========== criminal
> angel =========== animal
> spirit ============ flesh

It is also remarkable that a victim of this evil primitive creature is:

> a man
> a Christian
> a doctor

a healer of souls
a man of culture
a producer of cultural code

The conclusion which Maugham imposes on his readers is that:

a woman = an animal

a man = a human being

Again the familiar juxtaposition between Nature and Culture is employed to convey the expected **cultural stereotype**, to revive the traditional belief in female Otherness and to defend the conventional societal rule and order. The **semiotic message** which is communicated here is much more powerful. Women again appear more than "Dangerous Things," they stand as powerful, menacing predators who endanger other species, here, men. If that is the case, the highly misogynist note is the final note of this deliberately chosen system of signs. If Mrs. Crosbie ("The Letter") and Miss Thompson ("Rain") kill their former lovers, La Cachirra from the story "Mother" kills her son's beloved. She is the predator personified. Maugham even uses the word-signal "prey" to help the readers recognize her:[68]

> La Cachirra was forty, haggard and very thin, with long hands and fingers like a vulture's claws. Her cheeks were sunken and her skin wrinkled and yellow. When she opened her mouth, with its pale, heavy lips, she showed teeth that were pointed like those of a beast of prey. Her hair was black and coarse.

To intensify the atmosphere of danger, Maugham combines several familiar icons:

witch-cultural stereotype =	black
woman-animal-archetypes =	vulture-like
predatory animal =	a beast of prey, vulture claws
old woman =	40, bony, thin, yellow-faced

Before the **ominous sign** appears in the narration, Maugham gives the opinion of La Cachirra through her neighbors' eyes. They say:[69]

What an evil face! She looks like a murderess.

62 *Semiotics of Misogyny*

Then Maugham explains why his heroine has such a frightening *visage*:[70]

> La Cachirra had only come out of prison one month before, and she had spent seven years there – for murder.

Despite the fact that nobody in the neighborhood knows about the secret homicide, they all sense danger in her presence:[71]

> Her eyes, deep set in their sockets, large and black, shone fiercely. Her face bore an expression of such ferocity that no one dared come near to speak to her.

What surprises the neighbors is that this wicked witch shows deep affection towards her son. Nobody seeing La Cachirra "fondling her son with a loving gesture" thought that "she was capable of tenderness". Her neighbor Rosita falls in love with her son, and he returns the same feeling to her. His mother, La Cachirra is consumed by jealousy and kills her son's lover. She warns her before it happens:[72]

> "What do you want with my son?" "What do you mean?" replied Rosalia, assuming an expression of surprise. La Cachirra quivered with passion and she bit her hand to keep herself quiet. "Oh, you know what I mean. You are stealing him from me."

What could have been a typical scene between a mother and the beloved of her son, ends brutally:[73]

> If you don't leave Currito alone, I'll kill you! cried La Cachirra.

Then the drama develops further, Currito stops paying Sunday visits to his mother and sees Rosita instead. His mother waits for him in agony and even starts to hate him:[74]

> When he did not come, she hated him; she would have liked to see him dead at her feet.

When Currito comes she plays the role of an abandoned woman. Her love is not motherly, not human; it is some feverish maddening passion that she feels towards him. The climax occurs when Rosita, her son's beloved calls her a murderess. La Cachirra complains to Currito and explains that she killed her husband because he was abusing Currito. This does not stop Currito from loving Rosita. When they announce their plans to marry, La Cachirra kills Rosita:[75]

> La Cachirra drew a knife from her bossom, and with an oath buried it in the girl's neck. Rosalia shrieked.

When the police came she feels no remorse:[76]

> She looked at them scornfully. She deigned to make no answer. Her eyes shone with triumph.

The only question she asked was:

> Is she dead?

And when the doctor gravely confirmed it she managed to say only:

> Thanks be to God.

The female predator kills another female physically, but she spiritually destroys a man, her own son, Currito who becomes another victim of female violence. Although he never reappears in the story, his fate and suffering remain the tragic invisible background. A man is placed between two female species:

witch	man	woman
predator		seductress
LaCachirra	son	Rosita
old		young
animal	lover	human like
killer		killer

La Cachirra kills her beloved, kills him symbolically, while Rosita's love and bad temper also bury him tragically and kill him symbolically as well. A man in the Maugham's fictional misogynist world is a victim, a prey of female violence, aggression and even beastly love. Love brings him disaster, Currito loses a mother whom he never had (according to Maugham's fantastic rendering) and a beloved who did not love him genuinely, but simply wanted to possess him to spite the evil La Cachirra. The two killings are duplicated like cell division. La Cachirra kills literally twice and is imprisoned twice. The double-killings motif supports the basic sign-woman as predator:

woman-predator

	I	Rosita killed	II	Pepe Santi killed

woman-archetype

I	LaCachirra	destroys her son future daughter-in-law
II	Rosita	destroys Man's peace

The Women of Nature and Culture meet on the same semiotic ground, they both stand for evil, danger, destruction and the negative role in Man's life. The desire to naturalize the fantastic world is nourished by the existing **cultural stereotype**. The will of the fiction-maker agrees with the **collective archetypal consciousness** which forms a comfortable misogynist paradigm.

CHAPTER THREE

Women as Signs of Economic Exchange

3.1 Women as Buyers

> At one end of the scale, cooking fire and drinking water are included in the category of things that are shared between neighbors. At the other end, women form part of the good exchange between strangers.
> Claude Lévi-Strauss *Anthropology and Myth*.

The traditional universal myth accepts women not only as the elemental force, brutal Nature and primitive component of the human world but it also acknowledges them as the key factors in economic exchange. The motif of **women** *as* **financial symbols** and indicators of Man's prosperity is the prevailing motif in societal discourse. According to this myth, Man marries Woman to improve his financial situation. The ideal cultured man basically does not have to engage in sex. It is the woman who is primarily interested in such degrading activity. She as the source of "id," is the vessel of primordial shameful desires allegedly forces the man into repulsive intimate contact in exchange for her dowry. Woman of Chekhov's and Maugham's fantastic worlds buys man in exchange for "bedroom." She, a seductive creature and a powerful natural force, attracts a presumably weak male, the product of civilization, through his own sign money and enslaves him not intending to participate in any forms of cultural activity. In marriage woman exchanges her body for the cultural sign which may be attractive to man. "Man is forced

66 *Semiotics of Misogyny*

to marry due to economic circumstances," – this is the semiotic signal Chekhov and Maugham send to the readers.

In 1882 Chekhov published the story entitled *Nenuzhnaiia pobeda* (The Useless Victory). The main character of the story by the name Arthur, was unable to maintain the desired lifestyle, is forced to marry. Prior to marriage Arthur tried all kinds of activities, from borrowing money to teaching algebra, writing poetry and making French translations. Finally, he even reached the level of Doctor of Philosophy and Mathematics, but this did not help him to avoid marriage. Arthur marries hoping to improve his financial situation. There is another mini-story inside the story. It is the tale about the spider who wants to marry a fantastic young creature:[1]

> "I do not love you," said the spider. I do not like you, but I want to collect taxes from the insects you treat, clothe and teach to read ... I need money.

The story of a spider provides a **semantic coherence** not only to the entire macrostructure of *The Useless Victory*, but also to the entire Chekhovian semiotic universe. The phenomenon described by Greimas as **isotopy** is recreated by Chekhov within the story.[2] The spider tale and its key message "I do not love you, but I need money. Marry me!" falls precisely into the realm of those "semantic categories" which become visible signs in all Chekhov's stories. The spider tale is the key to decoding Chekhov's entire semiotic universe in reference to Women – Men. It is the semiotic point of departure in the realm of Culture. Women placed inside the cultural process, are still associated with the "id." They even defend their primordial instincts through the market system, buying men for satisfaction of their sexual desires. At the end of the tale the rich spider kills his wife, the fantastic creature. The spider is a metaphor for Chekhovian, cultured Man who really does not need a female, but just desires to possess her dowry. So he only temporarily compromises his culture and superiority to achieve financial stability. The characters in the story discuss the immorality of marriage for money, and the Doctor of Philosophy and Mathematics confesses with cynicism:[3]

> What can one do! I will be ready to commit a contemptible act. I need a million by all means, by hook or crook.

The cultured man who needs only money promises to marry a prostitute once she accumulates a million by selling her body. The goals of a man and a woman differ. The buyers and sellers meet at the cultural scene to exchange "natural products" for signs or material forms of civilization. Chekhov introduces a dialogue which discloses this encounter. Arthur, the million seeker, the unfortunate Doctor of Philosophy who is awaiting for a prostitute's fortune confesses to a rich countess:[4]

> You want to run away from your million to be happy, while I am seeking a million not to be included in the list of happy people. As you see our goals differ.

The countess who owns a million does not know how to get rid of it. She is unhappy in her marriage with an old man. Chekhovian woman, a child of nature, she does not value the material world of civilized man where she is deprived of her sexuality. She values the pleasures of her body more than money, the sign of financial prosperity or success in the world of man's civilization. Again, Chekhov, the semiotician, juxtaposes the two worlds. The two goals are symbols of the two different mentalities and two opposed semiotic worlds:

Nature	*Culture*
sexuality	prosperity
million-symbol of Nature	million-sign of Culture
sensuous love	contract
intercourse	signature
body	mind
Woman	*Man*

While the "cultured man" discusses the purposes of his desire to own a million, an actress Il'ka tries to collect a million as quickly as possible so that the poor Doctor of Philosophy can marry her. She does so by selling her young and beautiful body to some "weak" men who agree to pay 100,000 franks for a quarter hour of love. Her admirers would passionately say:[5]

> I love you! – everyone was saying to her, and everyone was promising her paradise. One hundred thousand! – she would reply briefly.

It is remarkable that Il'ka manages to raise 120,000 franks. A Frenchman Désiré, and a German Bach, agree to pay the exorbitant price for her love. It is remarkable that Il'ka manages to achieve her financial goal among foreigners, for the Chekhovian males who buy her services are not Russian. His paradoxical world is temporarily turned upside down. A woman who traditionally entices men to marry for dowry temporarily sells her body to 'other' men, so that she eventually can afford to "buy" the man of her dream. The men who usually are "not" interested in sex, are now willing to pay 120,000 franks each for a quarter-hour of love. These males who buy Il'ka's expensive caresses contradict the Chekhovian image of a cultured man; that is why he made them foreigners. The patina of otherness somehow protects the Chekhovian ideal man from disclosure. When he says:

> The omnipotent passion has won.

Chekhov implies that the Frenchman is not a symbol of his ideal man in his fantastic polarized universe where man is presumably immune to passions, female advances and pleasures of the body. His ideal man must be a Russian. Chekhov on numerous occasions stressed that Russian men differ from foreigners in their relations with women. Perhaps, it is a Frenchman or a German who is closer to Nature, while a Russian man, in Chekhov's view, is a symbol of ideal Culture, where man only exchanges sex for signs of economic prosperity. He desires only signs, but not women. The cultured ideal man of the story is also the confused Viennese Prince who becomes the victim of almighty Nature represented by a beautiful female, Il'ka. The story ends on a tragic note for a male who marries Il'ka but is tried for a crime he never committed. In her passionate hunt for a million, Il'ka is not careful and accepts some false valuable papers and her husband is tried for forgery. The two different creatures, who seek the same goal for a different reason, are again placed in opposition to each other:

She	He
Omnipotent Nature	Helpless Culture
Inferior	Superior
Winner	Victim

Il'ka's suicide at the end of the story somehow does not mediate the same sadness as Arthur's trial. Her end is parallel to the spider tale; the female is again destroyed. She disappears from the man's world. The cultured man from Chekhov's fantastic world does not even temporarily allow his body be bought. There are such humorous obstacles in the woman's fantastic hunt for a mate. Eventually, she fails because the superior male fools her with false signs, false papers which she, with her deficient intellect, is unable to distinguish from the real signs, real money. Consequently, she is unable to buy the desired mate. The final semiotic performance is completed and signs are rearranged as:

She	He
Nature	Culture
Loses	Outwits

The noble civilized man "outwits" the primitive female when he "avoids the bedroom" through the help of other males, the judges and judiciary figures who establish forgery. The "savage female" does not attain her goal, and the desired mate is saved from the humiliating sexual act. He is placed in prison, which is a symbolic victory for a man whom a woman failed to buy even with a million dollars.

Chekhov believed in harmony and balance of power. According to his own theory, he recreates this state in his fictional world where woman is a sign of omnipotent nature and is only temporarily stronger than man. "Nature cannot tolerate inequality," Chekhov once wrote to his brother Alexander on the topic. His fictional females follow his own and societal semiotic model—women = inferior creatures managing to control man only for a short period of time. Later the "natural" course of events takes place whereby man escapes from persistent hunt.

The same motif is in the story called *Brak po raschetu* (Marriage for Money), 1884. A widow, Mymrina, tries to marry off her daughter, Dashen'ka, to a telegraph clerk, Aplombov. She tries to buy a male for her

70 *Semiotics of Misogyny*

Dashen'ka for 1,000 roubles, three coats, bedroom paraphernalia and furniture. The wedding takes place, but the next morning the sleepy provincial town wakes up disturbed by an unusual movement of people and things. The excited servants gather at the street corners, the curious town-dwellers look out of their windows and the entire town is being covered by something white which looks like snow but turns out to be feathers and down from a duvet. The custodian explains:[6]

> "There was a dissatisfaction," he answers. "The Mymrins had a wedding last night and the bridegroom had been cheated. He had been given 900 instead of 1,000."
>
> "And What did he do?" – "He got angry." He says, "I, you know," – he says. He ripped the duvet in the spell of anger and let the down out of the window . . . so much down! It looked like snow storm."

The town-dwellers enjoy the procession when the unfortunate angry bridegroom walks triumphantly down the street, accompanied by two policemen:

> I am an honest man but I will not allow myself to be taken to the cleaners!

The bridegroom destroys the marriage contract because the bride fails to provide the promised amount of money. She offers only 900 instead of one thousand, but this is not the only reason. The groom, who happens to be a telegraph worker who discusses at the engagement dinner the problem of electric power which greatly displeases the bride and her mother. The bride is the epitome of ignorance and her only goal is to attain a mate. She gets a little annoyed when the topic of electricity is raised:[7]

> Dashen'ka, the bride, on whose face all virtues were written except one – ability to think – got upset and said: "They want to show off their education and always discuss the unclear."

Chekhov follows the familiar semiotic pathway, juxtaposing Nature and Culture:

He	She
telegraphist	ignorant female
civilization	nature
source of "ego," "super ego"	source of "id"
victim of economic exchange	dictates the exchange
producer of Cultural signs	producer of Natural signs
poor	rich

A female owns the stimuli for economic exchange: 1,000 roubles, three coats, duvet and furniture. She may buy a mate and exploit his body to satisfy her primitive needs. A clever civilized male presumably escapes from the tenets of this predatory animal whose ignorance is apparently intolerable. Chekhov's male hero again outwits the female and rejects her seductive offer.

The image of white duvet fluff flying over the little town is a caricature, a malicious portrait of a failing female. The article in the future bedroom is destroyed, and the dreams of sex-obsessed female are crushed. The woman who is interested only in the bedroom has her bedroom article publicly ruined. Dashen'ka will go down in the history of the townspeople as an eternal laughing stock. The story ends with the scene of the bride crying over the ruined duvet of high quality. Chekhov, the practitioner of psychoanalysis, exposes publicly the dreams and intentions of his anxious female. He laughs at her unsatisfied libido metaphorically represented in the storm of flying duvet fluffs. He proves to the civilized world what are the true interests of the average female. She is shown to have no interest in progress, or technology, that is Culture; on the other hand, her only obsession is her primordial desire to engage in sex.

Both Chekhov and Maugham subvert the traditional meaning of women as commodities depicting the reverse order of **semiotic exchange** in gender relationships. In their fictional world it is not men who buy women, that is obtain sexual favors for money, but it is the other way around. The traditional **woman-sign** exchanging her body for money is abandoned in favor of a new semiotic process where a woman exchanges her money for man's body. The semiotic transformation that takes places in the fictional misogynist world is the opposite of the historical reality:

72 Semiotics of Misogyny

Real World		Fictional World
Woman = Biological Body		Woman = sign of culture
Man = sign of culture	sex	Man = sign of nature
Man = holder of money		Woman = holder of money
Money buys sex		Money buys sex
Men = Buyer		Women = Buyer
Woman = Seller	money	Man = Seller

This transformation supports the initial claim at the centre of this artificial universe, namely, that women as carriers of "Id" govern the **sociocultural semiosis**. The traditional mythical male hunter seeking a sexual partner is replaced by a woman hunting for her mate:

Woman = hunter

Woman = "id" carrier

To summarize his discovery about feminine nature Maugham introduces a male character, Mortimer Ellis, who married eleven times. This notorious bigamist from the story "The Round Dozen" miraculously escaped his twelfth marriage. He sold his body eleven times for substantial sums of money, having discovered that "women have got a craving to be married" and that this craving may be used successfully by a man, Mortimer Ellis made a profession out of marriage. The seaside resorts of England became his working territory:[8]

> They were his hunting ground. His method was to go to some place and take apartments in one of the empty lodging houses. Apparently it did not take him long to make acquaintance with some woman or other, widow or spinster, and I noticed that their ages at the time were between thirty-five and fifty. They stated in the witness-box that they had met him first on the seafront. He generally proposed marriage to them within a fortnight of this and they were married shortly after.

To satisfy their "cravings" they would frequently entrust their savings to this man whom they had just met. What shocks Maugham is that:[9]

> They were women of a certain respectability; one was the daughter of a doctor, and another of a clergyman, there was a lodging house keeper, there was the widow of the commercial traveller, and there was a retired dressmaker.

All these respectable women were ready to give from five thousand to a thousand pounds to purchase a man and satisfy their libido. By sheer chance Mr. Ellis was deprived of his intended "symmetry"; he was arrested on the very day before his twelfth wedding. Maugham, who assumes the voice of Mortimer Ellis, feels that this benevolent man of heart was a victim of the court and law which protects women:[10]

> I wonder if the judge, I wonder if the jury, I wonder if the public ever thought about my side of the question. The public fooled me when I was taken into court and the police had to protect me from their violence. Did any of them think of what I'd done for these women.

Then the voice of another fictional character in the story tries to reason with him and makes a weak remark:[11]

> You took their money.

Mortimer Ellis Maugham energetically defends the man-victim of feminine desires and the legal institutions that guard those primitive instincts:[12]

> Of course, I took their money. I had to live the same as anybody has to live. But what did I give them in exchange for their money?

He asks rhetorically and answers with a great deal of romantic passion:[13]

> And I give them love. Why, many of them had never known what it was to have a man to do them up behind. Many of them had never known what it was to sit on a bench in the dark with a man's arm round their waist. I bring them change and excitement. I give. I give them new pride in themselves. They were on the shelf and I come along quite quietly and I deliberately take them down. A little ray of sunshine in those drab lives that's what I was.

If the traditional nineteenth-century romantic discourse depicted a woman as a victim of love, with pure feelings, seduced and abandoned by her lover, Maugham and Chekhov, fearful of the new gender hierarchy and different redistribution of societal roles between genders, transform the traditional meaning, the familiar sign, into the other so it is now a man and no longer a woman who is a victim. Maugham's women buy romance. They seduce men, not with their bodies that are no longer young, but with the other signs-money which are the symbols of a different value. These women are not producers of these desired objects. They inherit them from other men, their deceased fathers and husbands. Money appears to have procured the temporary object they possess. They use it to attract men. So money buys them men, love. When Mortimer Ellis is tried in court he is confused. The exchange of money for love seems to him quite legitimate. Maugham draws the map of this semiotic paradox when man is tried for performing this exchange, and women willingly exchange money for sex:

society's law	Maugham's law
attacks bigamy	defends the lover
bigamy = a crime	trial = a crime
Mortimer Ellis = criminal	Mortimer Ellis = a ray of sunshine

The archetypal exchange of the body for money traditionally performed by a woman either in the form of vulgar prostitution or a subtle one – of misalliance so much derided by feminists and defenders of women's rights does not take place in Maugham's or Chekhov's fictional worlds. Here the exchange is reversed. The male body is sold for money to women who possess them. A poor male has to make his living in exchange for sexual therapy to women 35 to 55 years old. Their sexual needs have to be satisfied by a man who needs money. The familiar archetypal prostitute with a golden heart, an amateur psychotherapist is now a male with endless "rays of sunshine" in his heart to warm the "round dozen."

Another "buyer of romance" is Jane Fowler from Maugham's story "Jane". She is introduced by her best friend, Mrs. Tower:[14]

> She's worthy, she's dowdy, she's provincial. She looks twenty years older than I do and she's quite capable of telling anyone she meets that we were at school together.

Then the narrator has a chance to check this introduction and see Jane for himself and this is his impression of Jane Fowler.[15]

> Mrs. Fowler looked a good fifty-five. She was a rather a big woman; she wore a black straw hat with a wide brim and from it a black lace veil hung over her shoulders, a cloak that oddly combined severity with fussiness, a long black dress, voluminous as though she wore several petticoats under it and stout boots. She was evidently short-sighted, for she looked at you through large gold-rimmed spectacles."

Obviously this future buyer of romance is past her youth, and this what the author is painstakingly trying to convey to the reader. With a solid gold chain on her neck and a locket with a photograph of her deceased husband she enters the drawing room and announces to her friends that she is about to marry again. A moment later her husband-to-be introduced to the guests. There is a slight shock among the guests:[16]

> There entered a youth in a very well-cut dinner jacket. He was slight, not very tall, with fair hair in which there was a hint of a natural wave, clean-shaven, and blue-eyed. He was not particularly good-looking, but he had a pleasant and amiable face. In ten years he would probably be wizened and sallow, but now, in extreme youth, he was fresh and clean and blooming. For he was certainly not more than twenty-four.

Her female friend is dismayed, amazed, exasperated and can hardly control her passion:[17]

> "Are you crazy, Jane?" she cried. He's penniless and you are rich, you can't be such a besotted fool as not to see that he's marrying you for your money.

Jane Fowler insists that her lover is fond of her and is not interested in her money. Then she mysteriously mentions Freud:[18]

> I dare say there's a great deal about human nature that I don't know. They tell me there's a man called Freud, an Austrian, I believe.

Thus, again another of Maugham's women follows Freud's prescription by taking on a young lover. Despite the fact that her middle-aged friends condemn Jane, she needs Freud to justify her seemingly undignified behavior. Despite her middle age and unspectacular looks she marries a young man twenty seven years her junior to satisfy her primordial instincts. Having buried one husband she does not agree to a grim celibate widowhood, but rather prefers a young passionate lover who is able to satisfy her needs. She is the symbol of a sexual monster who devours her partners. The photo of a deceased husband in her locket is a sign of her demonic power. Unlike the archetypal seduction where a fresh, young female attracts an old male, in Maugham's fictional world the opposite happens. A paradoxical **replacement of signs** marks this fictional misogynist universe:

> she - young, poor   she - old, rich
> he - old rich   he - young, poor

The traditional archetypal image of a young, beautiful woman undergoes a symbolic reversal and transference. The qualities of the archetypal female are imparted to the man-victim of female sexuality.[19]

Jane Fowler's new husband, a fashion-designer, transforms his old wife into an attractive female who can comfortably compete with his youth. This additional function of the young man adds on to the entire misogynist plot where a man acts as a sexual object and a creator of beauty, a role which has been traditionally ascribed to women.

Gilbert Napier, a man, is used by an old woman as a sexual object. He brings her his warmth, love and sense of the aesthetic. Thanks to his taste the dowdy provincial lady is transformed into an elegant *femme* whose wardrobe causes admiration and helps her to attract the attention of both sexes. Gilbert performs the noble function in their liaison. He transforms the ugly duckling into a queen. His love does wonders; he devotes his creativity to beautifying Jane. Gilbert has the role of a fairytale helper in Jane's metamorphosis:

>   she - beautiful
>   rich
>   Gilbert   youthful
> She - ugly   he
>   rich
>   old

Sex and the company of a young male transform Jane again into a marriageable woman who may hunt for another mate, and this is what she eventually does divorcing Gilbert to marry another man, Admiral Reginald Frobisher.

This new liaison is what the society based on Victorian morals requires, and Jane marries an admiral who is fifty-three. The young French designer, epitome of taste, sensuality and frivolity, is exchanged for a military man in command of the Mediterranean fleet. Freudian and Victorian recipes are combined together. Gilbert will still continue to design Jane's dresses and Jane "shan't lose sight of Gilbert," but she will be officially married to someone else. To maintain her mental stability and physical shape she needs young Gilbert, while the admiral is required to establish the respectable British middle-class facade.

Gilbert, the sex therapist and fashion designer, suffers immensely. He feels betrayed and used. The traditional *abandonata* is not a female, but a man. His portrait at the moment of the dramatic news is another sign of the male victim:[20]

> When he entered the room, pale and distraught, she saw at once that something terrible had happened. She knew what he was going to say before he said it.
>
> "Marion, Jane has left me."

The traditional cultural archetype is a woman betrayed and abandoned by man for another woman, but not in Maugham's world. In his imagined universe a man is a victim, Gilbert signifies a man exploited by a woman:

	man
	young
	vulnerable
Gilbert	seduced
	abandoned for another man
	suffers
	victim of love

If in traditional romantico-sentimental discourse the empathy was directed towards a woman and a man was hated as a destroyer of her happiness, in Maugham's world it is the woman who arouses negative emotions as the symbolic evil in man's life. She promises union and deceives the naive, gullible man who still continues to love:[21]

> I couldn't hope to keep her always. She was too wonderful and I'm a perfectly commonplace fellow.

The natural reaction towards Gilbert is that of commiseration while the woman who abandons the man is to be despised. Thus, the semiotic goal is achieved:

> Jane = sign of female evil
> She = object of hate

If Gilbert is the carnivalesque victim of seduction and female sexuality, Syd, the Spanish dancing gigolo from the age of eighteen is the grotesque prostitute. Syd spent his life in hotels, drifting from England to the Continent, working for women who used his body to satisfy their primitive desires. Occasionally this man was used as a tool in losing weight; he "danced with stout women who wanted to get their weight down," Syd makes his living selling his body to women either for simple dance on the dancing floor or for having sex with them:[22]

> Sometimes a rich woman, after dancing a good deal with one of them for two or three nights, would give him as much as a thousand francs. Sometimes, a middle-aged woman would ask one to spend a night with her, and he would get two hundred and fifty francs for that.

Again Syd, the dancing gigolo, is another victim of sexual abuse. He enters into it willingly in exchange for money. Maugham creates another male scapegoat to convince the readers that it is a typical proof of true relations between the sexes. The world is turned up-side down; women rule, dominate and forcibly engage men into sex seducing them with their money.

3.2 Woman as a Sign of Fluctuating Value

Following his idea of marriage as a source of social advancement and improvement of man's financial situation, Chekhov creates a humorous story based on various prices of women in marriage. The story called *K svadebnomy sezonu* (For the Wedding Season) and published in 1885 is the fictional catalogue of various suitable brides. The subtitle of the story, "From the Salesman's Notebook," leads the reader into the world of buying and selling peculiar items. Various men and different women are priced according to their age, social origin, appearance and some skills such as speaking French or playing the piano. For instance, a 42-year-old Ivan Kuchkin wants:[23]

> A girl of 18-20 years of age, who would come from a nice home and would speak French. It is necessary for her to be pretty and have a dowry in the range of 15-20000.

He is characterized as a "crook, but a rather decent one."

"A retired officer Feshkin who drinks and suffers from rheumatism is looking for a wife to take care of him." (148) He will settle for a widow but he stipulates the condition:

> as long as she is not older than 25 and has some capital.

A suitor by the name Prudonov, who works in a photo studio, who drinks "not permanently but goes on alcoholic binges," requires a bride with a photo studio and a steady income of no less than 2,000 a year. Young and pretty women before 25 are valued higher, and they may have less financial value on paper. Their appearance is the additional asset to their estate, and men take this into consideration, when they wish to improve their financial situation with the help of their wives. Ivan Kuchkin who works for the provincial government office seeks more social recognition and wider connections. His bride-to-be who can speak French and is in the "fresh attractive condition of 18-20" is a possible guarantee of Kuchkin's success in social climbing.

A widow priced at 100,000 roubles cash, with two houses is looking for a retired general. Her asset is her alleged virginity since her deceased husband got ill on the day of their wedding leaving her a virgin. Her only flaw as an item of wedding trade is her slight physical defect:[24]

80 *Semiotics of Misogyny*

> She has a hardly visible eye-sore in her left eye, and talks in a whistling manner.

A merchant's daughter with money is for an actor Zhensky "of an unknown social origin,"[25]

> who claims that his father owns a spirits' making factory but he, perhaps, is lying. He is dressed always formally in a tail-coat and a white tie, since he does not own any other clothing. Left the theatre because of his hoarse voice. He desires a merchant's daughter of any shape, provided she has money.

Chekhov's fifth marriageable item is less valuable physically since merchants' daughters are notoriously overweight. Actor Zhensky agrees to settle for an overweight mate because of his desperate financial state. He does not price the bride as high as the sixth item on the salesman's list. The last one is any female of aristocratic origin who can marry a criminal and follow him to Siberia. Chekhov, the salesman offers the following brides:

N	Age	Social Status	Wealth	Other Qualities
1	18-20	nice home	15-20,000	spoken French
2	25	?	capital	compassionate
3	?	business	2,000 yearly	
4	?	upper middle class	100,000, 2 houses	virgin
5	?	merchant	capital	full figure
6	?	aristocracy	?	orphan

All the six "items" on Chekhov's list are valuable from any buyer's point of view, since a man may benefit from marrying anyone of the offered brides. In each case a prospective bridegroom might improve his social status and gain financially. For instance, 42-year-old Kuchkin is offered a young bride, 18-20 years of age. His bride to be is the helping agent in his upward mobility. A retired alcoholic officer needs a guardian to look after his decaying body and depleting finances, he is offered a 25-year-old female with capital. A failing businessman, Prudonov, is desperate in his efforts to save his business. He may improve his affairs once he marries a bride who owns a photo studio and has a guaranteed income of 2,000 roubles. A penniless actor 35 years of age may receive a merchants daughter in exchange for his acting talent and youth. A former captain, sentenced to exile in Siberia for misuse of funds and forging, needs a female from an aristocratic family to marry him and share his miserable lot. The least expensive is this poor orphan from nobility but without any financial assets. Let us follow Chekhov's "matchmaking" strategy:

> an old failing government clerk +
> a young girl, nice origins, 15-20,000
> = X roubles + 15-20,000 + X roubles;
>
> an alcoholic + a 25-year-old female + capital
> = X roubles + X roubles;
>
> a failing retoucher + bride + 2,000 yearly +
> photo studio = X roubles + 2,000 + X roubles;
>
> a penniless actor + merchant's daughter +
> capital = X roubles + X roubles;
>
> a criminal + aristocratic female
> = X roubles (symbolic).

In each case a man somehow profits from the exchange of his body for some property or capital that a woman brings into the marriage. The basic semiotic signal to the reader does not change: a man is forced to engage in a relationship with a woman who may offer something in exchange for his loss of man's freedom. Men are allegedly victims of their unfortunate circumstances, but they may improve their lot choosing a proper item on the suggested list. Out of the six items advertised, five are selected by males, while only one, the most expensive Grusina, a widow with 100,000, is actively selling herself. Chekhov allows this expensive bride to seek her mate actively on her own. In the depicted marriage market women are mainly displayed, and only the richest widow is granted the right to sell and advertise herself. Even in his laughter, Chekhov observes the economic hierarchy and mythical gradation. Two types of consciousness are in the story: Chekhov's individual world and the world of popular myths which he shares with his readers. The story is gender-reader oriented since laughter is expected from the male audiences.

The inner semiotic layer reaffirms Chekhov's **concept of sexual authority** which the author persistently mediates to his readers: females imposing sex upon men. In exchange for participation in sexual liaison, men

82 *Semiotics of Misogyny*

are promised upward mobility, improvement or preservation of their economic status. As is usual and everywhere in his world, Chekhov's women seduce gullible men by their own sign, $-rouble. While in the real world, it was man who designated some material value to a female fresh face, youth, figure, virginity, spoken French and respectable social origins. However, his manipulative females simply display their assets both natural and man-designed to lure naive men.

Chekhov's laughter is directed at both men and women, but the males reinforce the comic because they cannot do without the corrupt, sensuous, lustful and primitive females. Chekhov who in 1885 was not yet married and successfully protected his bachelorhood for many years has an air of superiority over his male characters. His men still outwit the females and are not tricked by their schemes. Chekhov, a convinced bachelor in 1885, is laughing from the heights of his independence at all men who have left the privileged empire of bachelors. They are all pitiful, laughable victims of women, lust, marriage and money-signs. Chekhov, a happy bachelor, offers a better alternative, to withdraw from the marriage market and not to participate in the shameful money-marriage exchange. His ideal reader is a person who shares his views, a male who escapes the tenets of the seductive females.[26] It is, he who would understand the joke and appreciate the sarcasm of the author. It is remarkable that all the names of the buyers in the salesman's list are derogatory statements about them:

Kuchkin	-	originates from Russian "heap" (*Kucha*) which may imply "manure pile", or "dunghill"
Peshkin	-	alludes to (*peshka*) - pawn or the most insignificant chess figure
Prudonov	-	carries the association with Prudon, the famous economist, highly sarcastic in this case
Zhensky	-	stems from the Russian word (*Zhena*)- wife, also meaning "female," "feminine"
Butuzov	-	comes from the Russian "*butuz*" - meaning a chubby child.

Women as Signs of Economic Exchange 83

These names of men are signs of their mental, cultural inferiority and justify their search for women.[27] According to Chekhov, only Kuchkins, Prudonovs and Zhenskys could participate in this repugnant exchange.

Another caricature or modern marriage is the story (*Brak cherez 10-15 let*) "Marriage in 10-15 years". There a very promising sex object is on display:[28]

> In the living room there sits a maid of 20-25. She is dressed according to the latest fashion; sitting simultaneously on three chairs, one chair is taken by her while the two others are taken by her dress. There is a broach on her chest, about the size of a large frying pan. Her hairstyle is modest, as fitting an educated maid: two-three pounds of hair put up and a small staircase left for her servant.

The living-room is the scene of display, advertising and sale. The sex object is young, and valuable. The signals of her momentary worth are in her attire. Her dress, hat and broach are larger than usual:

dress	- occupies three chairs
broach	- as big as a large frying pan
hat	- decorated with a turkey size plumage
hair	- two-three pounds of hair, a staircase

The sex object is portrayed in a humorous way; it is a caricature on a "beautiful half of mankind." Nonetheless, the buyer's agent sent on behalf of a 52-year-old bankrupt male, intends to close a successful deal. He inquires about "the maid who sits on three chairs and whose "hat is decorated with a natural size turkey sitting on its eggs" and asks if she really could offer 40,000 and 50,000 of real estate. The overdressed maid coquettishly replies that she may offer only 20,000 roubles. In addition, her husband may get access to the money only on terms of a three year credit. The marriage agent is ready to leave in indignation:[29]

> No, Miss, – Balalaikin sighs, now nobody marries on credit. If you insist on one, you may have only one year credit. The maid and Balalaikin start bargaining. The maid eventually gives in and is satisfied with one year credit.

84 *Semiotics of Misogyny*

The credit terms actually imply that the female wants to have more security, warranty on a bought male. A three year-warranty looks more promising, but she has to settle for one-year.

Despite the fact that forgery, living on credit, and false pretenses are among the "virtues" of the future husband, the "educated maid" is quite happy:[30]

> How happy am I!—she utters, caught up in a new, unfamiliar experience.—How happy am I! I...love and am loved!!

Having never seen her future husband, she is instantly in love with the object she had purchased for 20,000 roubles on a one-year warranty contract. She exchanges her dowry for imagined sexual pleasures. Her hat is decorated with a natural size turkey sitting on its eggs. This decorative item on a female who exchanges her money and real estate is quite symbolic.

One may recall Chekhov's theory of sexual superiority again and his reference to "sitting" as the main difference between man and woman.[31] In this case, her eggs are her money and real estate; she is sitting on them to hatch her sex life for a year. Again the typical Chekhovian woman exchanges her property for sex and an old penniless crook "buys the whole package"—money—marriage—sex, all wrapped up in one "educated maid of 20-25." Somehow, despite the age, status and wealth difference, the authorial sympathy is with the pitiful old crook whose destiny has been decided between the flippant agent Balalaikin and the lustful bride to be. The narrator regrets that:[32]

> Nightingale, roses, moon nights, perfumed notes, romances... All this has gone far far away... It is now as old fashioned to whisper in the dark alleys, to suffer, to long for the first kiss and all the rest as to dress in armour and kidnap the Sabine women. All is being perfected!

It appears as if the practical lustful greedy female has destroyed the entire romantic part of the relationship between man and woman, leaving only the naked cynical triad:

money—marriage—sex

Maugham is also convinced that women protect their changeable economic value through the careful selection of males. He points this out to a protective network among women where older females stand on guard for the established societal order and rate of exchange in marriage. Whenever the young venture to disturb this order the older come to the rescue. This is the theme of the story "The Romantic Young Lady" where a twenty-year-old beautiful Dona Pilar falls in love with the neighbor's coachman, a love that disturbs the traditional marriage game. A young duchess blinded by her passion cannot see the danger of her feelings. Her mother, engaged in horse and bull breeding notices the market error, "the daughter of a duchess cannot possibly marry a penniless coachman." This is clear to older females. The duchess, her mother, approaches the coachman's master, Countess de Marbella, and the two older women save the societal hierarchy and the traditional exchange of a valuable female for a suitable male.

The duchess, "horse breeder" and the countess, the "cleverest woman in Seville" form a temporary alliance and destroy the unsatisfactory exchange. Maugham likens the entire system of human marriage to breeding of high pedigree 'species'. That is why the judges who preside in this symbolic courtroom are the two women:

horse breeder woman	matchmaker woman	
pairing	marriage	
proper		Duchess's + Marques
improper		Duchess's + Coachman

The two watchful females agree on the impropriety of the liaison between Dona Pilar and a servant. They plot a correction of this mistake which does not appear to be very difficult as the servant is totally dependant upon the countess; he is her slave.

Presented with a choice – horses or a young bride – he chooses his beloved horses; that is, he remains a slave of his female master. Jose estimates the value of the horses and of his young bride-to-be and comes to a conclusion that mules are more worthwhile; they possess a higher market value:[33]

> "There's not a pair of mules in the whole of Spain to come up to ours. They're almost human beings. They understand every word I say to them."

Thus, Maugham introduces a symbolic yardstick to compare horses and brides. Jose's final choice is the reaffirmation of the ancient stereotype about woman's doubtful value. Again the familiar misogynist feature plays the key role in the rearrangement of signs:

$$\text{horses = almost human}$$
$$S1 - \text{intelligent}$$

$$\text{women = not human}$$
$$S2 = \text{lacking intelligence}$$

2 horses in exchange for 1 woman or $S2 = 2S1$.

The S1 is obviously a **sign of greater semiovalence** then S2. The juxtaposition of the two is so vivid, that it is purely iconic, a "graphic representation" of the existing archetype in the collective consciousness. The penniless servant who practically fulfills the master's order pretends that he actually makes his own choice:[34]

> "One can get a wife any day of the week, but a place like this is found only once in a lifetime. I should be a fool to throw it up for a woman."

So the devoted servant remains in his old capacity of a slave, and the social hierarchy and the system of cultural values remain undisturbed. The horses, the "best mules in Spain," remain with the coachman, and Dona Pilar is made available for Marques de San Esteban:[35]

> She was twenty when I first knew her and she was very beautiful. She had magnificent eyes and a skin that, however hard you tried to find a less hackneyed way to describe it, you could only call peach-like. She was very slim, rather tall for a Spanish girl, with a red mouth and dazzlingly white teeth. She wore her abundant, shining black hair dressed very elaborately in the Spanish style of the period. She was infinitely alluring. The fire of her black eyes, the warmth of her smile, the seductiveness of her movements suggested so much passion that it really wasn't quite fair.

Women as Signs of Economic Exchange 87

The writer recreates the archetypal juxtaposition of values according to the varying gender perceptions of one's own market value on the "human breeding farm." The coachman's choice represents the male view of the other gender where:

>horses
>>are
>>>above
>>>>women

The duchess-countess alliance stands for the shrewd sale of women in marriage. The more beautiful the female the higher is her marriageable value. That is why

>Beauty
>20 Years Old
>Peach-like
>Slim is worthy of Marquess de San Esteban
>Red Mouth
>White Teeth
>Passionate
>Seductive

Again a female body is sold, it is apparently not worthy of two mules but will perhaps suit an aging Marquess. Thus, the traditional exchange takes place where female youth is exchanged for a noble title. The value of a female fluctuates depending upon the conditions of sale. If the buyer is a coachman he measures her in horses, if nobleman in money. However, Dona Pilar's mother is engaged in breeding horses so that her estate is measured in horses as well. Consequently, a woman is placed in between mules in any case:

2 mules	Pilar	a farm
coachman's		Duchess'
carriage		estate

Because the duchess possesses fighting bulls in addition to the peach-like beauty Pillar, the female's value is secured and guaranteed.

3.3 Marriage and Men

A different kind of exchange is involved in the story *Anna na Shee* (Anna on the Neck) published in 1895. The story begins as a tale about the wedding between a young 18-year old Anna and a 52-year-old government officer. Anna comes from an impoverished family whose tragedy was brought on her by father's unfortunate addiction to alcohol. Anna appears to be sold to an old wealthy man who owns 100,000 roubles and has some real estate property. Anna's beauty and youth are exchanged for money which Anna does not use herself. This is the archetypal surface plot where Anna is a valuable item sold by a desperate father, a widower with two small children.[36] Chekhov presents this familiar ancient tale about a young beautiful female who marries an old ugly man for money. She hates him, is fearful of him, and yet tolerates him for the sake of her unfortunate poor family. This is a traditional traumatic frame. In the course of the story the plot transforms it, and a metamorphosis of the central female character takes place. A woman who virtually acts like a prostitute is gradually redecorated in different **semiotic attire** and is given power to improve her husband's social standing. A wealthy respectable government officer. Modest Alekseevich is suddenly shown as a weak man who needs the help of a woman in his career. It turns out that it is not Anna who bought financial security and prosperity, but Modest Alekseevich. Her smile is the demonic seductive power which may help him to receive a medal.

The readers discover Chekhov's double-layered plot already on the second page of the story.[37] Initially the author attempted to evoke the reader's sympathy for young beautiful Anna in this prearranged marriage. First, the reader is introduced to the sad rushed wedding that ends in an unusual ceremonial trip to the monastery. The drunk father, running after the train with a pitiful, kind and guilty smile on his face, and three of Anna's brothers next to him create the biographical interlude about Anna's life before marriage. Chekhov, the impressionistic painter, does not actually speak. He paints these vague shadows from Anna's past with the most sparingly used **logo-materials**. For instance, the father is actually described in one sentence:[38]

> Peter Leontich, father, in a cylinder hat, teacher's uniform, already drunk and already very pale, was leaning to word the window with his goblet and was saying in a begging manner: "Aniuta! Ania! Ania, one word only!"

The entire history of their relations, the pain, suffering, guilt and remorse, is already there in one signal given to the reader in the second paragraph of the story.

While the moving train leaves the running family behind, Chekhov exposes the actual plot, the helpless male seeking Anna's special help. The author makes modest Alekseevich confess to Anna (and readers) about his actual hopes. It turns out that Modest Alekseevich is interested not in Anna's body, but in what it may buy for him, the price of her charms. He tells her an interesting story:[39]

> Five years ago when Kosorotov received the order of St. Anna, second degree, and came up to thank his Highness, then his Highness expressed himself in this way, "So now you have three Annas: one in your buttonhole, and two on the neck." One has to mention that, then Kosorotov's wife came back to him, a grouchy and flippant dame, called "Anna." I hope when I get the second degree Anna, his Highness will not have the reason to tell me the same. (162)

The mini-story inside the story contains the key concepts and key signs: woman as a burden, a medal instead of a woman. It leads the reader down the designed semiotic pathway, the other goal in marriage, Chekhov subverts his own **surface plot structure** and destroys the traditional expectations of the readers. Through Modest Alekseevich Chekhov exposes the otherness of man's motives in marriage.

Modest Alekseevich dreams of receiving the order of St. Anna as well.[40] He is looking at his acquisition, young fresh 18-year-old **Anna**, as a passage to the Order of **St. Anna**. Then, Chekhov, disguised as a narrator, adds more information to influence the image of the unusual husband. He is not only preoccupied with the possibility of getting a medal, but he seems to be very awkward with a woman, he *is* more interested in the **St. Anna** the medal, than in **Anna** a young beauty. This newly married man is portrayed as an unusual male who desires a medal more than a female. His passion for

90 *Semiotics of Misogyny*

the possible Order of St. Anna in the distant future appears stronger than his desire for the beautiful young wife on their wedding night. Soviet critics may have treated this scene as evidence of the career aspirations of the old tsarist bureaucracy. However, remembering Chekhov's fictional roles for his fictional men, one may assume that the author faithfully follows his own semiotic pathway. The contrast in male and female thoughts follows the tale:[41]

> Modest Alekseevich was touching her with the clumsiness of a respectable man who was too used to handling women, while she was thinking about money, her mother and her death. (163)

Chekhov again draws too contrasting images:

he	she
man	woman
naive	cynical
pure	corrupt

Nonetheless, the roles are reversed:

he	she
man	woman
nature	culture
belief	trade

The conventional Chekhovian, lustful woman is now a passive, cold but calculating female who analyzes the results of the business deal while his man appears as a sincere natural creature in love with the ruthless female. However, it is a temporary and misleading signal. The two messages corrected together produce the following text inside the text:

1. woman marrying for money
2. man marrying for medal
3. man not desiring a woman but Her
4. as a road to success
5. woman turning into a medal

While Anna undergoes **gradual metamorphosis** from a woman to a medal-a sign-Modest Alekseevich also changes.[42] Chekhov presents to the reader a double-pictured screen where the female and male characters evolve according to the **desired semiotic matrix**. At first, Anna appears as a victim of her father's sinful habit. The desperate alcoholic is unable to provide for his daughter and three sons and is forced to sell his daughter in exchange for some financial help. Anna is sold to Modest Alekseevich for his 100,000 roubles and rented property. Hating her husband, experiencing nothing but revulsion at the sight of him, Anna assumes the same role as the women of the oldest profession on Earth. She becomes a legalized prostitute, sanctified by a marriage license and church ceremony:[43]

> She would recall how painful was the wedding ceremony in the church when it seemed to her that everybody in the church including the priest and guests were looking at her with sadness: why, why does she, so nice, likeable marry this middle-aged, unattractive gentleman?

Anna herself feels sinful, laughable and guilty of something she had done only to save herself and her family. But for this shameful marriage, she would have been a slave to her drunken father and her brothers, mending their clothes, running to the market and feeling constantly embarrassed for the holes in her boots covered up with ink. So Anna exchanges her role of a slave for the part of a bourgeois prostitute. However, during this exchange and **semiotic metamorphosis** her partner reveals his true intentions. He announces his conjugal goal, to use his young wife's charm for the purposes of social advancement. For instance:[44]

> Occasionally Modest Alekseevich would go to the theatre with Anna. During the intermission he would not let her alone for a single moment walking with her in the halls and foyer holding her under his arm.

While displaying publicly his property, his young wife, he teaches her to use her sexuality, her feminine attractiveness. Very frequently Modest Alekseevich would command:

> Bow to this old lady!

And Anna would object, saying that she does not know her, and he would insist:[45]

> "All the same, this is the wife of the man who is in charge of the official chamber. Bow, I am telling you!" He would insist "Your head will not fall off."
>
> Anna would bow, her head would not fall off indeed, but it was painful. (166)

Little by little, Anna discovers that it is not she 'who has sold herself' but it is Modest who has obtained something more valuable than his entire estate. Modest Alekseevich, the buyer, had purchased an expensive doll who can be displayed, and whose charming smile may win him new connections and additional favors. He does not need the conventional favors from the woman. He needs her smile as a **powerful tool**. He expands his own social creativity at the expense of Anna's smile, while Anna, in fact, feels cheated. Let us compare the two character progressions:

He		**She**
rich	Stage I	poor
buyer		seller
client		prostitute
naive		calculating
in love		in despair
victim	Stage II	*winner*
he		she
seeker of medal		source of medal
"poor"		"owner"
prostitutes his wife		seller

Modest does not need Anna's sexual favours; he needs a medal. Anna's charm may bring him the happiness he seeks. But now he is at her mercy, and this is a humiliating situation of imitating the misery of a poor man. His plea to Anna is a metaphor for his new state. Modest Alekseevich is desperately trying to break through this metaphoric state of "poverty," i.e., the anxiety of social high-flying:[46]

> I have made you happy, and today you can make me happy. I beg you introduce yourself to the wife of his Highness! For God's sake! I may get the position of the Senior Officer through her!

The ball scene is the turning point in the plot and in characters metamorphosis. Anna discovers her power over men, the diabolical magical force of her smile and of her young attractive body. This discovery relieves her from the pain and anguish of the past. Anna is no longer a prostitute. She is the queen of the ballroom and the social circle is her little kingdom. She is now the benevolent charity giver who can bestow her selective mercy upon men of her own choice. Previously sold to Modest Alekseevich, she herself is now in a position to be generous, giving away what she did not need:[47]

> She had success with men, this was clear, and it could not have been different. She felt as if she would choke from excitement.

The intoxicating excitement of her metamorphosis imparts a completely new atmosphere around her. There is some Dionysian frenzy in the air. Anna's smile conquers, tortures and hypnotizes men who lose their minds at the sight of her dazzling beauty. They even temporarily change into young, agile males as do the huge, clumsy, middle-aged officer who is, Anna's dancing partner in a mazurka. Chekhov mediates an air of magical excitement created by Anna's smile at the ball. Men are hypnotized and seduced by the mysterious Anna. Finally, the goal of Modest Alekseevich is achieved. His Highness himself notices Anna:[48]

> His Highness himself was walking towards her, in a tuxedo with two stars in the buttonhole. Yes, his Highness was walking directly towards her, because he stared at her and had a sugary smile. He was chewing his lips which was his usual way when he saw pretty women.

Chekhov introduces his favorite semiotic signals to announce the coming metamorphosis. They are:

Two Stars   His Highness   Lips
Anna

The Russian word *Vysochestvo* (Highness) comes from *vysoko* (high) and alludes to the verb "to shine," placed next to the sign "stars," it provides an **alarm cluster** which alerts the reader about the coming glittering spectacle. Finally, his Highness utters:[49]

94 *Semiotics of Misogyny*

"Very pleased, very pleased," . . . he begins . . . but I will order your husband to be put in a punishment cell for hiding such a treasure from us for so long. But I am sent to you on my wife's errand. You have to help us. Oh, yes, we have to give you a prize for beauty . . . like in America . . . Oh, yes . . . Americans . . . My wife is eagerly waiting for you.

It is her victory and Modest Alekseevich is in ecstasy. At last, all his signals sent to his superiors have been properly understood. Anna's smile has finally been properly evaluated by his Highness, never mind the general success with all other, less important men. The female character has entered the stage of **utmost semiotic significance**. A poor victim of misery and sex-sale is turning the tables on the market place. A former "prostitute" is now granted the status of a beauty queen. The key sign in this portion of the message is "Americans and American." The dream about the society of eternal success and "pursuit of happiness" had already reached distant Russia in Chekhov's lifetime. The sign "American" enables the author to reconstruct the mythical world of utmost success which his male character is so desperately anxious to achieve.

Anna, noticed and invited by his Highness, participates in the flea-market at the ball where she presumably contributes to the prosperity of the municipality. She sells tea. This symbolic tea-party turns into a wild carnival. Men buying cups of tea from smiling Anna pay fantastic sums of money. She forces them to drink more than they can. One man an asthma-sufferer silently pays 200 roubles for a goblet of champagne. Tea, wine, money and Anna's smiles are being poured out in wild frenzy. It is the shower of gifts upon the newly born American beauty queen, a mad fever similar to the gold fever familiar in American history. Later at supper, one general eloquently summarizes the unexplained phenomenon of common craziness. He proposes a toast to the "force which makes even artillery give in." This force is Anna's smile which finally puts the Order of St. Anna on Modest Alekseevich's chest. He achieves the goal of his exchange. He made a clever purchase: he sold his estate for three insignificant symbols. **Anna, St. Anna** and the **American beauty queen** have changed his fortune. The fearful, guilty being, is now a conqueror who laughingly spends her husband's money. To her, any being who could so eagerly part with the signs of wealth and exchange them for the signs of ambition and fantastic social hierarchy is nothing more than a "blockhead." The Trinity Order which Modest Alekseevich now possesses includes Anna, a woman with a diabolic smile, the queen and the other Anna, the medal which he had longed to acquire.

The marriage deal is successful and satisfactory to both sides, for medal-hungry man and money-anxious woman each had pleased his/her pleasure-seeking self. Her smile and her body are the signs which regulate society ruled by men from within. As a sign of subversion of the patriarchal structure, the marginal creature, a prostitute, moves from the periphery of society to its centre and becomes the true ruler whose power is in her seductive smile. It is not his Highness who grants medals. It is smiling Anna who virtually has replaced the government official. Chekhov's theory of sexual authority works against his own principles. Unexpectedly, for Chekhov, his woman gains the position of higher authority. The representative of primitive Nature fuels the complex society of Culture.

3.4 Marriage and Women

Bateman Hunter from Maugham's "The Fall of Edward Barnard" is another archetypal man who marries to improve his economic status. His name "Hunter" suggests a certain iconicity, he hunts for a woman, but on the other hand he is a "bait" as well. His hunt is successful, because he allows himself to be used as a bait as well. His friend Edward fails to honor his commitment to beautiful Isabel, and Bateman happens to be a fortunate replacement. He himself a bait when he corrects the mistake made by his friend. Isabel is quickly lured to another male who can restore her status.

Although Maugham informs his readers that Bateman is attracted to Isabel whom he claims to love not only for her beauty "but still more the beauty of her soul," he in fact loves her for something else:[50]

> She seemed to him to collect in herself all that was most admirable in his countrywomen. But he saw in her something more than the perfect type of the American girl. He felt that her exquisiteness was peculiar in a way to her environment, and he was assured that no city in the world could have produced her but Chicago.

Much like Chekhov's Anna, Maugham's Isabel is also the American queen. America has become an archetype of wealth, a **cultural universal**, a sign of financial prosperity.[51] Isabel signifies "economic possibilities," the "real capital" of the United States, upward mobility and fulfillment of man's dreams. This woman who may bring prosperity to a man is allowed to be attractive. Unlike other of Maugham's women she is depicted with admiration:[52]

> Her delicate features, the aristocratic shortness of her upper lip, and her wealth of fair hair suggested the marquise again, and it must have been obvious, even if it were not notorious, that in her veins flowed the best blood of Chicago.

In fact, the feminine beauty in this case is just a mere sign of wealth, aristocracy and is nothing more than part of the material environment produced by **sign-makers**. She is a part of the rich landscape which is the ultimate desire of each male:[53]

> The dining room was a fitting frame to her fragile beauty, for Isabel had caused the house, a replica of a palace on the Grand Canal at Venice, to be furnished by an English expert in the style of Louis XV; and the graceful decoration linked with the name of that amorous monarch enhanced her loveliness and at the same time acquired from it a more profound significance.

She is the sign of luxury, grandeur, opulence and happiness which she may bring to anybody who wishes to marry her. Because she symbolizes wealth she is also allowed to be clever, unlike so many other of Maugham's women likened to primitive animals. Possessing money and material wealth she automatically acquires intelligence. It is significant how Maugham describes Isabel's mind: "It was richly stored." Her conversation, unlike the stupid chatter of her sister-characters from other stories, "is never flippant." She discusses either expensive concerts she attends, political situations her money may influence or art that her father purchases. Her conversation is abundant with the icons of prosperity that Bateman does not fail to notice. She does not bore him because her talk reveals her high financial value:[54]

> It comforted Bateman to hear her. He felt that he was once more in a civilized world at the centre of culture and distinction.

Consequently, a woman who traditionally was placed in the midst of Nature and the natural, is now a part of Culture. A wealthy female is a road to man's success, to his access to Culture.

Bateman's decision to take the place of Edward Barnard and marry Isabel is dictated not by love but by a desire to possess her wealth and to join her world of the rich. He may obtain the same material culture and distinction without having to produce his own wealth, without the effort of labour. All he has to do is to exchange sexual favours and pretend that he passionately loves her:[55]

> "Isabel, you know I wanted to marry you the very first day I saw you," he cried passionately.

He was sincere, indeed, for he had dreamed of marrying the "blue blood of Chicago." "Blue Blood" stands as an **ironic icon** against "Blue Stocking;" because Isabel is of blue blood she is allowed to possess intelligence, a quality traditionally reserved only for spinsters, ugly "blue stockings." His dream has come true:[56]

> And as he held her in his arms he had a vision of the worlds of the Hunter Motor Traction and Automobile Company growing in size and importance till they covered a hundred acres, and of millions of motors they would turn out, and of the great collection of pictures he would form which should beat anything they had in New York.

Bateman Hunter successfully accomplishes his wife hunt. Isabel is not a beauty he wishes to possess, but her dowry is the real magnetic force that draws him to her. He exchanges his freedom and bachelorhood for "Hunter Motor Traction and Automobile Co.", and other possible successful economic ventures. Holding Isabel in his arms, he actually holds keys to economic success. Maugham's semiotic plot is very simple:

98 *Semiotics of Misogyny*

he	marriage	Hunter Automobile Co., 100 acres of land millions of motors expensive art collection high material culture
she	marriage	sex dinners & dances entertainment

Like Chekhov's Anna, Maugham's Isabel is a sign of Power that causes a poor man's social metamorphosis and allows him to ascend and reach a level where he himself may produce signs and influence the traditional **economic exchange**.

Anna is valuable as a means of social upward mobility. By entering into an intimate relationship with a female body he, a male, begins to relate to something else, the "body politic" or the societal body of the complex interchange between signs and its producers.[57] Her body is a symbolic intermediate step on the man's passage from Nature to Culture:

he	Body	Body Politic
	Her	
	Nature = Culture	

Most of his men marry, but they seem to be doing it for reasons other than the traditional myth implies; they marry not because they are attracted to female bodies. They marry because they are attracted to the **semiotic value** of their chosen females who may help them to achieve prosperity. Under ordinary circumstances, Maugham's men fly away from marriage and from females whom they fear enormously. This behavior of his fictional characters recreates and revives the actual male anxieties exhibited by Kaulong men of Papua New Guinea who "are quite literally scared to death of marriage (and sex)" (J. Goodale, 1980: 133).[58] Kaulong males postpone intercourse and try to marry in their older days when they are ready to die. In the traditional mythical consciousness of the tribe, women are actual killers of men; Cannibalism practised among them is described as female ritual. Fear of being eaten by a woman underlies the perpetuated male anxiety. Maugham who travelled extensively and lived in the Pacific for some time might have been familiar with cultural myths of Micronesia, Australia and other tribes of the region.

For instance, Fred Manson ("Episode") prefers to stay in prison rather than marry his devoted fiancée who did not abandon him during his imprisonment and even went against her family. She, a woman of education, falls in love with Fred, a postman. He seems to be much enamored of her and they decide to marry. Gracie's family, working-class people, who tried to educate their daughter definitely prefer a "gentleman"; Fred, a postman, is not exactly the son-in-law they pictured for Gracie. The story of their love turns out to be a tragic repetition of the archetypal sacrifice on the part of the loving woman. She abandons her lectures in London and a teaching career, leaves her parents and works in a lingerie department while Fred, her beloved, serves a prison term for theft:[59]

> Fred was arrested for stealing money from the letters he collected.

The sentence and prison term does not make Gracie change her mind. She is convinced that Fred's deep love caused him to commit the crime:[60]

> He only did it because he wanted to give me a good time.

She remains devoted to her lover, visits him daily in prison, saves every penny for their future marriage and patiently waits for his release. When this day is about to come the man who before wanted to marry Gracie so much suddenly falls into depression and tells his friends that he has changed his mind. His fellow prisoners are bewildered:[61]

> "You can't let her down now. Her people have thrown her out. She's been working all this time to get a home ready for you. She's got the licence and everything."
> "I don't care, I'm not going to marry her".
> "But why, why, why?"

Fred cannot explain this unexpected change of heart. He even falls ill, but he is determined not to marry:[62]

> "I'll tell you, I've thought about her night and day for eighteen months and now I'm sick to death of her."

His friends did not want to believe Fred, until he finally announced his decision through a messenger. Gracie is devastated:[63]

> "There's nothing for me to do now but put my head in the gas-oven," she said.
> And she did.

Maugham concludes with a happy end to his story. His male is saved, and, instead of the expected feared symbolic killing or destruction of man in marriage, the woman is killed. Her head is in the oven. The archetypal symbolic cannibalism is reversed:

Maugham's myth and fictional ritual

> woman's head in the oven
> woman is killed
> ready to be eaten by males

Kaulong myth and tradition

> man's head is roasted in fire
> male is killed
> eaten by females

Fred, the intended sacrificial victim, escapes his destiny, saves his life and avoids the expected ritual. Maugham's fictional male is the victor in the traditional male-female encounter which was supposed to end in a cannibalistic ritual, the killing of a man through a **symbolic act**.

Gracie's "head in the oven" signifies the fulfillment of the misogynist desire, victory over the alleged female aggression. She is punished for her attempt to marry Fred. She is punished before the feared intercourse takes place. Much like in Kaulong culture, sexual intercourse is "intensely polluting for" Maugham's fictional males. Escaping it the male is saved from danger, pollution and death. (Goodale, 1980: 134).[64]

The same phobia is experienced by George (*Mabel*). He has not seen his fiancée for seven years; finally, their marriage which was delayed for various family and business circumstances can take place. However, when George receives a cable from Mabel who is supposed to join him in Rangoon strange emotions overwhelm him:[65]

> Then, suddenly, without warning, his nerve failed him. He had not seen Mabel for seven years. He had forgotten what she was like. She was a total stranger. He felt a terrible sinking in the pit of his stomach and his knees began to wobble. He could not go through with it.

His emotions are not considerations of heart, reasoning or doubts, it is the physical fear of a trapped animal. Mabel's cable is a **signal of coming danger**, it is the fear of being killed by a female since marriage and sexual intercourse with a woman are bound to destroy man.[66] His first impulse was to respond negatively:[67]

> But how could a man tell a girl a thing like that when she had been engaged to him for seven years and had come six thousand miles to marry him?

George decides to write and postpone the dreaded event. In the meantime he takes a ship to Singapore; then he desperately seeks refuge in Bangkok, Saigon, Manila, Shanghai. George is restless, his travel is a frantic flight from imminent danger. He flees from Mabel like a war refugee, apprehensive lion or a Kaulong man. He runs away to those places where a journey would be out of the question for a woman:[68]

> He went to Hankow and from Hankow to Ichang, he changed boats here and from Ichang through the rapids went to Chungking. But he was desperate now, he was not going to take any risks. There was a place called Cheng-tu, the capital of Szechuan, and it was four hundred miles away. It could only be reached by road and the road was infested with brigands. A man would be safe there.

Finally, when George reaches Tibet and rests peacefully there Mabel steps out one day:[69]

> Hullo George, I was so afraid I'd missed you again.

Mabel signifies the **omnipotent sign** or the sign of the highest **semiovalence**. She overcomes distance, physical danger, time and male desperate efforts to find refuge. She is invincible. Her power is demonic, mysterious, the Other force which enters man's universe with the desire to possess and destroy the male:[70]

> "I'm ready to marry him as soon as I've had a bath," and she did.

Thus Maugham concludes the "sad" story of unsuccessful flight. Mabel happens to be more powerful than the rivers, mountains, and forests of Asia, the rains of the Pacific. She crosses the globe, pursues her victim and eventually achieves her goal.

Maugham's Mabel is at the crossroads between Nature and Culture. She conquers Nature and subdues Culture. She stands above and controls both of them:

	Mabel	
	Woman	
Nature		Culture
Mountains		Transport
Rivers		Communication
Time		Customs
Weather		Government
Vigorous		laws
	Man	

Her vigorous hunt ultimately endorses her power to own, possess and "torture" her victim, a powerless weak male who is unable to escape.

CHAPTER FOUR

Women, Their Semiotic Value

4.1 Women as Symbols of Inferiority

> Everywhere, in every known culture, women are considered in some degree inferior to men.
> Sherry Ortner "Is Female to Male as Nature is to Culture?"

Dean MacCannell and Juliet F. MacCannell (1982:6) view culture as a multilayered semiotic structure where certain signs remain more or less constant while others undergo metamorphosis in time.[1] They pay significant attention to the so-called stereotypes or more or less stable cultural associations which may be observed in the course of the ongoing process of cultural production. Much like "Russians continue to have soul," blacks are inferior, Jews are crooked, women are less intelligent, "they are still believed to be incapable of abstract, theoretical thought" (1982:8).[2] Despite the fact that these two authors basically address the problematics of modern culture within the North American context, their summary of the cultural semiosis may be extended to culture in its broadest definition. The ranking and debunking of women as producers of signs is not limited to their immediate cultural milieu, but is rather indicative of a common cultural trend. If two modern semioticians state this cultural inequality, the two writers, Maugham and Chekhov, demonstrate how biased cultural values are produced.

Maugham and Chekhov, products of the gender-biased culture, have a natural obligation to the cultural tradition that produced them. They pay their cultural tribute by the fictional worlds they create which reaffirm the existing cultural values. Their texts are parts of a larger text, their utterances add to the discourse at large.[3] They say what is expected, what had been repeatedly said before them, and what their readers may be pleased to hear, namely, that a woman is intellectually inferior to a man.

The motif of female inferiority is the **semiotic constant** in their fictional world and a sign of the Other, the real world of signs where women are mainly excluded from the semiotic production. The two writers as producers and supporters of the existing signs, the accepted system of semiotic production, are entrusted with the mission of making certain signs more visible than others. Emphasis upon these selected signs, cultural values and popular stereotypes, is an act of **semiotic loyalty** to the culture and community which produced this semiotic product. The writers are free to choose their fictional worlds, but not free to abandon all the icons and signs of the reality. "The Empire" of the real signs rules and dictates the interactions inside the other signs, fictional worlds. Being programmed by culture to believe in female inferiority, Maugham and Chekhov, like any other writer, convey the existing cultural stereotype to their readers. To fulfil the desire of the reader, cultural community and the **semiotic imperative** of the cultural past, they have to revive the familiar sign:

woman = silly creature

The classical stereotype in Maugham is the young Lisette, a model from the story "Appearance and Reality." The readers who know, expect and crave for the familiar sign get it with the condescending portrait of Lisette:[4]

> Though Lisette was a philosopher only in the sense in which we are all philosophers that she exercised thought in dealing with the problems of existence, her feeling for reality was so strong and her sympathy for appearance so genuine that she might almost claim to have established that reconciliation of irreconcilables at which the philosophers have for so many centuries been aiming. Lisette was French, and she passed several hours of every working day dressing and undressing herself at one of the most expensive and fashionable establishments in Paris.

The reference "philosopher" is a paradoxical sign of the opposite:

  he = clever philosopher   she = idiot

The end of the passage discloses the intended meaning:[5]

> A pleasant occupation for a young woman who was well aware that she had a lovely figure. She was in short a mannequin.

Maugham recreates the expected opposition between the two genders:

    Man = philosopher = thinking being
    Woman = mannequin = unthinking, incapable of thought

Female stupidity in Maugham's view, could be even fatal as in the case of Marie-Louise, who also happens to be French and "stupid," so stupid that her husband kills her:[6]

> He knew now that she was terribly stupid. But of course, she was not to blame for that, she was not to blame.

Eventually, her stupidity bores him so much that he breaks her skull. The crime is committed over a very innocent exchange of words:[7]

> She put down her brushes and began to powder her face. She gave a nasty little laugh "What are you laughing at?" I asked.
>
> "Madame Renard, that was the same dress she wore at our wedding. She'd had it dyed and done over; but it didn't deceive me. I'd have known it anywhere."
>
> It was such a stupid remark, it infuriated me. I was seized with rage, and with all my might I hit her over the head with my Indian club. I broke her skull apparently, and she died two days later in hospital without recovering consciousness.

The semiosis thus created evolved in the following way:

   She = a creature of a different race, the Other
   She = stupid, unlike man
   She = deserves to be killed for her stupidity
   He = intelligent
   He = victim of female stupidity
   He - kills in self defence

If Chekhov "kills" his female characters in humorous stories, shielding the misogynist meaning with humorous narration, Maugham appeals to the notions of truth and verisimilitude. The confession is made by a prisoner and the story claims to be the real fiction. The author appeals to the actual experience and the readers' knowledge of this experiential world which may sometimes appear more improbable than a fictional universe may allow:[8]

> I know that this is a fantastic story; I am by way of being a realist, and in the stories I write I seek verisimilitude. I eschew the bizarre as scrupulously as to avoid the whimsical. If this had been a tale that I was inventing I would certainly have made it more probable.

Aware of the effect of the allegedly true bizarre story, Maugham – the narrator retreats into the cocoon of doubt. He cautions the reader that the story told should not be taken at its face value:[9]

> As it is, unless I had heard it with my own ears I am not sure that I should believe it. I do not know whether Jean Charoin told me the truth, and yet the words with which he closed his final visit to me had a convincing ring.

Nonetheless, the suggestion that the plot may be real carries a very dangerous message to the reader:

A stupid woman could be killed by a man.

Although the woman is not named other than stupid, the inner semiosis that takes place justifies the killing:

$$\text{She} = \text{stupid} = \text{killed} = \text{as a rodent}$$
$$\text{She} = \text{animal}$$
$$\text{She} = \text{has to be killed}$$

The message about female lack of intelligence here echoes visible zoological allusions, so much used in Maugham's discourse about women. Women - mannequins, women - incessant small talkers or merely stupid are the signs in their "dynamic phase," which evolved from the introductory zoo-signals such as "she was mouse-like; "there was something grey and mouse-like in her appearance which Peirce would have classified as signs in their firstness".[10]

Maugham's semiotic plot evolves within the Peircean triad. However, a certain replacement takes place. What appears as an intermediate stage in Peirce is the final semiotic phase in Maugham. The given, "something there," is the semi-fictional, semi-real product, the consequence of Maugham's distribution of signs. Having presented women as rodents or mannequins, he finds it very easy to justify their killed. The seemingly arbitrary signs are in fact logical consequences of the **semiotic intention** or disclosures of the suppressed aggression. Is it Maugham's individual idiosyncrasy or a symptom of a far more serious suppressed collective aggression which is not even hidden deeply in one's subconscious, but rather easily identified through the familiar semiotic code?

Chekhov's theory of sexual authority expressed outside his fictional world, and his misogyny inside this fictional universe support the archetypal myth about female inferiority which has become a real cultural universe. Like Maugham and many others before him, Chekhov exploits the familiar stereotype which has become almost iconic in most cultural traditions. The author similarly reconstructs this ancient stereotype, the myth about female inferiority, addressing a Russian audience at the beginning of this century. The most explicit repetition of cultural sacred profanity is found in his story *O Zenshchinakh* (About Women). Chekhov reiterates what has been established as undisputable truth by the old culture, namely, that women are basically useless in society except for their biological function, reproduction of males. Much like modern semiotician Umberto Eco, Chekhov chooses to pay attention only to the procreation of male species:[11]

> A woman is of no use to the Fatherland. She does not go to war, does not copy documents, does not build railroads, while hiding vodka in the cupboard she actually negatively affects the taxes.
>
> In short, she is shy, talkative, superstitious, petty, hypocritical, phony, stupid, flippant, profit-seeking and malicious. The only nice thing about her is that she produces such charming, gracious and terribly clever souls like men . . . For this virtue alone, let us forgive her her sins.

Chekhov repeats the old nickname which had been given to women long ago, the sign which had been constructed for centuries is represented anew:[12]

> Insignificance is her name!

The author states this, absolutely confidently expecting the approving laughter of the male reading audience. He reinforces the emblem of ignorance to the delight of his male readers who may have been amused again by the true portrait of their mothers, wives, mistresses, sisters and aunts. According to Chekhov, their mind is "no good":[13]

> She has long hair and small brain, while with a man it is the other way around. One can discuss neither ranks nor politics, currency rate with a woman. While the grader already solves world problems and college registrar officers study Book 3,000 of foreign words, clever and adult women discuss only fashions and military men.

The portrait of a woman drawn by Chekhov is highly ironic. It is a powerful caricature, but it is a desirable image, the expected picture of the opposite sex based on the legitimization of inequality and sexual polarity. Certain comic details concerning males simply support the main caricature. They are the semiotic background.

The prevailing signal – women are inferior – dominates Chekhov's discourse. He takes advantage of the familiar popular male mythology which is based on the idea of male gender supremacy and division of functions in the traditional culture:

he	she
creator of culture	producer of the human race
writes	wraps pastries in his writings

While proving female lack of intelligence, Chekhov introduces another fictional category, Man-idiot, whom he places also higher than a woman:[14]

> Men, even if they are idiots and cretins, may not only study, but may occupy university chairs, while women have only one name-insignificance.

In his semiotic universe this category is needed to lower the already low status of a woman:

>   he
>   creator of culture
>   consumer of culture
>   she
>   undermines Culture
>   asserts Nature

In the world of popular mythology a woman is incapable of being either a producer or a consumer of culture. "All the efforts to civilize a female are useless," – such is the semiotic case of the popular myths and Chekhov returns the same message to the expectant popular reader – consumer of these peculiar humorous stories.

In the story *Zinochka* (Little Zina) (1887) he depicts a little governess who is presumably an advocate of education and culture. Nonetheless, the little governess is still a walking ignorance. Apparently, the only thing she remembers from Chemistry is that "carbon dioxide is in mineral water and samovar smoke." She also repeats the scientific myth about the Dogs' Cave where even dogs suffocate once they enter it. The deadly cave is known to be near Naples, and his Zinochka is at least aware of the familiar tale, since none of the governesses go a step farther than this chemical wisdom. To emphasize her ignorance, Chekhov writes:[15]

> Zinoshka always passionately defended the usefulness of the natural sciences, but she hardly knew in chemistry anything more than this cave.

Even when Chekhov's women are portrayed as participants in Culture, they are usually unsuccessful, like this pitiful governess Zinochka. Chekhov mediates a common and shared sense of vexation when women dare to assume duties which lie beyond their natural and sole function – to "produce intelligent nice males."

Chekhov accepts women in their natural, i.e. passive state. He gives preference to Olen'ka from the story *Dushechka* (The Little Soul) which Barbara Heldt renders in English as "The Darling".[16] In Heldt's view,

Chekhov does not like this passive female, the vessel of love, lacking her own identity and living through her males and their social, cultural interests and functions. "Tolstoy and others may have liked Olen'ka, but Chekhov did not,"–she concludes in her chapter entitled "Woman is Everywhere Passive." (55).

In fact, my contention would be just the opposite. Chekhov prefers silly, helpless Olen'ka who does not have her own opinions and merely repeats the standard pronouncements of her three husbands. Her first husband was a theatre manager who used to say that "audience needs a circus," and that "it does not appreciate real art." Olen'ka would say the same. Married to a lumber-man, the "little soul" is worried about the problems of the lumber trade. Being in love with the veterinarian, she is concerned about the diseases that affect the animals. Having no interests, no intellectual occupation and no thoughts of her own, little Olen'ka mirrors the cultural world of the man she loves. The three lovers who eventually die symbolize the Other world which this female of limited intellectual capacity is unable to grasp. The triad of dead representatives of culture is used to emphasize how foreign this woman, a symbol of nature, is to the man's world. The three different occupations may stand for three major divisions of culture-Art, Industry and Medicine which Olen'ka's three husbands symbolically represent:

Kukin	Pustovalov	Vladimir
theatre manager	lumber house manager	veterinarian
Art	Industry	Medicine

and which are all foreign to her as a woman.

The utmost comic element of the situation reveals itself when, at the end, Olen'ka transfers her entire love upon the veterinarian's son, a ten-year-old Sasha whose interests she then shares and even adopts his childish vocabulary. Chekhov depicts a loving soul whose unused maternal instincts now find a natural outlet. Heldt maintains that Olen'ka's relationship with the little boy "has some impure overtones" (55). But it seems that Chekhov deliberately created such an atmosphere to prove to his readers again that a woman, sinful by nature, is incapable of producing her own signs and may simply be consumed in culture created by a male, be it an adult lover or a child of male gender. Although Sasha is not Olen'ka's own son, her feelings for the boy are very deep. Her natural longing for a child is satisfied, proving the main thrust in Chekhov's sexual theory, that a woman is only good in her natural biological capacity of a loving mother: This is how he proves his point:[17]

> Olen'ka talked to him, gave him tea, and her heart in her bosom suddenly became so warm and sweetly shrank as if this young boy was her natural son.

Olen'ka apparently lost all thought after her husbands died and her lover returned to his wife. This little boy became another source of new thought, a little source of culture:[18]

> My sweetheart, my little beautiful prince. My little child, what a clever and handsome little creature you were born.
>
> -A part of the land surrounded by water on all sides is called an island – he would read.
>
> -An island is called . . . she would repeat, and this was her first opinion after so many years of silence and emptiness in thoughts.

The semiotic message of Chekhov's story reaches its climax when the ten-year-old boy is shown to be intellectually superior to Olen'ka. Olen'ka occupies the lowest place on the scale of human intellectual achievements. She is not only below males in Art, Industry and Science but also below a male child in his early stage of development:

```
            Male
   Kukin    Male
            Pustovalov   Male
                         Vladimir    young male
                                     Sasha
                                                  Olga
                                                  Women
```

112 *Semiotics of Misogyny*

According to Chekhov, woman again is totally useless. Even this son was not produced by her. Chekhov takes away from his female character her most sacred and her only useful function. His Olen'ka merely consumes the child's wisdom, being unable to produce her own signs of Culture. In fact, she proves to be significant for neither Nature nor for Culture. "The Little Soul" symbolizes a thing which society can do without on the one hand, while on the other, she is needed to prove the importance of other women who reproduce males, producers of Culture.

Robert Hodge and Gunther Kress define "texts as social objects," and agree that "the production of texts involves social processes" (1988:160). The texts created after a long tradition of other texts incorporate not only other texts, but the social processes which were initially involved in their production. Thus, literary texts of the end of the past century and the beginning of this one are **social objects** of a very **intense semiotic value** having incorporated numerous other objects of the past. In the case of Maugham and Chekhov their texts share the most basic textual component, the archetypal text which established female inferiority long ago. Their new texts, new social objects so to speak, have deep discursive roots going back to the most ancient times, ancient human consciousness and archetypal myth which is at the basis of their textual production. There is a consensus among contemporary anthropologists, philosophers, literary critics, ethnographers, historians, psychologists and artists that "the secondary status of women is one of the true universals" (Ortner, 1974: 67).[19] All languages, and texts produced in those languages, reflect the Otherness of women, their subordinate position and segregation not only predetermined by their physical otherness, "biological determinism," but by the low evaluation of their mental faculties, their intellectual inferiority. The entire series of texts produced by mankind, including the Bible, Babylonian myths, Chinese folklore and Hindu tales carry the same message about female otherness, primitive nature, child like mentality and ultimately limited societal performance.

The story of woman's genesis represented in ancient mythology, such as Babylonian, Assyrian, Sumerian, Egyptian and finally Hebrew and Aramaic speaks of female secondariness, lesser significance. The archetypal

Eve made out of Adam's rib is, perhaps the best mythical DNA containing the entire program of the later discursive variations that mediate the same message, the ancient signifier of the older signifieds or the prototype of the older dynamic signs of the **similar semiotic valence**. Each new text was another system of signs which incorporated this nearly genetic semiotic code that devalued woman's intellectual capacity. In this respect Chekhov's and Maugham's texts are similar, identical social objects which reproduce the same archetypal text, meaning and sign. They continue to pursue the same policy of excluding women from the **valuable semiosis**, the truly significant production of signs.

Most of Maugham's women are presented as "stupid," intellectually deficient, narrow-minded beings who are simply not even interested in culture, nor in the production of complex signs other than those connected with their primitive significance through Sex, Libido and Procreation. For instance, Mrs. Davidson, the missionary's wife *(Rain)* has the "expression of foolishness," allusion to a sheep implies her stupidity. Maugham wonders in the story *The Wash Tub* that his female characters, American women, "can even read." Marie-Louise, a French woman, was terribly stupid *(A Man with a Conscience)*. So was Millicent Skinner, the English lady who slept while her husband Harold "spent an hour or two learning Malay" *(Before the Party*, vol. 1, 392, 1952 ed). "Women are simply bloody," concludes the consul *(The Consul*, 960, vol. 2, 1952 ed). The three fat women obsessed with their weight, lionlike appetite and food are no more than slaves of their own stomachs *(The Three Fat Women of Antibes*, 184-198, vol. 1, 1952 ed.). However, if this gallery of funny, animal-like silly creatures is merely a nuisance in the male universe and on his territory delineated by culture and **culture-oriented signs**, there are some other women whose stupidity is much more dangerous. These are women who are stupid patriots and women-spies. Maugham's Julia Lazari, a Spanish dancer who danced "in London, Birmingham, Portsmouth and other places" happens to be also a spy. (*"Julia Lazari*," 762, vol. 2, 1952 ed.). Nonetheless, she reveals her total inappropriateness in this role which requires male intelligence. For instance, she makes such silly mistakes as "slips a hundred franks" into the officer's hands for her release when she is once caught for espionage. Here Maugham pronounces his harsh verdict:[20]

> She must be a stupider woman than I thought," said Ashenden.

Moreover, this inapt spy cannot even spell or write a letter properly:[21]

> She hesitated an instant, but then wrote as he directed. "How do you spell, absolutely?" "As you like. Now address the envelope and I will relieve you of my unwelcome presence".

Another spy character is Miss Caypor from the story *The Traitor*, she is the newer sign among the archetypal women. Mrs. Caypor is German, educated at Heidelberg, a "woman of character," possessing "Teutonic superiority", becoming the icon of Germany:[22]

> It was not hard to see that her attitude was definitely hostile. It put Ashender at his ease. She was a plainish woman, nearing forty, with a muddy skin and vague features; her drab hair was arranged in a plait round her head like that of Napoleon's Queen of Prussia; and she was squarely built, plump rather than fat, and solid.

This "Queen of Prussia did not look stupid," as Maugham puts it, but he eventually proves that in fact she was. Her fanatic patriotism was on the verge of stupidity and irrationality. Her obsession with things that are solely German made her even dangerous:[23]

> Her ideal was a German world in which the rest of the nations under a hegemony greater than that of Rome should enjoy the benefits of German science and German art and German culture.

She stands for the stupidity of arrogance, blind belief and ignorance of a stereotype. Although she is a walking icon of Germany she is primarily an inferior female. As a spy she is detected by another male spy and is under constant surveillance. Her failure as a spy is her failure as a woman who is in the wrong position. She is an invader in the male "Empire of Signs."

There is a double semiosis in this story. Aside from the traditional debunking of a woman, her mental faculties and the archetypal inferiority myth, Maugham subverts Nietzschean male-female polarity. If Nietzsche used the feminine allusion in his low characterization of the non-Aryan, or non-German nations, Maugham here destroyed the **semiotic balance** created by Nietzsche to justify his dream about the Dionysean universe.[24]

When Nietzsche writes the Semitic and Aryan myths he associates the myth of the Fall with repugnant, inferior femininity:[25]

> Semitic myth of the fall – a myth that exhibits curiosity, deception, suggestibility, concupiscence – in short a whole series of principally feminine faculties, at the root of all evil.

On the other hand, the legend of Prometheus (a male) is granted equal importance for the Aryan people:[26]

> In fact, it is not improbable that this myth has the same characteristic importance for the Aryan mind as the myth of the Fall for the semitic.

Thus, Nietzsche proposes his anthropological theory of races, cultures and myths using the archetypal universal myth about female inferiority. In his typological system based on the familiar false proposition that there is archetypal gender and sex polarity:

male	female
high	low
culture	nature
civilization	barbarian
aryan	semitic
Prometheus	Christ
Hellenic	Judaic

Much as culture has accepted inferiority of female gender it has to accept the Nietzschean concept of semitic primitivism. Historical experience of this century has demonstrated the gullibility of the masses and how easily people become convinced that this classification of myths and cultures may be right. It was too flattering for German fascists to be perceived as the followers of the Hellenic mythical hero. The male, superior, iconic myth of Prometheus seduced many civilized Europeans of both sexes. The archetype of the most

116 Semiotics of Misogyny

ancient origin and highest semiotic valence exhibited its utmost demonic power when thousands embraced the concept of Aryan superiority.

Maugham, a post-Freudian, a post-Nietzschean and post-fascist, writer who reflected upon the past mythical consciousness in his own peculiar way. He dispensed with the idea of Teutonic superiority after the defeat of the Germans in the Second World War. However, he argued symbolically with Nietzsche as he had rejected the basic Nietzschean proposition. In his case, the Aryan race is associated with the feminine – Mrs. Caypor, the icon of Germany and a Teutonic symbol, is presented as a failure.

Maugham moves far ahead of Nietsche. He expands the universe of the inferior to include most of humanity. Everything that is negative, biased, narrow-minded, every evil among all the nations and people is of a female origin. It is the archetypal women who is the evil both for the people of Prometheus, and for Christ, Germany and Russia, England and China, France and Samoa, Spain and Japan. It is the woman as the universal demonic force whom Maugham condemns, despises, judges, mocks and attempts to isolate from the entire human universe. He fears that Nietzschean prophecy may come true and:[27]

> All that is now called culture, education, civilization will one day have to appear before the incorruptible judge, Dionysos.

Perhaps, Maugham intuitively felt what Nietsche did not mean by his sermon. If Nietzsche was fearful of the invasion of the inferior, foreign, non-Aryan "element" among the Teutonic race of Prometheus, Maugham knew who Dionysos actually was.

Maugham, a writer, and not a philosopher was perhaps more familiar with Greek ancient literature, history and mythology. He knew that Dionisos whose coming Nietzsche predicted was not the god of wine, celebration and festival, but that he was the God of women of Nijsa, the fairyland whose God *Dio* was Dionysos (Otto, 1915;61).[28] And thus he was the god of the feared, evil part of the human race whose coming he was not willing to hail.

Maugham could not embrace Nietzsche and the coming of Dionysos, as he sensed this god was not his. William Otto exactly described the causes of such pathological fear and anxiety:[29]

> We should never forget that the Dionysiac world is, above all, a world of women. Women awaken Dionysos and bring him up. Women accompany him. Wherever he is women await him and are the first ones to be overcome by his madness.

Ancient Dionysos is associated with feminine madness and desire to castrate man, deprive him of his power. Maugham experiences Dionysian anxiety while he speaks of female inferiority. By analogy with Nietzsche, he fears Aryan woman as much as any other because of the symbolic archetypal power she possesses. Maugham's subtextual prophecy may be read like this:

> Damned be the day when the judge Dionysos, the female god will come and mutilate the weak representatives of culture.

4.2 Pink Stocking as an Icon of a Female

> You can't send a girl into the drawing-room repeating the multiplication table.
> A Victorian mother.
> A sign is said to be iconic when "there is a topological similarity between a signifier and its denotata; examples, painting an algebraic formula."
> Thomas Sebeok, *Contribution to the Doctrine of Signs*.

Most of Chekhov's women are signs of Nature rather than Culture. They are the biological beings of inferior capacities who are unable to produce or grasp signs created by the opposite sex. Chekhov's semiotic message to the readers as to the function of women is summarized in the icon **Pink Stocking**, from the story under the same title (1886). Chekhovian **neometonymy** derives from the well known "blue stocking" which was associated with a "woman of much learning but little charm" (M. Phillips, W. Tomlinson, 1926: 247).[30] Chekhovian semiotic neologism acquires even more forcefulness and subversive strength if one recalls the origins of **protoicon-Blue Stocking**.

118 *Semiotics of Misogyny*

According to M. Phillips, and W. Tomkinson, "the wearer of the original blue stockings was Benjamin Stillingflee, botanist, athlete, verse maker, and conversationalist" (247).[31] Eventually the "title" served well both men and women and stood for their intelligence, art of conversation and capacity for learning. Later it became restricted to women who "were well-informed but ill dressed." They were the ones who paved the way to education for other women. They fought for the right of women to be educated. As the same authors put it:[32]

> We ourselves owe no small debt to the blue stockings. They made life a larger thing for women. They gave ample proof, and at a time when it was badly needed, that women were worthy of education, and although it was left for a later generation to devise an education more worthy of women, it was the blue stockings who first blazed the trail.

The familiar icon "blue stocking" is the precise antithesis to Chekhovian neologism whose semiotic effect ("pink stocking") is achieved through the strong semantic opposition. The newly created icon is the precise opposite of the old which is constructed on the two levels:

a) purely visual:

pink versus **blue**

b) associational:

blue stocking	**pink stocking**
female intelligence	female stupidity
capacity for learning	lack of learning
need to be educated	no need to be educated
lack of charm	charm
spiritual	physical

With the semiotic rhetoric of the visible, powerful signal Chekhov challenges the efforts of men and women directed at affirmation of women's rights. He defies the message of "blue stockings," as well as the established associations around the concept itself. His "pink stocking" is an icon in defiance of the women's movement and their achievements in the area of educating women. It is his response to the Russian "blue stockings" and their feminist efforts which Chekhov deliberately ignores and attacks with his seemingly innocent "pink stocking."

His "pink stocking" appeared after various women's clubs and societies sprang up around Russia and drew public attention to women's social worth and the improvement of their lot. By the time Chekhov was ready to take off "blue stockings" from Russian women, there were already great numbers of them who were educated and who actively participated in society. In 1863 a women's publishing cooperative was organized to coordinate the efforts of women engaged in publishing, translation, editing and journalism. Russian feminists achieved their greatest victory by 1870, having won the battle for higher education of women. At the same time numerous Russian enthusiasts flocked to Switzerland where they studied Law, Medicine and History. Women's graduate courses were organized in major Russian cities (Stites, 1978: 82).[33] The names of such women as Kovalevskaya, Suslova, Figner, Likhacheva, Konradi among others must have been known to Chekhov. Entire intellectual Russia was obsessed with the ideas of emancipation inspired by George Sand, John Stuart Mill and Chernyshevsky's Vera Pavlovna. The question on the Russian intellectual agenda was not whether or not to educate women, but how, and Chekhov's unexpected response was his subversive "Pink Stocking" which denounced the entire generation of Russian and Western feminists and their cause. The story reiterated the myth of the old culture:[34]

> Her calling is, let us say to love her husband, give birth to children and cut salads. Why the dickens does she need knowledge?

Chekhov returns the archetypal popular myth to its original producer – the male part of the crowd that had kept women at a distance from the domain of culture and education. To their delight Chekhov recreates the desired expected stereotypical female who is incapable of writing even a simple letter.

Mme Somova, "a pretty little dame in a light blouse and pink stockings" struggles with a letter to her sister on a grey rainy day. Her bored husband, having nothing to do until the next meal, expresses curiosity and reads his wife's letter. While reading the six-page letter his face changes. Somov's reaction to the letter written by a "pink stocking" undergoes various stages: from curious interest, surprise, confusion to bewilderment and even fear. Finally, Somov expresses verbally the meaning of his facial signs:[35]

> – No, this is impossible! he mumbles having finished reading and hurling the letter on the floor.
> – It is absolutely impossible!
> – What is the matter? frightened Lidochka asks.
> – What "is" the matter! You have wasted six pages, killed two hours on writing and to no avail! At least one thought? One reads and reads and reaches delirium, as if from deciphering Chinese, gibberish on tea cups! Eh!

Poor authoress Lidochka pleads ignorance of grammar and lack of attention while Somov, and simultaneously, all of Chekhov's male reading audience obtain the utmost pleasure. Lidochka is exposed in her sheer ineptitude as "a pink stocking," the parallel anti-symbol of the traditional "blue stocking." Lidochka has the charm, physical attractiveness, but possesses neither intelligence nor primitive literacy. This charming intellectual cripple attains her culminating point of ridiculousness when Chekhov permits Somov to disclose the paradox of her social origin:[36]

> By the way you belong to an educated intellectual circle, you are the wife of a university graduate, a general's daughter! Sister, have you studied anywhere?
> - of course, I did. I graduated from Von Moeubke's boarding school . . .

This embarrassing disclosure of Lidochkas social standing intensifies the point Chekhov is trying to make, that education of females is totally useless, if the general's daughter and the wife of a college graduate cannot write a simple letter. The concept of wastefulness permeates the story. Chekhov uses the keywords, key signs which allude to futility of educating females:

Von Moeubke's boarding school
rubbish
words and no meaning
wasted six pages
Chinese gibberish on tea cups

The name of the boarding school is German which gives the readers the idea of an expensive educational institution, in fact, the best perhaps in 19th century Russia run by a more advanced Westerner. It sends the message about the financial losses of educating a hopeless "pink stocking" whom even Von Moeubke cannot teach to write a letter. Chekhov attacks the Russian feminists with his graphic icon "pink stocking." The angry message stands between the two signs denoting foreignness:

Von Moeubke	Chinese
German	teacups gibberish
progressive	backward
clear	obscure
source of enlightment	symbol of darkness

no matter what
Lidochkas remain pink stockings

The author, a contemporary of the women's movement and rising female awareness among Russian women, stubbornly clings to the comfortable past, the kingdom of lace, drawing rooms, teacups and pink stockings. He sends a comforting message to the angry, bewildered male crowd frightened by the new woman, an educated articulate being, a "blue stocking," Chekhov, a "wise doctor," cures the anxiety of the male audience with a **soothing sign**:

pink stocking

as if saying, that despite the painstaking efforts to educate the primitive sex they would still remain "pink stockings," meaning pretty, petty, ignorant, illiterate, inept, and socially maladjusted. The "pink stockings," in his view will always need the protection and guidance of the traditional rulers of society. Chekhov comforts the apprehensive male audience whose anxiety and fear are proven to be groundless. The convinced misogynist in the face of **blue stockings**, Chekhov mediates his firm belief that the world will never be run by them, that the Old Order or the Grammar of the Old Culture will never be violated. The soothing pink color of primitive Lidochka's stockings is Chekhov's cure for the common male anxiety in the face of rising feminism. "Pink Stocking" gives hope to the myth producers, Chekhov provides this secure old world of dinners, salads and comforting pink amidst

122 Semiotics of Misogyny

nonsense and gibberish. The writer tries to convince himself and his male readership that, after all, biology and biological destiny will prevail.

At the same time the story about the primitive "pink stocking" is a hymn to the woman, a sign of the past. Chekhov conducts a humorous debate with feminists and male supporters of women's' education. He temporarily accepts their argument and realizes the problem of ignorant females:[37]

> How will you teach children if you do not know anything yourself?

But within one phrase Chekhov destroys this argument:[38]

> The hell with knowledge. Knowledge can be obtained by children even at school.

The benefit of educating a future mother outweighs the danger of producing a "blue stocking," a really dangerous species for society.[39]

> What is good in being a blue stocking? Blue stocking – this is devil knows what! Neither a woman nor a man, something in between, neither fish nor fowl. I hate blue stockings! I would never have married an educated one...

Instead, Chekhov offers a "pink stocking," charming, illiterate Lidochka:[40]

> Under the influence of vodka and a sumptuous dinner, Somov grows merrier, kinder and softer. He watches his pretty wife, who with a concerned look on her face, is preparing his salad, and a passion of woman loving, leniency and all-forgiveness flows upon him...

Chekhov proves the advantages of marrying "pink stockings", versus "blue stockings": His Somov recalls:[41]

> how demanding clever women are, difficult in general, strict and unyielding and how easy in contrast it is to live with a stupid little Lidochka who does not interfere anywhere, does not understand many things and does not bother with criticism. It is peaceful with Lidochka and one does not risk to be controlled.

A shrewed manipulator of the sexes offers to the male audience two female types:

I	II
blue stocking	*pink stocking*
clever	stupid
demanding	meek
critical of males	approving of males
unyielding	agreeable
difficult	easy
traumatic	peaceful
dangerous	healthy

He leads the confused anxious male to the comfortable choice of Lidochka, the "pink stocking," the source of health, long and peaceful life. Unsure if his readers will choose M-me Somova as the paragon of ideal marriage material. Chekhov turns into a pink stocking guru, promoter of *dolce vita con* Lidochka:[42]

> Forget about those clever and educated women! It is peaceful to live with the little simple ones," he thought, accepting from Lidvchka a plate full of chicken...

The **semiotic temptation** reaches its culminating point when the "pink stocking" advocate has to resort to gastropornography. The chicken plate signifies comfort, satiety and eternal bliss with the undemanding uneducated female, the convenient antithesis to the dangerous "blue stocking." If Chekhov the psychiatrist appeals to the cure through color, giving preference to soothing pink, Chekhov the preacher resorts to the basic gastronomic signal. The "chicken" is something so basic that its pleasure cannot be denied by anybody, including the supporters of John Stuart Mill and George Sand. Realizing that man can not live on chicken alone and may become bored with his comfortable "pink stocking," Chekhov condescendingly suggests using "blue stockings" occasionally:[43]

> So what? Somov thinks. If I am to chat about some high matters I can go to Natalia Andneevna or Maria Frantsevna .... Very simple!

He accepts that sometimes even a superior man may have a desire to communicate with the clever and educated women, i.e. "the blue stocking." Nonetheless, in Chekhov's prescription, the dosage of such communication is very minimal and extremely rare, only as the last resort. This "sin" of relating to "blue stockings" is accepted and forgiven, provided a man marries a "pink stocking," the bedrock of social stability, mental and physical health.

Chekhov's **semiotic neologism** is the summary of the old illusionary bliss, the nostalgia for the past, the dream about the old civilization where life was presumably seen in shades of pink, a comfortable order where woman exists as a seductive object, the source of one's natural biological satisfaction. Chekhovian **pink stocking** is the most all-embracing metaphor of womens' past history, a kinder version anticipating the more categorical Freudian verdict, woman as the embodiment of the "id". His soft metaphor was an attempt to seduce the males by the familiar icons of the Past Old World of contentment, sexual hierarchy where the male was privileged, superior and in control. "Blue Stockings" and the education of women introduced new signs which were anxiety-causing factors. Chekhov, a compassionate doctor and a sympathetic and interested defender of mens' rights, offered an old prescription, in the basic world of dinners, quiet empty chit-chat and boredom; boring stability seemed to him more healthy. The world of "pink stockings" had less stress and anxiety for a fragile male whom "blue stockings" intimidated and threatened to destroy with their intelligent conversations about "the lofty and the intelligent." On this note Chekhov concludes his sermon to males and particularly females whom he scares with a denial of marriage unless they are "pink stockings." This is how Chekhov views the alternative to the grave proliferation of feminism, womens' courses and "blue stockings."

4.3 Maugham's Soothing Sign-Woman as an Archetype

> Women are simple passive objects of male activity.
> Lévi-Strauss *Structural Anthropology*.

Chekhov's fictional universe inhabited by women may be basically divided into two parts: the territory of "blue stockings" whom he despises and the kingdom of the "pink stockings" whom he may even enjoy as pretty sex objects and useful creatures because they make man's life more pleasant and comfortable. The "pink stockings" are young, simple, silly, childish and loving. It is the kingdom of sweet, pretty Olen'kas, Zihochkas, Lialechka's who decorate man's world with their pretty bodies, nice clothes, babies they produce and prepare food. It is the Chekhov's comfortable female archetype.

In Maugham's case, his archetype is a complex construct, a sign with various meanings that undergoes a standard semiosis; it moves from a soothing, nurturing, peaceful state to a dangerous state when a man is victimized either by adultery or foolishness. Eventually, all Maugham's female characters appropriate negative, undesirable qualities or become, semiotically speaking, **ominous signs**.

Such is Margery Hobson ("*Virtue*") who pretends to be an ideal wife and eventually leaves her husband for another man. This woman-archetype undergoes two stages. At first, she appears as an attractive woman whom Maugham describes as "a lady." He does not grant her the privilege of an aesthetic object of high decorative value. Nonetheless,[44]

> She was not beautiful, but comely, with fine dark hair and fine eyes, a good colour and a look of health. She had a pleasant frankness and an air of candour that were very taking. She looked honest, simple and dependable.

At the beginning her marriage to a man by the name of Charlie was successful. As a matter of fact, Maugham claims that there had never been a more devoted couple:[45]

> Breakdowns never disturbed them, bad weather was part of the fun, a puncture was no end of a joke and if they lost their way and had to sleep out in the open they thought they were having the time of their lives.

It was a paradisical state when woman performed her expected functions with utmost obedience, eagerness and precision. She "typed his monographs," "corrected the proofs of his articles in the scientific magazines." Not only that, she did not interfere with his social life either:[46]

When a man marries, his wife sooner or later estranges him from his old friends, but Margery on the contrary increased Charlie's intimacy with them.

Thus, Margery appears first as the archetypal woman:

>
> She - nature
> passive
> submissive
> peaceful
> subservient
> virture

Then after sixteen years of devoted married life, she falls in love with a younger man who eventually leaves her. Charlie eventually dies from grief. Strangely enough, Margery, the sinning woman, "acquires a spiritual look" after her husband's death:[47]

> Grief and fear had worn her to a shadow, she seemed very fragile now and she had acquired a spiritual look that I had never seen in her before. She was very gentle, very grateful for every kindness shown her, and in her smiles unsure and a little timid, was an infinite pathos. Her helplessness was appealing.

This sarcastic portrait of a grieving Margaret is still a sign Maugham is most comfortable with. He forgives her for her adultery; after all, a creature of "id" she followed her natural instincts. She is still the woman Maugham can tolerate because she is gentle, non-aggressive and non-interfering in the Other Universe. She does not encroach upon the territory of civilization and does not express any willingness to produce men's signs. Even her hypocritical grief in her post-adultery stage is acceptable female behavior. The archetypal Maugham's woman whose obedience and submissiveness do not disturb man and support the traditional peace and order is allowed to sin quietly. After all, she cannot tolerate "sexual starvation," hers are the needs of a more primitive being. Where Margery fails is in her flight from Charlie. Her honesty or "virtue," as Maugham describes it, eventually kill Charlie. He criticizes her for this open, direct violation of the marriage, although he would have forgiven her had she kept her affair in secret, Maugham condemns Margery for leaving Charlie:[48]

> Good gracious, she could have remained faithful to him in spirit while she was being unfaithful to him in flesh. That is a feat of leger demain that women find it easy to accomplish.

In her second stage, Margery is not the ideal woman. She is transformed into the expected treacherous female, victim of her sexual instincts. The traditional Maugham's woman, she cannot be faithful to her husband. During this secondary semiosis:

<pre>
She -   Nature   He -   Culture
        violent   civilized
        immoral   moral
        sinful   saintly
</pre>

Charlie, a civilized creature, would have been satisfied had Margery been faithful to him at least "in spirit" if she could not be faithful "in flesh." After all, he, a man of culture, may not need intimacy, unlike her he requires love. The semiosis takes place in the traditional archetypal fashion:

<pre>
He   = embodiment of Spirit
She   = embodiment of Flesh
he
        above
                her
</pre>

Margery symbolizes the expected, but **unsympathetic sign**, the sign Maugham fears, dislikes and mercilessly mocks. His subtle message to the male audience is:

> Watch out! You may become Charlies!

On the other hand, Pritchard, the maid from the story "The Treasure", stands for the **pleasurable sign**. She is thirty five, an age which Maugham finds "reasonable." Her appearance suits her expected function of a maid:[49]

> She was on the tall side, nearly as tall as he, but he guessed that she wore high heels. Her black dress fitted her station. She held herself well. She had good features and a rather high colour.

Unlike Chekhov's "pink stocking," Maugham's iconically favoured type of a woman is traditionally dressed in black, the colour of a servant's uniform and the colour of the night, witchcraft and mystery. Unlike Chekhov, the aesthetically inclined dreamer, Maugham is not concerned about female beauty, on the contrary, he is apparently embarrassed if a woman is beautiful. Beauty of the other, inferior sex, bothers him, and Maugham prefers women not to be strikingly pretty. That is why he is pleased with Pritchard's appearance:[50]

> She was neither fat not thin. In a proper uniform she would look very presentable. She was not inconveniently handsome, but she was certainly a comely, in another class of life you might almost have said a handsome woman.

Maugham introduces another dimension to this sign, her societal low function which is a convenient condition when Pritchard, a maid, should not even be given a beauty appraisal unlike the other women. Had she been a representative of another class, a woman-buyer of romance and a mate-hunter, she could have been regarded as "handsome." However, she is merely a working woman applying for a maid's job. So she is placed in the class of "comely". Beauty, as an item of exchange, a tool of seduction and manipulation of males, is perceived by Maugham as an endowment of the societal "better" members. Beauty as an item of wealth, albeit natural, is reserved for the upper classes. Pritchard, a maid, is just comfortable in her appearance, to the extent that her looks do not irritate the master she must serve without being visible. Her invisibility makes her ideal. The traditional value applied to children (they must be seen but not heard) is merely reserved for a woman. As a servant she is in the same class as other beings who are inferior to men:

```
                                        Men
                    Children
                    Servants
        Women
        Animals
```

Pritchard who "had been trained under a butler and appeared to be well acquainted with her duties" is the ideal female, the "treasure":[51]

> And that is precisely what Pritchard turned out to be. No man was ever better served. The way she shone shoes was

marvellous, and he set out of a fine morning for his walk to the office with a more jaunty step because you could almost see yourself reflected in them. She looked after his clothes with such attention that his colleagues began to chaff him on being the best dressed man in the Civil Service.

In addition to her skills as a cleaner, "she knew by instinct with whom he wished to speak and with whom he did not." She began to guard his peace like a devoted dog. "She was quick, silent and watchful." Finally, she became even his most envied possession. Her most valuable quality was her silence. Her master marvels at the fact that in four years of service "she's never volunteered a remark of her own." Maugham glorifies this perfect woman who speaks only when she is spoken to and marvelously attends to her master's physical needs. He writes a panegyric to this perfect woman-maid:[52]

> Pritchard became an institution. She was known very soon to be a perfect parlour maid. People envied Harenger the possession of her as they envied nothing else that he had. She was worth her weight in gold. Her price was above roubles.

He did not see Pritchard as a gift or an ideal creature of God, but as a product of good male training:

> Good masters make good servants.

Pritchard was a valuable item because she was originally trained by a male butler, then by her master. Maugham's idealized woman-sign is a desired object, a useful tool that a society must possess. He is even critical and didactic, subtly reminding men that a Pritchard could be created with the proper effort on the part of males.

The climax of the story is that Pritchard and her master Robert Haringer eventually become intimate. Robert panics fearing changes in his life, anxious not to lose an ideal servant and lose his bachelorhood. However, the saintly Pritchard pretends that nothing had happened and Robert Haringer is again the happiest man on Earth. In fact, he is the only happy male in the entire three volume collection and 1,576 pages of misogynist discourse.

The didactic message of this happy tale is that woman should be only in the subservient position. Only a properly trained maid, serving the man, and looking solely after his bodily needs, is the desired form of female presence in the world. Maugham reiterates Michelet's perspective on women that approved the ancient **archetypal exclusion** due to "women's potential for disorder" to maintain strict "social boundaries." (Jordanova: 1980, 67).[53]

Maugham, however, moves even farther. He proposes to institutionalize Pritchard, the maid because it is the only acceptable status to preserve male happiness and harmony between the sexes. Not an ideal "pink stocking" tied to a man by marriage, but a servant in a black uniform this is Maugham's **soothing archetype** capable of curing him of his **misogynist anxiety**:

man
master
owner
happy man
in
control
served
by
woman
an obedient slave
faithful like a dog
invisible like a child
efficient like a robot
eternally ready
to serve his body

The master-maid contract is preferable to a marriage since it does not involve the economic losses of a divorce in case of a traditional exchange, so that man remains free and superior, content and victorious. Unlike the traditional liaisons with women, this is the most pleasurable since all the pleasures are bestowed and all the miseries of marriage are spared. The semiotic message to men is:

Let us create Pritchard, the perfect parlour maid.

The extreme solution and bold advice given by Maugham is intensified by the visual signalling of his text. If Chekhovian ideal woman is dressed in pink, Maugham's idol is clad in black. The juxtaposition of the two colours symbolizes the degree of isolation the two authors are willing to propose. Maugham's version is much more radical and hostile than Chekhov's. He tolerates only maids, in black uniforms, while Chekhov accepts the comfortable and soothing "pink-stockings."

CHAPTER FIVE

Women as Signs of Otherness

5.1 Jews and Females – Signs of Equal Value

> Generally the people in the town of S. used to read very little, and they would say that only young ladies and Jews keep the local library alive, otherwise one had to close it down.
> Chekhov, *Ionych*.

This is Chekhov's verdict in the story where he depicts life and customs of a small provincial town and condemns its boring monotony and dull stillness. Chekhov passionately hates all that is associated with provincial Russia where the only consumers of culture happen to be "young females and Jews." Chekhov's fictional world that generally excluded females from culture and consumption of cultural products is now strikingly open to the "inferior beings", women and Jews. This is unusual for the creator of "pink stockings", the Chekhovian, charming sex objects who were very unlikely participants in cultural exchange, sign the production and the consumption of cultural signs.

Traditionally young ladies were valued by Chekhov only for their beauty and sex appeal, while in this story the collective portrait of the town dwellers seems to praise their intelligence. Usually women were regarded as inferior beings of limited innate capabilities, while in this story they happen to be the only cultured persons educated in the small provincial town. Most of the Chekhovian women are flippant, superficial beings who are preoccupied with their appearance, material comfort and sexual indulgence. Unlike his archetypal fictional females who fall asleep while reading, his women of the town S. are the only users of the local library. What could this unusual shift signify in the otherwise misogynist Chekhovian world?

Jews are placed next to the active female readers of the local town library. This is a new motif and a new sign in the Russian literary discourse where Jews were seldom associated with the main stream of culture. A persecuted and disliked religious minority they were barred from Russian cultural life through geographic and political restrictions. The geographic boundaries of the pale did not allow them to settle in the Russian capital and in important urban centres while a strict quota guarded Russian institutions of learning from this undesirable minority. Petty craft and commerce were mostly the only traditional outlets for the majority of the Russian Jews. The general attitude of Russian society towards this visible ethnic and religious minority was marked by hostility, indifference or, in the best instances, pity.

Chekhov's position on the Jewish question was tolerant and humane. His biographer Ronald Hingley recalls the incident from Chekhov's childhood when the future writer, then a seventh-grader, organized his classmates to prevent the expulsion from the school of a Jewish student, Wolkenstein.[1] The student slapped a classmate who had called him a *Jyd* (pejorative name for a Jew) and was to be expelled from the Taranrog Grammar School. According to the biographical legend, Chekhov took a very strong stand in this case:[2]

> Bursting into the victims classroom, "like a bomb," he persuaded the pupils to unite in protest. Unless their Jewish comrade was reinstated, they would, he induced them to threaten, quit grammar school *en masse*; whereupon the authorities, terrified, quickly countermanded the expulsion.

Hingley believed that this childhood episode was a good preparation for Chekhov's future position in the Dreyfus case. Chekhov admired Zola's stand in the Dreyfus affair and was ashamed of the "loathsome" and "disgusting" treatment of the French writer by the reactionary Russian journals, including Suvorin's *Novoe Vremia* where he continued to publish his work. His relationship with Suvorin "never regained its former cordiality" after the Dreyfus Affair (235-6).[3] Thus Chekhov always associated Jews with a weaker sex, a tribe to be protected. Together with women they represented the strange world of the Other, beings who were frequently abused and needed help and understanding from the rest of society. Throughout his life, from Wolkenstein, Taganrogue classmate to the Dreyfus-Zola case, from love affair with Dunya Efros to friendship with Levitan, Chekhov had thought of Jews as defenceless creatures who required protection. Their status as second class citizens legitimized their societal inferiority. Along with women, they could form a suitable **semiotic pair**, women and Jews could be equated since both groups were affected by the traditional stereotype of inferiority, innate fault and vice.

In this respect, the semiotic pair "young ladies and Jews" as the regular library borrower creates a paradoxical effect in the story "Ionych". They are needed to emphasize the negative collective portrait of the little provincial town. If these traditionally inferior creatures, women and Jews, are the only library visitors, very sad conclusions may be drawn about the town as a whole. Chekhov successfully employs the structural elements of the prevalent social mythology to pass his artistic judgement upon the sleepy provincial town. He uses two dominant prejudices--sexism and anti-Judaism, to support his negative image of its provincial boredom.

His early life experience in the small Russian provincial town of Taganrog filled him with the utmost contempt for everything outside the capital. Moscow and St. Petersburg which were the main centres of Russian cultural and socio-political life were the Chekhovian ideal habitat. Longing for Moscow is the running motif of Chekhov's plays and stories. His numerous characters express passionate nostalgia for Moscow. They suffer in the stifling atmosphere of the Russian provinces. Sleepy life of Russian urbanites receives the strictest sentence in Chekhov's stories. It is not incidental that to condemn it vividly and with the least "discursive matter" Chekhov resorts to the original semiotic pair "young girls and Jews." The semiotic signals which are being sent to the readers are:

town dwellers	-	dull, ignorant
young girls	-	dull, ignorant
Jews	-	inferior beings

the young girls of the town S.		-readers, library users, civilized
Jews of the town S.	-	readers, library users, civilized

and if so, the inhabitants of the town S. are even more ignorant, boring and uncivilized.

"Young girls and Jews" metaphorize the inferior Russian society members and simultaneously represent a satirical portrait of the little town S. Having made Jews and females the most enlightened inhabitants of the town, Chekhov presented a mythical paradox to the crowd that reproduced the popular mythology in the first place. Since it is the average town-dweller who would like to see the "Other" as inferior, evil or useless, the "Jewish myth" is returned in its reversed form.[4] It is turned upside down:

I crowd = myth producer   II Jew = metaphor
II Jew = mythical target   I   crowd = target

Similar transformation takes place regarding the female inferiority myth. The familiar accepted stereotype about a woman, "pink stocking" is introduced in a totally unfamiliar fashion. A striking metaphorical exchange substitutes for the traditional symbol of female naiveté, superficiality and undeveloped intelligence:

pink stocking = blue stocking

The name is implied rather than given, since a female who uses a library regularly may be justifiably named a "blue stocking." Thus, the semiotic pair "Jews and young ladies" is combined on the basis of several semantic qualities:

a) sense of inferiority;
b) reversed mythical meaning;
c) purpose of debunking the "Other".

The myths of ethnicity, religion and gender are coupled or equated not with the purpose of pleasing the original myth producer, but rather for the sake of criticizing him. Quite unexpectedly for the popular reader the crowd is not present, but is still challenged with its own mythical products. The idea of a notionally inferior or evil being, the "Other", transformed into a heroic character is an utterly shocking fictional possibility. And yet, Chekhov expands the **mythical boundaries**-and challenges the expectations of the popular reader to achieve his narratological goal; that is to create a satire or to produce a humorous effect.

As in any carnival, the beautiful may parade as the ugly, the stupid as the intelligent or vice versa.[5] The **grammar of the laughing ecstasy** foresees the paradox between a mask and a mask-wearer. In the story "Ionych" the mask of the educated, civilized and culture oriented belongs to the characters who traditionally are not expected to wear it. The satirical, semiotic and humorous effects are intensified with the help of a **mask-changing device:** the method of reversal which is based on the interplay between the expected and traditional and the unexpected and innovative **semiotic constructs**. Consequently, the reader obtains the humorous depiction of a little sleepy town S. where the only library users are "Jews and young ladies." The carnival parade is in full swing; after all, it is only a mask which may be easily taken off, in case somebody is offended or disturbed by the unusual.

Chekhovian **inversion of mythical pairing** undertaken in the story "Ionych", namely Jew female as a mask, reaches its apogee in the story "*Tina*" (Slime) (1886). The story, seldom mentioned by the foreign and Russian critics, is the most controversial in plot, character and **semiotic signalling**. The plot evolves around an act of forgery presumably committed by a daughter of the deceased money-lender Rotstein against two cousins, Russian officers, Sokol'sky and Kriukov. Both cousins are unable to cash their valuable paper because the seductive Jewess somehow destroys it. This outrageous act, however, does not disturb them. Both brothers are unable to condemn Susanna Moiseevna, nor do they feel any negative emotions towards her. The two brothers are both under the spell of her demonic charm, and the story ends when the two brothers see each other in Susanna Moiseevna's drawing-room, embarrassed to admit their weakness and mysterious attraction to the wicked Jewess. Both are ashamed of something immoral, other than pure forgery. They are afraid to acknowledge that both are in love with this woman. There is an attempt to judge each other, but also there is open resignation:[6]

> What can I say to him? What?-Alexander Ivanovich thought- What kind of a judge am I, if I, myself, am here? Without saying a word, producing some noise, he slowly left.

The keywords or key signals that appear throughout the story are "how unusual!", how strange!"

Indeed, everything in the story is unusual and unexpected. The evil is neither punished nor moralistically condemned. The villain, Susanna Moiseevna, who commits a complicated crime (forgery and seduction) is not represented as a negative character. On the contrary, she manages to arouse love in the two individuals and evoke confused emotions in the readers. There is a consistent attempt on the author's part to tone down the negative aura around this strange character. Chekhov resorts to persistent embellishment of the notionally negative character.

Susanna Moiscevna is a villain by definition. As a Jewess, she carries the traditional stigma of contempt, and as a forger, she is supposed to provoke the reaction of strict condemnation. None of this happens; in fact, what the reader observes is a strange authorial position. Chekhov takes the role of the "devil's advocate," which in a way contradicts his traditional attitude to women. Chekhov's Susanna Moiseevna is an absolute antithesis to his other female characters. Despite the fact that the character is a woman, she is endowed with enormous charm, intelligence, wit and, what is most unusual, she is treated with humour, warmth and empathy. First of all, Chekhov makes Susanna Moiseevna rather young and attractive. Even in the first scene when she appears in the story, with her migraine and in a totally unpresentable way, the Jewess is not described negatively:[7]

> Exactly against the entrance, in a large old man's armchair, there was sitting a woman, with her head back on the cushion, in an expensive Chinese robe, her head wrapped up. One could see only a pale long nose, thin pointed and slightly

aquiline and a big black eye. The wide robe masked her height and shape, but judging by her white beautiful hand she was not more than twenty-six to twenty-eight years old.

Even the physical appearance bears some signs of controversy. On the one hand, Chekhov provides the reader with the expected stereotypical details such as her black eye and long nose, some presumably non-Russian face features. On the other hand, the author introduces certain quite flattering features, such as "white beautiful hand" and "young age." Any other Russian bourgeois lady experiencing an attack of migraine may not have even accepted a guest. Chekhov's unusual character acts "heroically", agreeing to see a visitor at an inconvenient time. He refrains from describing the rest of her body; the woman's robe does not reveal her height and shape, which later in story are found to be very slim and attractive.

The first introduction of this controversial character, bears some semantic complexity. Chekhov manipulates the expected and the unexpected, definitely playing with the two principal myths:[8]

myth about the other group	*myth about the other sex*
Jewish	female young
black eyed	beautiful
thin nosed	possessing the utmost
rich	riches-beauty

There is an interesting detail in the portrait of this exotic female--she sits in the old man's chair, presumably the inheritance of the deceased old Rotstein. The chair acquires greater significance when the visitor announces the purpose of his visit. He came to collect the old debt of her father. Thus, Susanna Moiseevna inherited not only the antique furniture, but some "ancient" debts as well. This discovery takes place in her bedroom which bears all the signs of the poetic morning disorder: women's clothes, lace, shoes, caramel candies, cigarette butts. The visitor, however, is not disgusted, he is simply haunted by the smell of jasmine in the room. During the conversation, Alexander Grigorivich Sokol'sky discloses the purpose of his visit, but he fails to collect the money. First of all, Sokol'sky is overwhelmed by the exotic atmosphere of the house:[9]

140 *Semiotics of Misogyny*

> ... From his first step he was struck by the abundance of blossoming flowers and sweetish, thick and nauseating smell of jasmine flowers covered the walls like draperies, overshadowing the window, they were hanging from the ceiling, weaving in the corners, making the room look like a greenhouse rather that a place to where one lived. Tomtits, canaries and goldfinches were squeaking and romping in the greenery hitting upon glass windows.

The author emphasizes the exotic origin of the character's dwelling, which looks more like a greenhouse. Does the description bear some truthfulness or does the author simply laugh at the prejudice of the crowd who expect the "Jewish house" look strange and unpleasant?

The most expected part of the myth would have been the signal "dirty," since any disliked ethnic minority is described as such. Chekhov does not resort to this most expected mythical component; instead, he merely denotes its exotic character. The signals which contribute to it are:

Birds   Flowers   Green   Lack of Light

Smell of jasmine

They are united under the mythical umbrella "exotic," without implying "repulsive." There is more of the myth of the exotic Orient, the mystery of the unknown, than any sense of dislike. What apparently is done by the author is the **myth fusion**. Chekhov separates the structural components of the myth about the Jews and utilizes only the least neutral. The familiar myth had to bear the following:

Jewish
non-Russian
foreign
dirty
exotic
strange
Oriental
repulsive

Chekhovian version contains only:

Jasmine	-	Oriental
Flowers, Birds	-	exotic
Jewish	-	Other
greenhouse	-	unusual

During the entire discourse, the author seems to be willing to defend his female heroine. Despite the fact that she is Jewish, she is not presented as "repulsive". Chekhov prepares his readers to accept this exotic creature who lives in a greenhouse, smells of jasmine and talks very intelligently and unusually boldly. "How strange she is" the visitor repeats. Chekhov makes him to repeat it several times, thus intensifying her strangeness ever more.

When Susanna Moiseenna finds out that Sokol'sky's demand to collect money early (he comes two weeks prior to the maturity date of his draft) is due to his marriage, she engages in a long tirade:[10]

> Why does a young man need money, honestly? Whim, games. What have you overspent it on? Parties, lost in gambling or are you marrying?
>
> --Your guess was right!--The officer smiled and lightly getting up, tinkling with his spurs--I'm marrying, indeed ..
>
> But listen, are you marrying a poor one? Or because of passionate love? And why do you need necessarily five thousand and not four or three?

Nonetheless, Chekhov makes him apologize for his intended marriage:[11]

> The matter is that legally an officer cannot marry earlier than at an age of twenty eight. If he wishes to marry, he has either to resign or pay five thousand roubles deposit.

And a few moments later, he "exotic creature" takes the mask off a misogynist and utters:[12]

> I definitely don't understand how a decent man can live with a woman? Just don't understand, even if you kill me.

The strange, sharp-tongued female temporarily poses as a representative of the opposite sex:[13]

> I have been living, thank God, twenty-seven years already, and I have never seen a bearable woman in my life . . . All are pretentious, immoral, liars . . . I can tolerate only maids and cooks, and the so-called decent ones I do not allow near me, within a gun's range.

The Chekhovian **mask-changing device** is again at work. What was a combinatory semiotic pair in the story "Ionych", is a completely reversed structure:

female	male
engineer of marriage	denounces marriage
loves her own sex	hates the opposite sex

This female Chekhovian character assumes the authorial voice which remarkably echoes later Maugham's voice. If Maugham proclaims that he can tolerate only maids, Chekhov does the same through Susanna. The author transfers his own fear of women and marriage to the female character and at this point is faced with the contradiction, that the misogynist is a woman herself. The "exotic Other" may be even as intelligent as a man, a non-Russian woman is endowed with male-like reasoning. The Jewess denounces women as if she were a man! The strange woman parades as a cynical man who contemplates marriage. Then she suddenly transforms into an advocate of the entire persecuted group.

She vehemently attacks the imaginary majority, which presumably hates all Jews. Now Susanna, the Jewess, is a metaphor for all Jews:[14]

> Oh, I perfectly understand their hatred! Why not! I openly expose what other people do their best to hide from God and other people. Why not hate me after that?

Chekhov here makes another attempt to defend Susanna, but not as a character who needs empathy from the reader. Instead, the author, resorting to the metaphor--Susanna=Jewish minority--deals with the reasons for racial and religious hatred. The author leaves the mythical territory of the stereotype and cautiously steps into the unexpected world of unpopular thinking. What the artist undertakes is the leap from popular fiction into a less popular analysis of a collective mass consciousness[15]. The question which he asks is, "Why is the Other hated?" The question is less shocking than the answer:

Because the Other is honest!

The reply to the unusual question is close to condemnation of the majority, and this is not what the reader could have expected. After all, the Jewess commits the stereotypical crime. She withholds the money from the presenter of the draft; she evades payment just like her father and her mythical forefathers in the past. And the paradoxical occurs. Instead of the expected outpouring of hate, the readers find an outrageous proposition that there is no reason to hate someone who is open. Chekhov dares to challenge the prevailing stereotype with another controversial idea that the hated minority is equal to the producers of the popular mythology. He suggests that there is no difference between the essential behaviour of the hated minority and hating majority; where the difference lies is in the manner of expression. Chekhovian critique of the hypocrisy of the secular and religious crowd is self-contained in Susanna's utterance. He takes off the **mask of disparity** between Jews and Gentiles implying that both commit sins. The semiotic signals that he sends to the readers are:

Jews	Gentiles
crooks	crooks
sinners	sinners
admit their sins	hide their sins
honest	hypocritical

The artist turns upside down traditional stereotypes, sending a provocative message that popular belief is based on a wrong premise.

Chekhovian semiotic strategy in this instance has somewhat of a familiar form of reference. A similar device was used by John Stuart Mill in his work on *Subjection of women*.[16] Talking about the ideological paradox in popular collective thinking, for instance, Mill writes the following:[17]

> Because the Greeks cheated the Turks, and the Turks only plundered the Greeks, there are persons who think that the Turks are naturally more sincere.

144 *Semiotics of Misogyny*

Temporarily the voice of the fictional character transforms into the open authorial one. The discourse is interrupted by a digression which is not immediately recognized as such. When Susanna says that she is hated, the readers may still think that it is the character's vocal part. However, when the female character questions the institution of marriage they may see a remarkable connection between Chekhov's own philosophy, and personal life experience and Susanna's passionate denial of marriage:[18]

> I don't understand why people marry! -she said, looking around for her handkerchief-life is so short, so little freedom, and they add to it extra ties.

"Marriage as slavery" is the central idea of Chekhovian life strategy. He avoided it in his personal life till very late years, and his characters frequently are proponents of the same idea. In the story "*Tina*" (Slime), Susanna, a woman who must have been a defender of this social custom, ironically is the authorial spokesman. She voices Chekhov's own opinion when she speculates about the shortness of life and inappropriateness of life and marriage. Chekhov, the vehement defender of his bachelorhood and misogynist, had an artistic sensibility. He sensed the paradox of his female character assuming his own voice. Chekhov, the artist, acknowledged this irony and he made his male character utter the following:

> You are a woman and such a woman-hater!

This remark made by Sokol'sky after Susanna's long anti-marriage tirade is a sign of the authorial discursive awareness. The flaw in the plot is noticed and acknowledged; nonetheless, the artistic pathway is rather unpredictable. The artistic instinct helps Chekhov not only to admit the flaws of discourse, but it also assists him in changing his traditional philosophical stand. Once the female character became his own voice he managed to forget that "she" is a woman.

Chekhov, the convinced bachelor, misogynist and believer in women's inferiority, surprises the readers with the following:[19]

> A woman, . . . smiled Susanna--am I guilty that God had sent me such an outer shell? I am as guilty of that as much as you of having moustache. The choice of a container does not depend upon the violin.

Temporarily he defends the other sex and even suggests that differences are purely superficial, like the "violin's container" or "any shell." How could this have occurred? What Chekhov suggests here is that all humans are equal despite their gender or other external characteristics such as religion or ethnic background. This conclusion comes unexpectedly for the readers and the author himself, whose unflattering opinion of women is voiced so frequently throughout his entire works. Thus, the discursive digression causes the shift, albeit temporary, in the philosophical make-up of the artist, whose fictional characters force him to accept another point of view. His own creation-a woman, a Jewess-forces him to reconsider his own views, along with the criticism of the popular views of the crowd. The denunciation of one stereotype, antisemitism, led to the abandonment of another, misogyny. His fictional character, a product of his own imagination, adopts a feminist stand, and by the irony of creativity, Chekhov is swept into the ethos of feminism. Like the despised feminists, he proclaims that the differences between the sexes are insignificant external peculiarities which may or may not be there. He sends the outrageous message to his readers:

> men = women
> sex = an external. variable
> religion = an external variable
> Jew = non Jew, an external variable

The critique of the religious stereotype goes hand in hand with the ridicule of the relationship between the sexes.[20] Having said through Susanna that gender is an arbitrary quality given by God, Chekhov leads the readers to another controversial idea that Jewishness is also an external insignificant quality. Moreover, he tries to prove that the latter is even more superficial than gender. He offers to consider the entire class of external characteristics, such as:

146 *Semiotics of Misogyny*

moustache	- optional physical feature
sex	- physical variable, God given
shell	- optional feature, God given
container	- optional feature, man made

These serve as a preliminary semiotic map which prepares the readers to examine the phenomenon of Jewishness. After Susanna's bedroom smelling of exotic jasmine, he takes Sokol'sky and his readers into her drawing-room. Object by object, glance by glance, step by step, he examines his unfamiliar surrounding:[21]

> The drawing room where he stood now, was richly furnished with pretension for fashion and luxury. One could find dark bronze dishes with design, views of Nice and the Rhine on the tables, antique brass, Japanese statues, but all these efforts to create the aura of luxury and fashion only overshadowed the lack of taste which was screaming loudly from the golden curtain-holders, flowery wallpaper, bright velvet table-cloths, cheap oil imitations in heavy frames. The lack of taste was compounded by the sense of incomplete and avoidable crowdedness when it seems that something is missing and a lot has to be thrown away. One could see that all the furniture was not obtained at once but in parts, during accidental purchases and sales.

What he finds there is basically and a lack of taste, nice decorative touch. The owner is depicted as a person who chaotically purchased her furniture at various sales. The narrator helps the character to establish the gender of the owner by emphasizing the cold and inhospitable air of the room, like a railway station, a club or a theatre hall. He claims that neither luxury nor fashion can hide one of the most striking features of the room, the lack of feminine touch. Chekhov, surprisingly, regrets that woman's hands did not touch this room, thus depriving it of "warmth, poetry and cosiness." Here Chekhov returns to the popular myth of a woman as an aesthetic regulator of household. But Susanna who lives in these rooms lacking the feminine touch is a woman. Does Chekhov insist on her otherness even in this respect? Or does he want to emphasize that she merely inherited an old man's house?

In any case, the readers are prepared to believe that there is nothing specifically "Jewish" in the room. Sokol'sky finds there Japanese statues, pictures of Nice and the Rhine and numerous objects that evidence nothing characteristic of a particular taste, but rather lack of any. He constructs a rather confusing **semiotic maze**, neither Sokol'sky nor the readers are able to establish a traditional stereotypic judgement about the owner of the room by merely cataloguing the objects. Any person could have bought Japanese statues or pictures of Nice and the Rhine. Chekhov prepares the readers to accept the next statement:[22]

> In fact there was nothing Jewish in the room, with the exception of a large picture depicting Jacob's meeting with Isaac.

The last may be perceived as irony since a Biblical plot could be found on any other picture in any other house. Moreover, if a reference to the Old Testament on the painting is the only sign of one's religion and ethnicity, then one may be mistaken more than once. Basically, Chekhov takes again a carnival mask and laughs at the narrow-minded provincial town-dwellers who would have liked to see the reaffirmation of their traditional stereotypical thoughts.

Having examined every object in the room, Sokol'sky or, rather Chekhov through Sokol'sky, returns to the hostess, Susanna Moiseevna who appears dressed for lunch:[23]

> But here the door opened, and she herself appeared, slender in a long black dress, with tightly belted, as if curved, waist. Now the officer could see not only her nose and eyes, but her pale thin face, black curly lamb-like head. He did not like her, although she did not appear unattractive. He harboured general prejudice towards non Russian faces, and moreover, found that the hostess's black curls and thick brows did not go with the pale face which somehow reminded one of the smell of jasmine, and her ears and nose were strikingly pale, as if dead or made out of transparent wax.

Despite the fact that Chekhov stresses Sokol'sky's negative impression of his hostess's appearance, the readers are provided with the missing flattering features of her portrait that was begun earlier in the story. If earlier Susanna's head was wrapped and in a migraine fighting pose, now the readers may see her "black curly lamb-like head." While her housecoat five pages earlier was hiding her young body, now her slender figure is revealed in a long black dress. Sign "slender" is a cryptic flattering description, later negated by the repeated signal "dislike." Neither Chekhov nor his character Sokol'sky can admit that his woman is attractive. She symbolizes a negative **actant** in the story and carries the burden of **dual mythology** as a sinner on the one hand, and, a Jewess, on the other. Presenting a non-Russian character to his provincial narrow-minded public and myth-enslaved readers, the author controls his artistic impulse. Following his own artistic instinct, he presents this most controversial character as unexpectedly a human being, vivacious, intelligent and attractive both physically and spiritually. He challenges the stereotypical expectations of the popular and most unsophisticated readers when he allows the Jewess a certain amount of praise although she is traditionally expected to be only ugly, vicious and dirty.

However, taking into account the reaction of the "reading majority" and lack of general sympathy towards a non Christian in a predominantly Christian society, Chekhov suppresses his most natural artistic intention to subvert the mythical image and compromises his artistic ingenuity with civic conformism of an individual who represents the religious, and secular majority. This conflict between the artistic impulse and loyalty to the group manifests itself in the conflicting semiotic signals which the author consistently sends to his readers:

> myth-defying and myth-supporting

In defiance of the myth Chekhov describes this epitome of Otherness as a young, attractive, female creature who is even endowed with male-like intelligence. Supporting the prejudice, the author endows her with the characteristics which are most expected from the "Other" and also preserves negative attitudes toward this symbol of Otherness. That is why, even having presented a pleasant physical portrait of the woman, Chekhov makes Sokol'sky express his displeasure on the ground that the face is "non-Russian." His reaction to Susanna's appearance in the drawing room is:[24]

> Pale anaemic . . . he thought. Perhaps, as nervous as a female turkey.

Appealing to the Slavophiles, racists and believers in the Russian superiority, Chekhov imparts to the "Other" those unflattering features. According to the grammar of the stereotype, the "Other" is the epitome of the familiar evil. Following it precisely, the author confirms that:

>Russian = beauty, attractiveness
>Non-Russian = ugliness, unpleasantness

The positive characteristic "slender" is taken away by the next unflattering label "pale, anaemic" and the association with a "nervous turkey". The zoological allusion removes any positive associations which could have been constructed earlier in the discourse. Having pleased the most staunch supporters of the myth, Chekhov undertakes the artistic task of dismantling the myth and pleasing himself. Not without an obvious pleasure, he writes about the notorious Jews and the "garlic myth." Sokol'sky and the readers follow Susanna in her rooms where she provocatively asks:[25]

> Do you like my rooms? Local ladies say they smell of garlic. Their entire wit is limited to this kitchen joke. Let me assure you that I don't keep garlic even in the basement, and when once a doctor came who smelled of garlic I asked him politely to take his hat off and spread this pleasant smell somewhere else."

The "local ladies with their kitchen jokes" may be easily recognized by nearly every provincial Russian little town-dweller who naively shares the same mistaken belief about the Jews as the major consumers of garlic. Despite the fact that garlic was grown and used by the Russian peasants the stereotype insisted on this **semiotic pair**. The "Other" or its stereotypical notion is associated with strong unpleasantness, Jew standing for "ugly" and garlic for "strong." Together they formed a strong negative image which appealed simultaneously to the auditory visual and olfactory senses:

Jew	Garlic
unpleasant to see	unpleasant to smell

The combination of the visual and olfactory signals was responsible for the symbol which was meant to arouse aversion. The readers who follow

Sokol'sky's journey into Susanna's kingdom may be disappointed, since the expected part of the mythical structure does not function in the traditional manner. "Garlic" appears as a **myth-subverting symbol**. Since Susanna does not keep garlic in her quarters, the expected strange odour in the dwellings of the Rotsteins is explained as a medicinal smell which remains after the death of the old paralytic father.

Chekhov preserves some components of the myth, such as smell, but he challenges the old stereotype with a possible other explanation. The remedies the old man used for his disease which could have given a peculiar smell to the house cannot be perceived in the same manner as "garlic." The stubborn plant with a strong odour is the symbol of a "strange" custom, a habitual act by collective choice, of a certain group while disease, old age and medicine cannot be perceived as a matter of cultural preference. They are **universal signs**. Death, old age and physical decay are transnational, universal human experiences, rather than choices made by a certain religious or ethnic group. Paralysis in old age is not an inherent ethnic characteristic. Chekhov the physician assists Chekhov the artist who intuitively seeks truth. He doubts the traditional mythical image of a Jew as ugly, dirty, smelling of garlic and hoarding money for no sensible reason. His Susanna is the mythical antithesis. She is not the same as the stereotypical Jew nicknamed *Shmul'*. Chekhov makes her a church-goer, who speaks "pure" Russian, attractive and not keeping garlic. Moreover, to emphasize her Otherness, he makes her speak the utterly unexpected:[26]

> Why does one need money?
> What nonsense it really is
> or
> One has to live and enjoy, and they (Jews) are afraid of spending extra coin. In this respect I am much more like a hussar than Shmul'. I don't like money to sit long in one place. And in general, it seems I have little in common with the Jews.

Chekhov makes his Jewess denounce the Jews, and in doing so reinforce her own originality. She is a member of the despised minority, and yet she possesses many qualities which defy her belonging to this group. On the contrary, the "Other" has much more in common with the Russian national group. Chekhov even endows her with this stereotypically Russian quality:

parting with money easily like a Russian *hussar*. He creates a **semiotic paradox** when the symbol of the "Other" is actually "other than that:"

Jews	non-Jews	Susanna
dirty	clean	not dirty
ugly	attractive	attractive
garlic eaters	"allergic" to garlic	"allergic" to garlic
greedy	generous	does not hoard money
	church-goers	church-goer

His unexpected defence of this controversial and unusual character is accompanied by the reassurance of other characters. The voice of the narrator and guest complement each other, and together with the utterances of the central character form an organic semantic whole:

Chekhov	Susanna	Sokol'sky
author	central character	character
narrator	authorial spokesman	authorial spokesman

The characteristic feature of this semiotic entity is its provocativeness, a subversion of the traditional stereotype. What the author-narrator suggests, the central character develops further and the passive characters, manipulated by both, confirm.

For instance, Susanna's confessions, her tirades about nations, languages and Jewish traits, as well as the narrator's introduction to the disruptive image, are inescapably followed by Sokol'sky's short approving remark:[27]

> How lovely she is.
> or
> Honest to God, she is lovely.

Sokol'sky approving reaction is needed to verify the effectiveness of the authorial efforts directed at construction of the **character-sign, character-puzzle** and **character-paradox**. If other Chekhovian characters were more colorful and had to be visualized, Susanna had to be also believable. Unlike other characters, she had no mimetic prototype in reality. Therefore, she had to be constructed on a purely intellectual ground. She was more of a **character-desire** which appeared after the elaborate weaving together of myth, stereotype and fear of female power.

5.2 Woman as a Sign of Otherness – Maugham's Russian Woman

To produce an alarming woman-sign Chekhov turned to a Jewess, Susanna, a strange creature full of sex appeal, demonic power and the epitome of utter alienation. Maugham, fearful of women, displayed his own utterly neurotic reaction to **women-signals** of danger when he created his Anastasia Alexandrovna Leonidov. The male character, Mr. Harrington, attracted to this exotic "mad Russian" is killed on the streets of Petrograd. He is a respectable businessman with wife and children in his native Philadelphia, who falls prey to the seductive Anastasia. He is another victim of feminist demonic power. But the most distinguished feature of this story is that the female protagonist is the symbol of extreme Otherness. Anastasia standing vis-à-vis English consul and American businessman epitomizes the analogous alien universe. She may be treated as a metaphor of the new Russia which the West had recently discovered and has all reason to fear. The action takes place in Petrograd shortly after the October revolution. On the other hand, Maugham is far too sympathetic to Russia as a country to express a negative collective sentiment and to burden his Anastasia with a mission too unusual for the female character. Maugham sets the time described in his story "Mr. Harrington's Washing" onto a particular period:[28]

> It was at the time when Europe discovered Russia. Everyone was reading the Russian novelists, the Russian dancers captivated the civilized world, and the Russian composers set shivering the sensibility of persons who were beginning to want a change from Wagner.

To imitate the Russian style, everybody "changed cushions in the sitting-rooms, hung an icon on the wall, read Chekhov and went to ballet." Maugham sees nothing dangerous in shaking hands with Diagilev or Pavlova drinking vodka, and imitating Russian colours and ways. He clearly states that those are not the "dangerous things."

Apparently the **sign of danger** is the woman, a Russian Delilah whose fine eyes, and voluptuous figure are capable of bringing disaster to men. One victim is Mr. Ashenden sent on an important spy mission to Russia who is already transformed, and in his euphoric state is ready to do and believe anything Delilah says. She is very successful at her seduction:[29]

> In her dark melancholy eyes Ashenden saw the boundless steppes of Russia, and the Kremlin with its pealing bells, and the solemn ceremonies of Easter at St. Isaac's, and the forests of silver birches and the Nevsky Prospect; it was astonishing how much he saw in her eyes. They were round and shining and slightly protuberant like those of a Pekinese. They talked together of Alyosha in the *Brothers Karamazov*, of Natasha in *War and Peace*, of *Anna Karenina* and of *Fathers and Sons*.

This female seduces men, creatures of culture, with allusions to the legacy of Russian men, their culture. Anastasia's eyes carry the associations with Dostoevsky and Turgenev, St. Petersburg architecture and Tolstoy. Unlike the other females he knew, his own, this one attracts Ashenden with all she does and does not posses. "These Russians, what fun they have," exclaims enamored or seduced Mr. Ashenden. He forgives her her hearty appetite attributing it to the Russian national trait. Mr. Ashenden is even willing to marry her, the biggest sacrifice Maugham's man can make, but what stops him from this heroic deed is Anastasia's maddening daily breakfast routine. Her diet invariably consists of scrambled eggs. He cannot see himself eating scrambled eggs every morning for the rest of his life, and he escapes marriage by going to America. Maugham describes the triumph of a wise man who does not fall into the trap set by Delilah:[30]

> No immigrant, eager for freedom and a new life, ever looked upon the Statue of Liberty with more heartfelt thankfulness than did Ashenden.

Ashenden meets Anastasia again, several years later. Maugham analyzes his feelings and past involvement and claims that all was nothing but an emotional confusion:[31]

> Of course, he knew now that he had not loved her, but Tolstoy and Dostoevsky, Rimsky-Korsakov, Stravinsky and Bakst; but he was not quite sure if the point had occurred to her.

Maugham tries to persuade the readers and himself that it is not love that his character feels towards Anastasia. She, a woman whose primary duty is to "produce sons", cannot be loved. Men love Anastasia as a sign of exotic Russian culture which she stands for, but not for what she really is. Later, Ashenden discovers that she is not a woman of traditional making at all. When they meet after several years of separation, Anastasia shocks her former lover with an announcement:[32]

> "He (her husband Vladimir) is going to have a baby."
> "I am not a mother," she said with a laugh. "I am not interested in that sort of thing."

A man who feared scrambled eggs for breakfast and children discovers that Anastasia is a totally different creature. She is not the familiar woman. Her voluptuous figure and fine eyes mislead Mr. Ashenden.

It turns out she is far more dangerous:[33]

> She seemed to be on intimate terms with the leaders of the various political parties and Ashenden made up his mind to sound her on the possibility of her working with him. His infatuation had not blinded him to the fact that she was an extremely intelligent woman."

Her danger is in her intelligence. This is a very revealing semiotic feature, and the readers may understand why Maugham's intelligent woman is called Anastasia. To persuade the readers that a woman is the **sign of danger** Maugham made her carry the **meaning of Otherness**; consequently he achieves a highly effective **semiotic field**:

she = a woman	Anastasia
traditional alien creature	Russian
not intelligent	intelligent
dangerous	dangerous
produces sons	does not produce
fertilizes eggs	eats scrambled eggs
passive in society	active in politics

The images of scrambled eggs or signals of imminent danger are supporting or auxiliary semiotic structures which assist Maugham in conveying his desired message: "This is a woman = **sign of danger**." She is dangerous even more than a traditional woman, because her behavior is unknown and unpredictable. In traditional intercourse when a woman behaves naturally and has children, eggs symbolize archetypal fertility, and usually stand for female reproductive power. In Maugham's case, when his fictional female Anastasia lets other women perform this role, "scrambled eggs" are transformed into a semiotic device employed to emphasize her Otherness, the danger of her unpredictability. Instead of the expected reproductive act when egg is in a woman's womb, Maugham shocks his readers by letting Anastasia eat them. He exchanges the expected icons for the unexpected:

egg	egg
sign of fertility	sign of danger
nursed	destroyed
in	in
a	a
womb	stomach

The exchange of this single archetype for the non-traditional discursive function is subordinated to another archetype, the woman = sign of danger.

Maugham in effect performs an act of **discursive sacrifice** when one archetype is destroyed for the sake of the other. The balance of semiotic power is shifted towards a transcultural, archetypal concept which is primary, and global within Maugham's discursive universe. The **pendulum of semiosis** moves towards the signs of Culture, leaving the signs of Nature with a purely functional role. Maugham's woman, a sign of danger, is even more ominous then than the traditional female, precisely because she is more powerful. She is able to participate in the production of signs herself. This possible inference bothers Maugham, when a woman abandons the traditional territory of sex and family in exchange for societal public play. When he writes about Anastasia:[34]

> She had a passion for intrigue and a desire for power. When he hinted that he had command of large sums of money she saw at once that through him she might acquire an influence in the affairs of Russia.

he actually sends a warning to his male readers: "Intelligent women may ruin more than a single man, a single family, they are capable of destroying a state."

5.3 Taking the Mask off a Character-Desire

While Maugham never takes on the liberal mask of a broad minded thinker, Chekhov occasionally does it with his character-desire, icon of Otherness--Susanna. In the first part of the story, he teases his readers, the provincial Russian dwellers, and even plays with a mask of a liberal who protests against prejudice, inequality and injustice. He temporarily plays the role of a progressive, enlightened Westerner and challenges the stereotypes and mythical beliefs about the Other.[35] However, this does not last long. Eventually, in the second half of the story, Chekhov returns to the more familiar traditional, mythical universe where Otherness is reaffirmed, despised and explained simplistically, crudely and in full loyalty to his misogynist myth:[36]

> You, obviously, do not like the Jews. I won't argue, there are many flaws, just like with any other nation. But are the Jews guilty? No, not the Jews, but the Jewish women. They are narrow minded, pitiful, lack any poetry, boring . . . You have never lived with the Jewess and do not know what a "delight it is."

Here, Chekhov returns to his favorite stand where woman is the culprit for all evil. The attractive creature who was earlier denouncing marriage and was the general authorial voice is now again a despised female. Chekhov now repeatedly focuses the readers' attention on Susanna's "malicious feline" expression. The carnival of the first part is over, the parade of joyful masks is transformed into a circus performance of a predatory animals. Susanna, with the evil feline expression, performs a risky action. She hides or somehow destroys (Chekhov is not quite clear in this part of the narration) the valuable paper which Sokol'sky presents to be exchanged for cash. After a scene of staged fight for the paper, Chekhov leads his readers to the implied name "tigress." Susanna's victory confirms this. If previously the readers were informed about Susanna's evil "feline" expression, now they can see how a vicious cat may turn into a tigress.

Surprisingly, the shocking disappearance of a draft does not make Sokol'sky hate her. He not only fails to fight physically, but looses spiritually. The vicious tigress manages to win his heart, and to his own amazement he realizes that:[37]

> Instead of thinking about the drafts, he somehow was greedily anxious to recall his brother's stories about the Jewess's romantic escapades, her free way of life, and these memories only encouraged his audacity. He rushed to sit next to the Jewess, and not thinking about the drafts began to eat...

Thus, the female predatory animal wins, lowering the man to her own primitive level. Chekhov is again on familiar **semiotic territory**:

   Woman = creature of lower order
        powerful animal
        controlling a man
        returning him to a primitive state

Sokol'sky's peaceful enjoyment of his lunch next to the Jewess is his surrender to her. Partaking of food symbolizes the taming of an animal by a stronger Other, who in this case is the detested Jewess. Her power is so great, that she makes a man totally defenceless. Evil reigns in its utter boldness. The thoughts about Susanna's romantic escapades euphemistically suggest another name, "prostitute." Virginia Llewellyn Smith takes this suggestion literally and describes Susanna Moiseevna as a "superior prostitute," ignoring the enormous semiotic complexity of the character.[38]

Chekhov, on the contrary, emphasizes her power to control a man without engaging in sex. Sokol'sky surrenders, but the seductive creature merely forces him to eat. The feast is also a metaphor of woman's victory; she celebrates the taming of a male. There is no other indication of physical intimacy with her than a battle for a piece of paper. The seduction ends in an utterly unexpected fashion, leading to a trivial lunch, and ending in the dining room instead of the expected bedroom. The readers and Sokol'sky himself are left in a torturing suspense. A actual sex is logically expected

158 *Semiotics of Misogyny*

after the battle scene, and yet it does not occur. Sokol'sky loses his male pride; after the expected overture, he is asked to join the "tigress" for lunch. He is also robbed. He forever loses the opportunity to receive money that is destroyed in a fight with the "tigress." The female-tigress is shown in her entire viciousness. The scene of the feast ends the first part of the story which could have been the ending. Chekhov could have stopped right there.

Nonetheless, the story then would have lacked semiotic complexity. To emphasize the tricky power of the mysterious Jewess he introduces similar experience of surrender by Sokol'sky's cousin. Chekhov creates another paradox when Sokol'sky's cousin, Alexey Ivanovich Kriukov, a person totally unlikely to be seduced, becomes another victim of Susanna's seduction. He stresses his calm, lazy disposition, likening Kriukov to an "immobile dolphin" and a person who "knew women and horses quite well." (485)

At the beginning, Alexey is indignant when he finds out that his cousin failed to cash the draft. He is furious that the treacherous female managed to cheat Sokol'sky. Listening to his confession, Alexey cannot comprehend how Sokol'sky failed to defend himself. His cousin's weakness infuriates him more than failure to collect the money. He angrily promises to punish the villain:[39]

> No, I won't leave it at that!--he started talking, shaking his fist. Drafts will be mine. Will be! I will put her in prison! One does not hit women but I will maim her . . .I won't leave a trace! I am not a lieutenant! I will not be touched by boldness and cynicism! No, the devil take her!

Chekhov prepares his readers for the most comical outcome when the indignant and belligerent cousin fails to collect the money, and also falls under the witch's spell.

Exactly like Sokol'sky he returns home the next day and Chekhov mentions, not without obvious delight:[40]

What happened was absolutely not what they expected.

Instead of the promised money and punishment of the criminal there is a laughing revenge. In reply to Sokol'sky's question about money, Kriukov laughingly reports:[41]

> "What a broad!"-he continued, *Merci*, brother, for the acquaintance. This is a devil in a skirt. Well, I arrive there, enter like a Jupiter, so angry that I am scared myself . . . I frowned, knit my brows, even made fists for significance . . . "Lady, I say, I don't joke!" and all this of the sort. I threatened with court and governor . . . She cried at first; then she said she had joked with you, and even took me to the cupboard to give me the money, then began to argue that Europe's future is in the hands of Russians and French cursed women . . . I, much like you, listened and let myself be duped. She first sang a panegyric to my beauty, touched my hand to see how strong I am and . . . and . . . as you can see, I have just left her . . .

The cousins joke about the provincial "tsarina Tamara" and their own weaknesses. Kriukov tries to give Susanna a more suitable name:[42]

> What a devil? One cannot find another chameleon of the kind in the whole of Russia! I have not seen anything like that since I have been born, and am I not a specialist in this area? It seems I have lived with witches but have not seen anything of the sort! Precisely, boldness and cynicism is her strength. What is so attractive in her are the sharp shifts, color play, this devilish impulsiveness . . . Brrrr and drafts-are gone.

Kriukov's indignation and fury is gone, what is left is a confessed loser, another victim of the devilish beauty. He is totally under the spell of her vicious charm. Some weeks later, he confesses to his cousin Alexander that he is haunted by her jasmine scent. He secretly decides to indulge in visiting Susanna once a month. Having collected all his courage, he goes to visit her. He finds the same conversational topic about the destiny of Europe and the same sweetish, seductive scent of jasmine. To his surprise, his cousin is also there and Kriukov thinks in resignation:[43]

> What can I tell him? What? What kind of a judge am I when I am here as well?

The story ends with the distant singer's voice singing:[44]

> Do not call her heavenly and do not deny her a place on Earth...

Earlier Chekhov promised his readers to expose the Jewess, allegedly the true culprit of Jewish tragedy and the genuine cause of the dislike of this group. However, during the course of the narration, the author somehow abandons this original goal. The readers fail to find any definite behavior pattern which deserves their condemnation. Both Sokol'sky and Kriukov conclude that Susanna is an extraordinary female creature, neither heavenly nor ordinary. They respond to her colorful personality. Sometimes she makes them angry; occasionally they recognize her devilish power calling her a "devil," a "vicious cat," a "chameleon," a "witch," but both cousins fall victim of her inexplicable charm. Susanna is their common secret adventure, a pleasant memory which they keep amidst their boring lives. Susanna shocks, infuriates, entertains, puzzles and introduces an unusual gaiety into the boring provincial life of the two cousins. Susanna is represented as a bubbling, joyful, remarkably intelligent creature. Even her forgery is not described as the vicious act of a greedy Jewess, but rather as some mysterious magic and sign of intelligence. She, a female, outwits two males, for Chekhov needed both Sokol'sky and Kriukov to prove Susanna's devilish wit. However, instead of angry exposure, the author seems to enjoy the fruit of his own creative fantasy. Much like Kriukov, he refuses to judge Susanna since she managed to charm him as well.

There is a definite character metamorphosis. At first, the readers see Susanna in her bedroom, suffering from migraine, appearing in the moment of weakness and in the most unflattering attire. A sickly Jewess who tortures the guest and refuses to pay a debt alerts the readers to expect a stamp of strict judgement. Little by little, Chekhov introduces a new description of the character. Instead of the simplistic function of a negative character, Susanna acquires various semiotic functions. First, she occasionally leaves the "character chamber" and invades the **authorial space**. Chekhov makes her his own voice; she becomes the **extra-narrative route** which an author may acquire through the character. Having imparted the character with the **mission** of an **authorial spokesman**, he gives another fictional life to Susanna who temporarily takes on the mask of a man. As a **pseudo-man-sign** she denounces women, and marriage. Occasionally, Chekhov forgets about the character's temporary function, leaving aside the male mask even when Susanna is already back in her own character's space. He lets her decide the destinies of Europe and discuss the national qualities of various European people.

Susanna is a character-paradox. Unlike other women in Chekhov's story she is portrayed as an intelligent creature. Chekhov repeatedly informs the readers that the secret of Susanna's mysterious power over men is her "utter cynicism," implying her bold, intelligent criticism of provincial life. Even her crime is presented as an evidence of her brilliant mind. Promising to explain the malicious nature of Jewish women, the alleged cause of anti-Jewish feelings, Chekhov does exactly the opposite. He has proven in his unusual triangle of characters that Susanna is the antithesis to the existing stereotype.

In the middle of the story Chekhov has reintroduced the concise characteristics of the women of the despised group. Chekhov-Susanna explained that all Jewish women "lack poetry, are narrow-minded, greedy and boring." And yet his character-desire is precisely the opposite of the stereotypical image. Susanna is portrayed in a complex way, as an enormously imaginative, clever, broad-minded, exciting and poetic individual.

Her entire, seemingly negative role is the negation of the introduced stereotype. It is not incidental that the story ends with a song line which highly poetically describes the controversial character as a heavenly creature. Thus, Chekhov deliberately fails to recreate a Jewess as **a sign of danger** and a cause of hatred. What he does is the act of subverting the traditional stereotype. The semiotic message of his complicated narrative strategy may be interpreted as:

                a woman   = face of any nation
                Jewish woman   = the other woman
                                  carrier of hatred
                                  heavenly creature
                Jews   = are not to be hated

Chekhov the artist manages to convey the message which judges and corrects the popular collective myth, as well as his own contradictory messages. Through the creative arguments, he arrives at a remarkably atypical conclusion, that Jews are neither "chosen people" nor a group to be persecuted.

The conclusion is made after a lengthy labyrinth of mythical pitfalls. Chekhov wrestled with the image of the "devil," "siren," "witch," "queen Tamara." He wanted to share the more expected, and the familiar and failed. Susanna's sharp contrasts, her mood swings, reflect Chekhov's own artistic vicissitudes, philosophical doubts and historian-like obligations to history. Finally, the **character-desire** prevails over the expected familiar mythical caricature. One may be tempted to search for the roots of Chekhov's controversial character in his own personal life, in topics of his day and increasing ethnic tensions in the South of Russia. The story *Tina* (Slime) was published in October, 1886. Around the same time Chekhov was engaged to Dunya Efros, a Jewess. In his letter to V.V. Bilibin, dated January, 1886 he spoke about his matrimonial intentions and on February 1, 1886 he wrote the following to the same addressee:[45]

> My *she* is a Jewess. Courage is necessary for wealthy Jewess to accept Orthodoxy with its consequences--well, it is not necessary and not needed and we have already quarreled over this. Tomorrow we'll make it up and in a week we'll fall out again. Vexed that religion is a problem, she has broken pencils and a photograph on my table--this is characteristic of her. She is a terrible spitfire. I shall undoubtedly leave her within one or two years of marriage.

Susanna may be easily juxtaposed against Chekhov's fiancée, the scene of the fist fight for the paper in the story echoes the episode in the letter. One may consider Dunya Efros as the prototype of Susanna, but awareness of this fact is important in the establishment of the ideological ethos of the story. Chekhov's contemplation of marriage to a woman of the despised minority in Russia is the best testimony to his rather advanced views. He obviously did not share the prejudices of the Slavophiles and the stereotypes of the predominant majority. This helped him to support Zola's stand in the notorious Dreyfus affair. While French Press condemned Zola, and his friend and publisher Suvorin participated in the wave of anti-semitism, Chekhov took the side of the most progressive and "educated people" and supported Zola. Like most biographers, Simmons refers to Chekhov's letter to F. D. Batiushkov where he wrote:[46]

> The immense majority of educated people are on the side of Zola and believe Dreyfus innocent . . . *New Times* is simply repulsive.(Jan. 28, 1898)

Chekhov admired Zola and called him a man who possesses "purity and moral elevation which no one had expected" (413).

Chekhov's own philosophical system had provisions for respect of another fellow-being. According to him "people of culture, respect human personality and are therefore forbearing, gentle, courteous, and compliant" (Simmons, 1962: 111-3). Following his eight main principles which define a "man of culture," Chekhov could not share trivial popular mythology based on ignorance, hostility and lack of human empathy. Like a true "man of culture" Chekhov relied on knowledge, discarding quite tempting collective generalizations. As a "man of culture" Chekhov was on the side of the oppressed, falsely accused and unjustifiably disliked.

Chekhov who took Zola's side in the Dreyfus affair would have protested against the anti-Jewish actions in 1905. On the eve of the enormous upheaval that was about to shake Russia, a man of culture could sense polarized nationalist sentiments and would have felt it his duty to protect men of culture from ignorance. It is not surprising that the story was met with mixed sentiments and disliked by many readers. Mme M. Kiseleva wondered why Chekhov had to rummage in the "muck-heap," to which he replied:[47]

> Writers are children of their age, and therefore, like the rest of the public, they must submit to the external conditions of social life. Thus, for instance they must be absolutely decent.

He also regrets that individuals would like to suppress the writers' voice:[48]

> Sad, indeed, would be the fate of literature, great and minor, if it were left to the mercy of individual views. That is the first thing. Secondly, there are no police who would consider themselves competent in the matters of literature. I agree it would not do to dispense with the bridle and the whip, since cardsharpers crawl even into literature; but, however you try, you won't invent a better police for literature than criticism and the author's own conscience.

Chekhov was obviously very hurt by the reaction to his story which was waiting until critics had acquired courage to deal with the unpleasant matters of *Slime*. The analysis of the story cannot be complete without focussing upon its title. The Russian word *tina* (slime) is close to the English "mire," Koteliansky chooses this more precise version while Y. L. Smith prefers "slime." The latter is much more metaphorical and even bears the strong negative attitude to the central character which the critic happens to have. Her choice of the translation has its roots in the general dislike of Susanna whom she naively perceives as a merely "superior prostitute," failing to discover the semiotic complexity of the story and multifacedness of its central character. She devotes just two sentences to the "unpleasant" story, which in her view, perhaps, does not deserve more.

The correct choice of the title by Koteliansky reflects his more cautious translation tactic. After all, the Russian original implies "marsch," "bog," "soft Earth." The original title deals better with Chekhovian perplexity about the unpopular and the despised. Kiseleva's reaction to the story symbolized the predominant readers' reaction which was that of pathological sensitivity to the theme of the despised minority. The title encodes the entire gamut of the authorial and readers' emotions that *Tina*-Mire-Slime may have evoked in his own time; and later the original intentions of the author are irrelevant. What is significant is that the interpretative potential of the successfully chosen title increases with time. It now uncovers what the Russian 19th century reader may have missed or was unable to see, bogged down in stereotypical popular mythology. The artistic sense of orientation led Chekhov outside the intractable territory of popular myth. He discovered exciting mystery in the trivial story about money lost to a Jewess.

Metaphorically, on the subtextual level, he offers, if not a solution, but at least another perspective on the "Other", Jews and Russians and Otherness. He tries to find poetry in those who were proclaimed "unpoetic," discovers a lack of peculiarity in the "Other" and refuses to pinpoint the odious features in the despised. Instead, Chekhov suggests leaving the "mire" of the stereotype and not dening the "Other" the right of being. The line from Glinka's romance:

Do not call her heavenly nor deny her place on Earth.

is an artistic verdict and a prophetic precursor of the ideological climate of the next century, which would be bogged down in the same mire of hatred and stereotype.

CHAPTER 6

Women, Slavery and an Interim Sign

6.1 Women – Dynamic Signs

The Chekhovian world of female characters would have been rather "boring," and his perception of human relationships would not deserve close attention had his gallery of women's portraits consisted only of "little souls," shallow inferior creatures, primarily needed as sources of procreation or aesthetic objects for daily admiration. Paying tribute to the traditions of the old patriarchal culture, Chekhov exhibits the gallery of charming, amusing "pink stockings": this is Naden'ka who could not even write properly, Nina who "scribbled her entire life" and died uneducated, stupid governess Zinochka, Olen'ka who had no thoughts of her own, and many others. He pleased his male readers with these funny, pleasant-looking creatures who were too lazy to use their intelligence, if any, whose primary concern lay in the preservation of their beauty and whose main preoccupation was entertainment and the adornment of their bodies. Men must have appreciated these stereotypical women's portraits which were even occasionally becoming grotesque caricatures.

However, he would not have been "a man of culture," the philosophical category from the system of his own making, had he confined his view of women only to these popular images. As a man of culture, Chekhov, the grandson of a serf, who became a physician and prominent Russian man of letters, believed passionately in self-advancement through education, culture and the general betterment of the self. Chekhov challenged the prevalent misconceptions about the social determinism. He proved with his own achievements that one's current misery should not become one's permanent destiny. He believed that one's unfortunate lot could be improved through education, hard work and inner creativity. In other words, Chekhov totally rejected the social imprisonment to which all previous history and philosophy confined millions of people. He was convinced that one's unfortunate birth into an oppressed and impoverished class did not imply a life-time sentence of misery and social isolation.

Chekhov restructured the Tolstovian idea of spiritual self-improvement, demonstrated with his own personal experience how his own philosophical system works, and how it is possible to extend the world of social possibilities. In other words, Chekhov rebelled against the social hierarchy, defended the concept of upward mobility, and defied societal prejudice. If he and members of his family could leave the class of the uneducated, oppressed and despised, the rest could do it as well. His famous letter to his brother is a philosophical manifesto where he proclaims the revolutionary idea of self-advancement and defines his ideal man of culture. Among the eight basic qualities which constitute a "man of culture" Chekhov valued the constant attempt to "exterminate a slave in oneself." Almost every biographer recalls Chekhov's famous letter dated Jan. 7, 1889 and addressed to Suvorin:[1]

> Do, please, write a story of how a young man, the son of a serf, who has been a shop-boy, a chorister, a pupil of a secondary school and a university graduate, who has been brought up to respect rank and to kiss the priest's hand, to bow to other people's ideas, to be thankful for each morsel of bread, who has been thrashed many a time, who has had to walk about tutoring without galoshes, who has fought, tormented animals, has been fond of dining at the house of well-to-do relations, and played the hypocrite both to God and man without any need but merely out of consciousness of his own insignificance-describe how that young man *squeezes the slave out of himself*, and now, drop by drop awakening one fine morning, he feels running in his veins no longer the blood of a slave but genuine human blood . . .

If he believed that the slave may be "squeezed out" of oneself, did he extend it to women who predominantly were in the position of slaves? A slave was not only a male ancestor who was in the state of misery, but also a despised female and she also required the same Chekhovian style "therapy". Despite his famous condescension towards women, disparaging characterization and flirtation with the popular stereotypes, the "man of culture" had to rebel against the despicable condition of women-slaves as well.

Although Chekhovian women are predominantly upper-middle class in the 19th century provincial Russia, there are some colorful characters of Russian peasant women, as well. They are the most oppressed among the oppressed, the best examples of those slaves whom he condemned. Chekhov, the misogynist, could not help sympathizing with the women-slaves, be they peasant women, wives, widows, in the poor families of little Russian clergymen, officers, or clerks. The very existence of this "other slave" amongst men was repulsive to Chekhov. His empathy for the woman-slave partly comes from his general feeling of disgust and anger at the very possibility of such a condition per se.

According to the Chekhovian perception of human society, slavery of any kind had to be eliminated. "One has to squeeze a slave out of oneself drop by drop,"-he passionately proclaimed in his manifesto. One may draw a semiotic conclusion out of his passionate motto:

> man = a slave
> woman
> inferior to man = more of a slave

If slavery was appalling to Chekhov he had to permit women to participate in the process of "squeezing out a slave." After all, mothers, mistresses, daughters and companions of free men could not be slaves. Their condition could harm men striving for inner freedom. First, however, he had to acknowledge women's subservient and oppressed condition, and he did it in his own contradictory fashion where a misogynist had to be reconciled with the humanist, compassionate physician diagnosing the condition of women.

Much like any other human being, Chekhov was full of contradictions. Within the span of a single passage he could express genuine empathy and utter dislike. For instance, Zhmukhin from the story *Pecheneg* (1897) exemplifies this complex Chekhovian voice which simultaneously bears the notes of sentimental meditation and indignation. At first, Zhmukhin sounds very sympathetic to the destiny of women, recalling his wife's youth and their marriage:[2]

> She is from a poor family, priest's daughter, church-bell, so to speak, I married her when she was seventeen years old, she was given away. Mostly because there was nothing to eat, want misery I have, as you can see, some land, property, no matter what, an officer; it was flattering for her to marry me, you know. On the first day of our marriage she began to cry, she cried and then had been crying for twenty years.

Zhmukhin gives a typical story of a young innocent woman who was practically exchanged for property. Married to a man, obviously older than her, totally strange to her she is the archetypal woman-victim. The husband's recollection of her reaction bears mixed feelings. On the one hand he realizes that his wife married him not for love; on the other, there is some sorrow that a seventeen year old woman, nearly a child, was given to him in despair. Zhmukhin acknowledges her tragedy, and there is no bitterness when he claims that their marriage meant upward mobility for Liubov' Osipovna. He recognizes that misery forced her parents to give their seventeen-year-old away. Her tears for twenty years do not irritate him; he accepts them as the natural response of a woman who is forced to submit to the brutal reality of family, order and tradition.

However, at the end of the passage Zhmukhin surprises the listeners with the angry conclusion:[3]

> And she sits and thinks, thinks. What does she think about, one may ask? What can a woman think about? Nothing, as far as I am concerned, a woman is not a human being.

Unlike other stories, here Zhmukhin's voice cannot be taken for Chekhovian traditional mask, because the story ends with the narrator's utterance which possesss unmistakable force. The narrator diagnoses his wife's pitiful state. She is a slave:

> Zhmukhin's wife, pale and even paler than the day before, looked at him attentively, not blinking, with a naive girl-like expression on her face, and her sad face would tell that she was envious of his freedom,--oh with what delight would she leave this place!

Chekhov juxtaposes the image of a woman-slave and husband-free master without actually naming her "a slave." "His freedom" is a signal or a marker of the sign "he, man" which implicitly suggests to the reader the **semiotic antithesis**-"she, woman," a "slave."

What has been implied in the beginning obtains its full semiotic value at the end of the narrator's utterance:[4]

> How pitiful she is! She is neither a wife, nor a landlady, not even a maid, she is more of a poor relative, poor, nobody's kin, a burden to all, nothingness, insignificance.

The reader is given a choice of powerful signals which finally lead them to the intended sign, a slave:

> a martyr
> a victim
> neither a wife
> nor a landlady
> not a maid
> poor relative
> burdensome person
> insignificance
> nothingness
> silent slave

Her movements are the picture of a frightened being, almost a caged animal. A new feature is Chekhov's obvious acknowledgement of woman's misery. Unlike Olen'ka, Ninochka, or Varen'ka, Zhmukhin's wife manifests very unusual behavior: she analyzes her husband's freedom and is aware of her own lack of freedom. She is far away from the hated *emancipé*, she is neither a "pink nor blue stocking" yet, but rather a creature in between, a strange Chekhovian female specie which may perhaps eventually produce another. She is the **sign in between other signs**. This instance of a new **woman-sign** in Chekhov's short stories is not limited to Zhmukhin's wife, Liubov' Osipovna. The story *Aniuta*, written eleven years earlier, strikes one as an antithesis to the entire gallery of female caricatures presented earlier. Aniuta is the unusual Chekhovian woman's image which reveals the change of a misogynist heart. Unlike the amusing, attractive but despised "pink stockings," his Aniuta is "a small slim, pale, grey-eyed twenty-five year-old seamstress who touches Chekhov's "disharmonic nature." She is different from his traditional women's characters in all respects. First of all, she is not a member of the Russian upper middle class, but a poor working girl who earns her living by selling her embroidery. She is also a part-time model for a medical student who uses her body to memorize human anatomy. Unlike other seductive, voluptuous females whose primary concern is the bedroom, Aniuta is an unwilling participant in everything which is done to her body. She obediently allows third year medical student Stepan Klochkov to mark her ribs with a charcoal so that he can better memorize the bone structure. She, perhaps, as obediently submits to the other, more traditional uses of her body.

If, in the past, Chekhovian females were authoritarian, capricious, domestic tyrants, clad in white and pink lace, who ruled the servants and husbands with iron fists, Aniuta is the other Chekhovian woman. She echoes much more a French woman from Zola or Maupassant, a typical new woman earning her living by monotonous, dull sewing. What makes Aniuta uniquely Chekhovian is her sadness, despair and lack of spirit. Unlike her French character-counterpart, Chekhovian Aniuta does not dream of marrying a rich man. She is not naive, neither is she cheerful at her tender age of twenty-five. Stepan Klochkov is her master, a slave-owner who may dispense with her as soon as she is no longer needed for his anatomical studies. She had already had five of such masters who had been using her body as a model, sex machine, and technical equipment, beyond using her services as cleaner, cook and seamstress. Chekhov writes about her:[5]

> During these six to seven years of wandering in such furnished rooms, she knew about five men like Klochkov. Now they had all completed their studies, established themselves, and of course, as decent people, forgot about her long ago. One of them lives in Paris, two have become doctors, the fourth one is a painter, and they say, the fifth one is even a professor. Klochkov-is the sixth . . . Soon he will also graduate and will make a career.

Aniuta is described as the victim of a man--this is a strikingly novel and unexpected shift in Chekhovian sexist portrayal, in contradiction to his misogynist theory, and is a manifestation of his changing attitude to women. Contrary to his own beliefs, this woman is no longer an idle, lazy "pink stocking," but a tired working-woman. Instead of a habitual parasitism on a man, it is she who supports her Klochkov. Her small income is an important contribution to the meagre allowance of twelve roubles that he gets from his father. He may become a successful doctor afterwards, but so far Aniuta's hands earn him money to buy his tea and tobacco, Chekhov stresses that this woman helps to make the future doctor Klochkov:[6]

> Undoubtedly the future is marvellous, Klochkov will perhaps become a great man, but the present is absolutely dreadful; Klochkov has no tobacco, no tea, only four lumps of sugar are left. It is necessary to finish the embroidery, deliver it to the client and to buy tea and tobacco for the received twenty-five copecks.

While Aniuta is portrayed as the positive, vital force in Klochkov's life, the student exhibits the ugliest features of the user-man. Stepan resents her services and her presence. He dreams about the day when he can live in decent quarters, drinking tea in the company of a wife or a "decent woman." Chekhov exposes Klochkov's nature: a man who drinks the tea which Aniuta bought for him with her hard earned money, but still does not see her as a "decent woman." He abuses her young body, treating it not even as a human flesh but as artificial matter, a board, a tool, or a visual aid. To Klochkov, Aniuta lost her femininity, her body is no longer a sacred source of life, but only his technical equipment. While cramming anatomy he complains that Aniuta's ribs do not protrude enough:[7]

> Well, well, you won't die, don't move, so this is the third rib and this is the fourth. To the eye you are skinny, but one cannot feel the ribs . . . This is the second . . . this is the third . . . No one can get confused like this and cannot imagine it clearly . . . I will have to draw . . . Where is my charcoal?

Aniuta has to stand in a cold room, naked, waiting until he finds the location of a proper rib. She may not touch her own body, or take off the charcoal

174 *Semiotics of Misogyny*

until the future "successful doctor" finally remembers where her ribs are. The male and female characters are clearly juxtaposed according to the changed semiotic map:

man	woman
negative	positive
parasite	giver
abuser	victim
calculating	loving
position of power	powerless
master	slave
cruel	caring

The Chekhovian sexual roles are finally reversed, for the previously calculating, cold, tyrannical creature is no longer a woman. Unlike, doctor Dymov, victim of his flippant wife, *Poprygun'ia* (Butterfly) (1892), Stepan is the abuser himself, the immoral indifferent being who is using his companion as a servant, a piece of equipment, and abusing her kindness and generosity. When Klochkov decides that her services are no longer needed and that she may be an obstacle in his career, he even praises her:[8]

You are nice and kind, and not stupid; you will understand.

Through Klochkov, the combined voice of the narrator-author presents an alternate view of a woman. Aniuta is not yet recognized as a being who is equal to Klochkov in her intelligence, but she is regarded as simply "not stupid;" it is not only an approval of her mind, but also a symptom of the significant shift in Chekhovian thinking.

Instead of an idle parasite living at the expense of a man, Aniuta is the new woman who supports her lover. She is the precursor of the new twentieth century woman who becomes a bread-winner in anticipation of lover's successful future professional career. Chekhov endows her with a sense of moral responsibility for Stepan's present well-being, a certain sacrifice for the sake of his future medical career.

The two characters in the story perform an important semiotic function. Stepan and Aniuta are the complex **signs-composits** which may finally be assembled by the readers, once they have all the required **semiotic parts**. During the course of the story, Chekhov gradually provides the readers with all the required character-components, so that a final image of the sign may appear. The established meaning of the sign implies "portrayal, replacement" of something for something else, be it Eco's lie or Voloshinov's ideology.[9] Aniuta and Stepan finally appear as two **opposite signs** that are associated with contrasting expression, meaning, two opposite ideologies or streams of the signified, **male and female:**

Aniuta   Stepan
sign of the oppressed   sign of the oppressor
she   he
woman   man

Chekhov not only constructs these two signs, but he also influences their reception by the readers. For instance, Aniuta is presented as a **sympathy-evoking sign**, while Stepan consequently appears as a **condemnation-deserving semiotic construct**. The emotional atmosphere is saturated up to its climax when Klochkov decides to dispense with Aniuta. He provides aesthetic reasoning to this decision. As a future "man of culture," and a successful physician, he finds his relationship with Aniuta, a poor woman, repugnant:

Aniuta also appeared as unattractive, untidy and pitiful . . .
And he decided to part with her at any cost.

Hiding behind the notion of beauty, Stepan merely tries to justify his anxiety. Aniuta is a woman at a low socio-economic level. He will not be able to marry her once he becomes a doctor. While in his third year of medical school he already pictures himself with another woman, a "decent" one, as he puts it.

Aniuta is blamed for his present poverty, the unaesthetic character of his apartment which is used simultaneously as a study, a studio, kitchen, shop and bedroom. The "tea" mentioned several times in the story has a semiotic function as well. Aniuta earns money to buy Stepan's tea, but he dreams of another tea, in a living-room, nicely furnished, presumably the future home of the well paid future doctor. The **sign** "tea" performs two contrasting functions:

tea 1	tea 2
Aniuta's tea	other woman's tea
present	future
poverty	well being
students life	physician's life

The omniscient narrator informs the readers about this other tea, the "tea" of his dreams which appears as an **ominous sign** one of the signifying Aniuta's coming trauma, the end of her love affair.

When Klochkov announces that he decides to part with her, the reader is prepared already to condemn this male character. Even when he temporarily changes his mind and permits Aniuta to stay, he still remains a villain. In his thoughts, which are exposed to the reader, Stepan decides to let Aniuta stay for another week only. The story ends with the familiar scene of anatomy lessons when the stool is prepared for Aniuta, for her body to be used a little more. A slave is allowed to serve longer for her master.

Aniuta is a **sign of economic exchange** of a different order. She possesses no property, no inheritance. At present, she satisfies Klochkov in his humble position of a student. In fact, they are equal at present. His father's allowance is combined with Aniuta's income, her part-time jobs as an artists' model and piece-embroidering work help them both to survive. However, her meagre income would not be needed in Stepan's future when a prosperous doctor would rise to the heights of a professional. Aniuta is also a threat to Stepan's future since a successful bourgeois would not want to be reminded of his poor past. Aniuta has to be eliminated as a trace of the embarrassing past, an obstacle to Klochkov's upward mobility.

Chekhov's exposure of this male character is rather unusual in his creative biography. As if the author undergoes a **semiotic metamorphosis**, his ideas are drastically transformed. Chekhov, the admirer of convenient **pink stockings**, is ready to accept the other woman. On the eve of the acceptance of the **blue stockings** in his later works, Chekhov introduces a very intriguing image, "blue legs." This could be classified as the Greimasion **pre-symbol**, a **sign-symptom** of another sign or the second stage of the familiar sign, "pink stocking." When Kochkov's friend, an artist, comes to "rent" Aniuta for his modelling sessions, he tells a funny story about a blue-legged woman:[10]

> Yesterday, I used one (model) with blue legs. I asked her, "Why are your legs blue?" She says, that is from the stockings, they lose color.

This Chekhovian image of a blue-legged woman is symptomatic of the new women in literature and in life. If these "blue-legged" women allowed being used, the "blue stockings" would later insist on participating in life, using their intelligence. However, Chekhov, the semiotician, had to introduce his "thirdness," another category between the other two signs:[11]

                                              free blue stockings
     pink stocking   blue-legged
     object   victim

Otherwise, the transition from the flippant sex objects to the intimidating "blue stocking" would have been too drastic. Chekhov needed this **intermediate semiotic category**, another interpretation of a **woman-sign** to reflect upon the newly appearing "blue stocking." Dealing with his own and readers' stereotypes, Chekhov had to prepare a sufficient ground for another female character. Until now, they were accustomed to see the "delicious pineapples" or Little Souls, Olen'kas who were aesthetic fixtures to the man's world. Despite their purely aesthetic function, they were regarded as immoral parasites who exchanged their beautiful bodies for economic stability and sex. Unlike these predominant characters Aniuta metaphorizes the "Other" woman, a woman-victim whose body alone serves a different purpose. She does not benefit from the liaison with the man. On the contrary, it is Stepan, a future doctor, who needs Aniuta to survive in the world. She is the backbone of his present and a promise of his better future. Even Aniuta's body is used for man's education, Stepan's anatomy lessons on Aniuta's ribs vividly symbolize the new distribution of roles. Unlike Dymov, the victim from *Butterfly*, he is the one who abuses one's love, devotion and generosity. It is not Aniuta who needs Klochkov for material support but vice versa. She and the "blue-legged" model" in the story convey a new message to the reader. It is the novel idea of a woman who offers moral, physical and financial support to a man. She not only lost her past inferiority but acquired intelligence. Klochkov's scant praise of Aniuta is a certain recognition of her worth. Belittling the male character Chekhov achieves his goal; he prepares for the reception of the new female character. Eventually he even will occasionally recognize traces of woman's superiority, but in between he has to prepare himself and his male readers for the coming of the ominous "blue stockings."

6.2 Women as Alarming Signals

> Women were therefore conceptualized as dangerous because less amenable to the guiding light of reason.
> Their potential for disorder can be minimized by drawing and maintaining strong social boundaries around them.
> J. S. Jordanova, *Natural Facts*.

Despite the fact that most of Maugham's women in his fictional world are sex objects, powerful predators and manipulative primitive creatures, there are a couple of female characters that actually compete with men-producers of cultural signs. They are Maugham's "blue stockings," Mrs. Albert Forrester *(The Creative Impulse)* and Eva Katherine Hamilton *(The Colonel's Lady)*. Both females are engaged in the same profession as Maugham himself, they are successful writers. Maugham is visibly alarmed that women enter professions other than those traditionally reserved for them by men, and he presents these characters as dangerous predators of a new breed, hunting not for marriage and sex, but for success and publicity. To intensify the air of fear and anxiety, he does not spare dark verbal colors for these unusual women.

First of all, he secures the visual perception of these signs. His Mrs. Forrester is larger than a woman usually is:[12]

> She was large-boned and her bones were well-covered; had she not been so tall and strong it might have suggested to you that she was corpulent.

Not only this woman's body is presented as "large," "tall," "strong" and "corpulent," but her face strikes one as, befitting her large body:[13]

> Her features were a little larger than life-size and it was this that gave her face doubtless the look of virile intellectuality that it certainly possessed.

Maugham uses one signal "larger than life-size" which reminds the reader that the depicted female is actually highly fictional. This woman imagined by Maugham is a fictional construct, a **woman-sign** which is intended to alert the male readers to possible social changes in the real world. It is an artistic warning, and he does not wish his readers to have any possible allusions of reality. His woman is not a typical specie whom one is accustomed to see in real life; she is larger than "life-size."

To prove that she is dangerous and that her "virile intellectuality" may harm men, Maugham also presents her as "dark as a Gypsy":[14]

> Her skin was dark and you might have thought that she had in her veins some trace of Levantine blood: she admitted that she could not but think there was in her a Gypsy strain and that would account, she felt, for the wild and lawless passion that sometimes characterized her poetry.

Thus, despite her proven success as a producer of cultural signs-poems, she is still portrayed as somebody who is inferior. She is a "Gypsy" and that alone permits Maugham to speak about her substandard creativity. This new woman causes anxiety with her sheer physical presence. Her big size intimidates and Maugham does not spare **verbal icons** to mediate this strictly visual effect. It is not enough that Mrs. Forrester possesses a large body and face. Her nose is "as large as the great Duke of Wellington's but more fleshy," her mouth is "big as well," her lips are "full," and hair is "thick." The entire physical description recreates the meaning of a large object which stands out among other people and things:[15]

> Her hair, thick, solid and grey, was piled on the top of her head in such a manner as to increase her already commanding height. She was in appearance an imposing, not to say an alarming female.

Maugham uses the traditional icons which attract one's attention: they are color and size which are superimposed upon the anthropological icon "Gypsy." The **semiosis** which takes place inside the portrait-passage is constructed on two levels:

I	visual (nature)	dark big	woman
II	mental (cultural-stereotypes)	Gypsy	

All Gypsies stand for theft, crime, witchcraft, danger, as well as dangerous women. Mrs. Forrester combines the two as a Gypsy and a woman, and as a biological rarity, which makes her presence among men even more alarming. In addition to her purely visible distinctiveness, she is a writer whose success is bothersome. He gives the prehistory of this alarming female:[16]

> Mrs. Albert Forrester began to write early. Her first work (a volume of elegies) appeared when she was a maiden of eighteen; and from then on she published, every two or three years.

She not only published in various genres, but used very enigmatic Latin titles such as *Felicitas, Pax Maris* and *Aes Friplex*. Her range of topics was extremely wide, and despite the fact that she exercised her pen in odes, sonnets, elegy, and essays, Maugham presents her as a master of prose, and a master of the English language:[17]

> She wrote several volumes of brief, but perfectly constructed, essays on such subjects as Autumn in Sussex, Queen Victoria, Death, Spring in Norfolk, Georgian Architecture, Monsieur de Diaghileff and Dante; she also wrote works both erudite and whimsical, on the Jesuit Architecture of the XVIIth century and on the Literary Aspect of the Hundred Year's War.

Her visible, strikingly big body befits the wide body of her works, also in the realm of fantasy as Maugham implies. He suggests to the reader that a person who writes on *Autumn in Sussex*, that is in a genre of travelogues, and then attempts to deal with Dante, switching to Renaissance studies, is either a superficial caricature or an alarming literary rival. Maugham tries to mock her style which he finds "sonorous but racy" and "humorous." The alleged grotesqueness of her writing is in her enormous publicity that is paradoxically combined with some infelicities in her grammar:[18]

> It was not a humour of ideas, nor even humour of words, it was much more subtle than that, it was a humour of punctuation: in a flash of inspiration she had discovered the comic possibilities of the semi-colon, and of this she had made abundant and exquisite use. She was able to place it in such a way that if you were a person of culture with a keen sense of humour, you did not exactly laugh through a horse-collar, but you giggled delightedly, and the greater your culture the more delightedly you giggled.

Thus, this prolific writer is even dangerous as she subverts the standards of culture and literacy, turning serious writing into one big **sign-displacement** exercise. Despite her troubles with grammar and playing with semi-colons:[19]

> Each work she published, a slender volume beautifully printed and bound in white buckram, was hailed as a masterpiece.

Maugham's "alarming female" continues to be alarmingly successful. At the age of fifty-seven she manages to write a novel, *The Achilles Statue*, which becomes so popular that:[20]

> The publishers, both in England and America, were hard put to it to fulfill the pressing orders of the booksellers. It was promptly translated into every European tongue and it has been recently announced that it will soon be possible to read it in Japanese and in Urdu.

Maugham mediates the sense of outrage that this illiterate authoress manages to reach world publicity. To prove that it is all ill-deserved fame Maugham claims that the "best minds in America were sensitive" to Mrs. Forrester's "talent," "America" and "American" are the cultural stereotypes of inferiority placed next to Europe and Britain. The fact that this "alarming female" is recognized, accepted and praised in America implies that she is not a real writer, the producer of genuine cultural signs. Maugham uses the stereotype about Euro-centricity of culture where America occupies as less significant place. He semiotically destroys the fame of his own fictional character:

Europe	Woman	America
Superior	inferior	inferior
producer of Culture	producer of signs	producer of signs

Then he makes a semiotic conclusion, if an "alarming female," a "producer of inferior culture" invades cultural space, she is dangerous. He warns about possible deterioration of culture when women, these "alarming females", become active participants in the **production of signs**. Despite her "male intelligence" and deep interest in politics, "she did not know which party to choose" which attested to her absolute confusion.

Her other danger was in oppressing her husband, Albert, who "made Mrs. Forrester's luncheons," fetched her books, and "passed her pencils" so that "she could make a note of an idea that had occurred to her." He was like a "well-trained, well-bred, and well-mannered Persian cat." His role was to keep her in touch with the concrete world. Their roles are reversed; what was traditionally a woman's job is done by a man. Albert cooks, serves, reads her manuscripts, in passive, submissive and shy, the traditional icons are misplaced:

he	she
passive	aggressive
shy	bold
cooks	writes
small	big
Persian cat	alarming female
nature	culture
nurturer	nurtured

Maugham, the misogynist experiencing pathological anxiety in the company of "alarming females" or "blue stockings," is not satisfied with the grotesqueness of his character-icon.[21] He has to punish her, and her punishment is depriving her of her mate. At the end of the story, Albert "elopes with the cook," a youngish female whose mother was "half-French." Mrs. Forrester experiences great shock at the loss of an obedient maid, servile pet and loving "Persian cat", Albert. However, their open discussion about their separation is nothing more than a farce where Mrs. Forrester again parades in Maugham's mask. She says to Albert in her deep grief:[22]

> Does the fidelity of five and thirty years count for nothing? I have never looked at another man, Albert, I'm used to you. I shall be lost without you."

This atypical female, primarily engaged in writing, she was indeed faithful to her loving mate, which makes her so different from other Maugham's women. She temporarily plays the role of a helpless female who is afraid of loneliness, and Albert humorously comforts her using his new lover's words:[23]

> I've left all my menus with the new cook, ma'am. You've only got to tell her how many to luncheon and she'll manage.

Thus, she, the "alarming female" is not grieving because she has lost a sex partner, but she is at a loss without a cook, a butler. Albert is the image of a man-victim who rebels against this new predator and finally refuses to perform these mundane unmanly duties. His place is taken by a female maid, and the traditional order is restored. Albert abandons his unnatural role and leaves Mrs. Forrester with a "fluent, a fertile and a distinguished pen." "Pen," his former wife's only love, is a **subversive sign**, metaphor signifying her otherness:

she	he
pen	penis

He leaves her and takes away his "pen" (penis) while she is left with her fluent"pen to substitute for the male organ. Maugham humorously employs Freudian phallic symbols to debunk his atypical female.[24]

The story ends happily with Mrs. Forrester busy writing a detective novel, a genre which she previously resented since it was Albert's favorite literature. The abandoned wife forgets about her former attachment and the only trace of the past is her new infatuation with writing detective novels. It is a new stage in her life, and Albert is forgotten as a part of her "semi-colon period," or her humorous exercises in illiterate pseudo-literary discourse.

"Semi-colon" is also a metaphor for utter indifference to the males as sexual beings which is a characteristic feature of this **new alarming female**.

Another alarming female is Eva Hamilton *(The Colonel's lady)* who starts in life as a "pink stocking," "a nice woman, a good wife" and a "woman you simply did not notice." She married George Pelegrine and they led a peaceful normal married life:[25]

> She had never bothered him. There'd been no scenes. They had no quarrels. She seemed to take for granted that he should go his own way.

However, Eva who starts as a "normal" woman eventually happens to be a different female, a disappointment," as Maugham puts it. Her otherness is in her infertility:[26]

> He could not understand why she'd had no children.

Although he understands that it was not her fault but the fact that Eva is "barren" puts her into a class of Other females. Later this fault and flaw in her body is aggravated by her unusual interest in reading and writing:[27]

> Eva had a lot of high brow books in her sitting room, not the sort of books that interested him.

To show the differences between George's and Eva's interests Maugham uses book titles as **distribution icons**:

his books	her books
farming	high brow
gardening	art
fishing	achitecture
shooting	philosophy
on the last war	literature
he	**she**
simple	complex
ordinary	other

On day, George discovers in the *Times* that his nice wife has written a book of poetry. He reads it and does not think highly of it. "Poor Evie", he says:[28]

He shared Edgar Allan Poe's opinion that poems should be short. But as he turned the pages he noticed that several of Evie's had long lines of irregular lines and did not rhyme.

George denies poetic status to his wife's work:[29]

"That is not what I call poetry," he said.

Then eventually he discovers that the book which he labelled as lacking poetry happens to be the "talking and reading item" among all his friends. He becomes the husband of a celebrity who is compared to Heine and Sappho. Evie's books are reviewed by *The Times Literary Supplement*, the *New Statesman* and *The Spectator,* published in England and the USA. His "homely, desiccated little woman" is being photographed for American publishers. He is very uneasy with her success and finally seeks revenge and divorce having read one of her books describing passionate love. Unable to distinguish between the real and fictional worlds. George accuses Evie of adultery. He consults a lawyer and after long talks decides to drop the suit. However, the story ends on an angry note:[30]

What in the name of heaven did the fellow ever see in her?

It could be read literally and metaphorically:

What did the critics find in Evie's work.

What did the man find in Evie's body.

The husband of a celebrity is presented as a victim of a "barren" female who cannot produce sons, but is able to create art. Adultery is not proven, but the accusation remains in the air since the traditional order is disturbed:

sign of danger
She
barren
creative artistically
self-sufficient

She
female
fertile archetype or
foolish soothing sign

186 *Semiotics of Misogyny*

With the invasion of female writers into the creative sphere men are left in simple occupations, such as:

Men	farming hunting fishing gardening	Nature

while women become the producers of culture. This phenomenon is seen as a symptom of the general societal malaise. Maugham's anxiety has some apocalyptic overtones. His prophecy warns about the doomsday when women become Sapphos and no longer produce children, but poems. The sense of catastrophe is intensified by the allusions to female perversity. This **new female** is the sexual and societal "Other" whom Maugham fears. What does she stand for? A Sappho, a sexual rebel, a barren woman, or a poet, a rival? Whom does he fear more, the sexual or the cultural "Other?"

Traditionally culture guarded its territory of **semiotic production** from the female gender. Discourse was divided into biological and logical, female and male. However, when societal performance became a sharable activity when females acquired *logos*, the artificial boundaries were no longer there. Both males and females had to face each other in an open competition, and then some retreated in fear or predicted cultural apocalypse. "What did they find in her?" asks Maugham on behalf of the angry men who cannot accept *Bios* and *Logos* all in one, that is in a speaking woman.

6.3 Blue Stocking Anxiety

> Talking with her made me feel like a jackass.
> Chekhov, *My Wives.*

Chekhov acknowledges that "blue stockings" possess intelligence, they can spell, read a great deal, study but, having admitted this, he had to make them unattractive. His early images of *emancipé* were always grotesque. For instance, such is his wife N5 from *Moi Zhiony* ("My Wives") (1885). Following the stereotype she is:[31]

> Long-nosed, plainly combed with a severe unsmiling face, she was myopic and wore glasses.

Deprived of beauty she is lacking taste as well:[32]

> Having no taste and no vain need to be liked she used to dress plainly and strangely: a black dress with narrow sleeves, a wide belt . . . some squareness, smoothness-not a single curve or careless pleat!

Nonetheless, the author mediates his attraction to this strange creature:[33]

> She attracted me with her originality: she was no fool.

This confession appears to be a new motif or a new "representamen" of a **familiar sign**, "woman."[34] N5 is a new female specie, an educated woman who "studied abroad and dreamt about an academic career." (130). The man acknowledges her intelligence, is overwhelmed by the knowledge:[35]

> She spoke only about high flown matters. Spiritualists, positivists, materialists were raining down her tongue. Talking to her for the first time, I was blinking and felt like a jackass. She could guess by the expression on my face that I was stupid, but did not start looking down, on the contrary naively began to teach me now to stop being a jackass . . .

He concludes his flattering portrait of a typical "blue stocking" with a striking remark:[36]

> Clever people are extremely pleasant when they are patronizing the ignoramuses.

What strikes the reader in this new portrait of a woman is that a man appears bluntly inferior to her. Nonetheless, the superior female does not abuse his pride and treats him rather generously. The traditional roles are reversed even more drastically than in *Aniuta*. If Aniuta symbolized a changing social and economic designation between the sexes, Raul's wife N5 stands for the shift in cultural values. To recognize woman's economic contribution to the social advancement of man was an achievement in itself. However, to place a woman higher than man meant a complete transformation in Chekhov's thinking and fictional strategy. On the semiotic level one may observe a total exchange of functions and displacement of signs. If initially Chekhov's fictional world totally relied on the established gender stereotype which did not require either criticism, or correction, this new sign, wife N5 required some appraisal and supportive argument. One may again recall that the prevalent interpretative versions of the Chekhovian woman-sign were highly negative. For instance, she predominantly was:

>an inferior specie
>a psychopathic being
>a sex object
>a shrewd lioness
>a timid cat
>an object of economic exchange
>a parasite
>a source of sin
>a useless creature
>doomed to natural extinction

In relation to man she was portrayed as the source of his misfortune while man appeared as a victim of her despotism, stupidity and whims. On the positive side, she was an attractive "pink stocking," but an epitome of ignorance and primitivism. Raul's wife N5 signifies a complete reversal of the designated functions. She appears as:

>woman sign of   intelligence
>   knowledge
>   kindness

Chekhov used the basic negative mythical premise and transformed it into a new proposition. He departed from the basic accepted notion that all educated women, "blue stockings", are unattractive. That is why Raul's wife N5 is "nearsighted, wears glasses" and strange black dresses.

However, having made her to fit the accepted gender stereotype, Chekhov turned the gender mythology upside down and gave the traditional male characteristics to a woman. Contrary to the habitual meaning the sign surprised the readers with a totally new ideology. It appeared that a woman could be:

> intelligent
> educated
> goal oriented
> generous to humanity
> rich in interests

What was originally expected and associated with a man now was imparted to a woman.

And yet, the most striking feature of this **semiotic shift** was the male anxiety *vis à vis* a female. To recognize that a "blue stocking" was no fool was rather simple, but to make man experience inferiority in her presence was much more daring. What had happened to Chekhov, the misogynist? The sense of humour prevailed. He found it more amusing to portray a "blue stocking" on her wedding night, discussing wedding customs in China and measuring her husband's skull, than to continue to put down the pathetic "pink stocking."

Raul's wife N5 demonstrated another new function, unlike other Chekhovian women she is no longer a passive listener anymore. It is Raul or the man who listens:[37]

> I was listening, listening . . . our entire later cohabitation consisted of my listening. She was talking, and I was blinking my eyes, afraid to show my failure to understand . . . If I had to wake up at night, I saw two eyes concentrating either on the ceiling or on my skull . . . Do not disturb me . . . I am thinking- she used to say, when I used to bother her with my coddling.

A Chekhovian woman whose primary interest is the bedroom, feels rather out of place in Raul's bedroom. Raul confesses that her presence makes him feel anxious as if he has to pass an exam every time. After a week of marriage to a "blue stocking" Raul admits that clever women are too difficult a burden for men.

Chekhov creates the atmosphere of a fantastic world where everything becomes possible, including a chance of a "blue stocking to marry" and to discuss phrenology on her wedding night. In this fictional world a woman is more intelligent than a man, but, quite interestingly, bores a man who is interested neither in philosophy nor in phrenology. The outrageous possibility of woman's intelligence and originality is rejected with a more expected man's reaction, boredom. The **changing semiotic policy** may be represented by a system where:

Man	Woman
animal	human being
sex-oriented	knowledge-oriented
primitive	educated
bored	interested
stupid	intelligent
inferior	superior

Nonetheless, Raul's wife N5 is still a caricature, not a new belief properly supported, and argued. Chekhov demonstrates his own and reader's uneasiness with the new image of a "blue stocking." The author and reader display the **blue stocking anxiety**, the reader is not ready to accept what the author has no courage to defend. Chekhov who proposes a new interpretation of a **familiar sign-woman** hides behind the old laughter at the sight of the convenient "blue stocking" clad in a tasteless black dress and decorated with glasses.

Chekhov was firmly convinced that in the sphere of creative activity a woman "is a goose," despite the fact that she can become a good doctor or a good lawyer. This comparison with the lower natural species became his permanent descriptive device in presenting women. In Chekhov's view, women occupy a lower position on the evolutionary scale. Even the examples of female creativity that he could witness in his own time fail to dissuade him:[38]

> The perfect organism creates, and woman as yet, has not created anything. George Sand is neither a Newton, nor a Shakespeare. She is not a thinker.

6.4 Origins of "Blue Stockings"

Chekhov once expressed an opinion that artist's intuition and scientist's brain have the same goals. Having presented his own fictional world to the readers, he was always seeking explanation. This quality was noticed by many critics, but Abram Derman summarized this artistic feature of Chekhov's in his book *On the Writer's Artistic Portrait*:[39]

It was a rare breed of sober positivist, convinced materialist, enamoured in Darwin and natural sciences, who did not believe in anything except what had been scientifically proven and tried to discover everything on his own, using his own mind and personal experience; a person who applied scientific methods even in his art.

Having created a character-caricature of the emancipated woman in Raul's account-"My wives", Chekhov recorded the appearance of this unpleasant animal in reality. While eight years later he tried to establish the causes of its origin in the story "Volodia, the Grown Up and Volodia, the Little One" (1893). Sofia L'vovna, the central female character, exemplifies such an attempt. She is a young woman of twenty-three, married to a fifty-four-year-old colonel. Marriage is described as a typical *liaison par debit*. Sofia , a daughter of a poor military doctor, was totally dependent upon him and marriage was a way out of this unhappy situation. She coldly analyzes the benefits of the change in her life:[40]

> She thought: the restaurant bill was one hundred twenty, and the Gypsies were paid a hundred, and tomorrow, if she pleases, she may blow even a thousand roubles, while two months ago, before the wedding, she did not even have three roubles of her own, and she had to ask her father for every trifle. What a change in her life!

However, despite the obvious material gain Sofia does not feel happy. Unlike other Chekhovian heroines she does not despise her husband, she even admits his physical attractiveness, youthful energy and optimism. Volodia "the grown up," is not blamed for her unhappiness. Sofia enjoys the financial freedom which she has acquired with marriage, as well as the pleasant company of a contented man. A short love affair with a friend of her childhood, also named Volodia, does not bring any happiness either. Neither does Sofia L'vovna find any solution to her mental state in religion. Her visits to the monastery, another possible alternative in life, do not help her to resolve her dilemma about how to live. She is caught among the three possibilities which do not seem to offer any happy solutions. Sofia L'vovna is bored, bored with perennial festivities, restaurants, Gypsies, and riding troikas. To Volodia, the grown up, her husband symbolizes the leisurely world where feast, joy, entertainment and endless socializing are a norm. Her role in this never-ending carnival is the typical role of a **pink stocking**, to entertain, to amuse the aging male until her beauty fades away.

Unlike the typical Chekhovian "pink stockings," after two months of successful marriage Sofia L'vovna already criticizes Volodia's world and this life. Moreover, she suffers. Her present life appears unfulfilling, the never-ending holiday bores Sofia. Chekhov imparts this female character with intelligence, and a critical mind capable of analyzing her existence in a calm, scientific fashion. She ponders, thinks and seeks a solution.

The visit of Volodia, the little one, her old childhood friend, and a young scholar, offers another life opportunity. A thirty-year-old, writing a thesis in foreign literature, leads a different life. He stands for the world of impoverished intellectuals who even at his age of thirty still has no financial freedom, lives in the barracks of his father a military doctor and is totally dependent upon him. However, Volodia, the little one, has to be an interesting person, a *mélange* of ideas whose life must be so different from the empty party-going. If Sofia's husband symbolizes wealth and boredom, her lover metaphorizes poverty and intellectual excitement. Sofia is drawn to Volodia, the little one, not because he is a younger male, but because he is an intellectual and not an officer. The readers are familiar with the Chekhovian formula of woman's happiness husband/lover. However, this story registers a definite shift. The woman is not portrayed as an impulsive female governed by the primordial desires. Sofia is not the source of "id," "lust" and animalistic behavior. Surprisingly, she analyzes her own feelings, cautiously expressing them to Volodia, with a sense of pride and human dignity. She even hides her feelings from him and feels certain humiliation. She is embarrassed about her marriage to an older man of means and about being now attracted to Volodia. Sofia fears his judgement, for morality is very important to this "innately immoral" woman. Sofia questions the motives of this man and is not comfortable with the idea of being used in a typical affair with a married woman:[41]

> In her situation the most degrading was the fact that Volodia, the little one, suddenly began to notice her after her wedding, while it never happened before. Now he silently spends hours

> with her or talks about trifles, and now, sitting in the sledge next to her, he does talk, but slightly presses her foot and shakes her hand; perhaps, that is all he needed. He wanted to see her married; and it was obvious he despises her and she arouses interest in him as a certain woman, as a fallen and indecent woman.

Chekhov prepares the readers for the atypical love affair where a woman has a different role to play. The semiotic implication of the statement is that Sofia L'vovna is the "other" woman and not the usual indecent, immoral woman, seeking the ordinary bodily pleasure. And five pages later, she emerges again as the "other" woman who begs her lover to teach her how to live.

Chekhov requires the love affair to demonstrate the otherness of the female character. It is not love that she seeks, but knowledge, purpose in life and a way out of boredom. Perhaps exchange of ideas, other themes of conversation, is the purpose of her relationship with another person, a man. Unfortunately, Sofia L'vovna does not find an interesting companion in Volodia, the little one. Nor does he intend to talk with her at all. Chekhov makes the lover hum constantly the same boring sounds:

Ta-ra-ra-bum-bia

When this angers Sofia and she asks him to utter at least one word, Volodia responds with the same meaningless sounds. She pleads to hear at least something meaningful, but Volodia does not intend to talk with her. He considers conversation to be the domain of "philosophers" while he wants to "kiss her little hands." Sofia L'vovna discovers that both Volodias, her husband and her lover want to treat her as a sex object. They both need only her body and she angrily rejects their attitude:[42]

> Volodia, why do you despise me? She asked vivaciously. You talk to me in some special, forgive me, clown-like language; one does not speak in such a way with friends and decent women. You are a successful scientist, you love science, why do you never discuss knowledge with me? Why? Am I not worthy of it?

Volodia's response to this tirade is the typical reaction of a man who is not accustomed to deal with "blue stockings," but sees a woman only as a source of sensuous pleasure. This unexpected complaint displeases him:[43]

> Volodia, the little one, vexedly grimaced and said: Why do you so suddenly want science?
> Perhaps, constitution? Or perhaps, little stellate sturgeon with horseradish?

Volodia is annoyed, this unusual conversation and sudden unfamiliar request is treated merely as a whim of a "pink stocking" or worse the craving of a pregnant female. Volodia is frightened; not prepared to deal with the woman's question, he dismisses it in a trivial manner, and tries to pacify her with a traditional kiss. Sofia L'vovna does not stop, moreover, she reprimands Volodia for her current misery:[44]

> I was grieving before your eyes, and if you wanted you could have made anything out of me, even an angel. But you . . .

She blames the intellectuals who denied her education and betterment. Sofia's reaction is a logical conclusion of a thinking individual, an attempt to improve her life, as well as to change the societal attitude towards women:[45]

> You despise me, and I wish you had known how I suffer from it!--she said awkwardly, knowing in advance that he does not believe her.

Sofia suffers, unable to stay locked into the societal stereotypes about family and gender, and wants to change her miserable condition:[46]

> I wish you had known how I wish to change myself, to start a new life! I dream about it with delight,--she spoke and cried from real delight,--to be a nice, honest, pure human being, not to lie, and to have a purpose in life.

This new Chekhovian woman, unexpectedly for herself, readers and author himself, desires another purpose in life! One may recall that in most of the Chekhovian fictional world women did not dwell on the purpose of living. They used to accept their archetypal roles. Sofia's longing for a different life contradicts Chekhov's earlier theory of sexual authority. This character is a trapped human being who is unable to fulfill her spiritual and intellectual needs. She raised herself above the state of a "pink stocking," a sex object, source of lust and sensuous pleasures Sofia possesses the ability to reject the given, to rebel against the existing Law and Order, but society is not ready for her. Her strivings for purpose in life, knowledge, education and equal participation in human activity are met with laughter which acts in the text as the best semiotic summary of the societal response to women's question. It is dismissed with senseless "ta-ra-ra-bum-bia."

If Volodia, the grown up, controls her life of a "pink stocking," the idle existence of a beauty and social butterfly, Volodia, the little one, denies her advancement. She is left with another alternative, to join her friend Ol'ga in the monastery, "to harness the flesh." According to the grammar of a stereotype, women are more prone to religiosity, than men, and Ol'ga symbolizes this societal belief. She chooses to become a nun instead of an idle "pink stocking." Sofia is not a believer. Her atheism makes her akin to little Volodia, perhaps a materialist and atheist himself. Thus, monastery and the role of a nun seem totally alien to her as well. Spiritually, she is ready to leave her comfortable "doll's house," and abandon the life-style of an idle "pink stocking." Intellectually, Sofia is already a new woman; she is longing for education and a change in societal role distribution. However, she feels trapped. To emphasize her despair and dead-end situation Chekhov resorts to a witty semiotic strategy, juxtaposing the two pairs of signs:

2 females	2 males
Rita	Volodia, the lover
Ol'ga	Volodia the husband

Rita is another woman whose life Sofia does not desire to emulate. Rita, Sofia's cousin, a spinster over thirty, summarizes the stereotypical features of a modern female. Having been denied the fate of a "pink stocking," she is described as a strange being, unattractive to both men and women:[47]

> Rita, Mrs. Iagich's cousin, was a girl already beyond thirty, very pale, with dark brows, wearing pince-nez, a chain smoker; even

> outside in freezing weather, ashes were always on her chest and knees. She spoke in nasal tones, stretching every word, was cold, could drink liqueurs and cognac in any amounts without getting drunk, and tastelessly tell ambiguous jokes. While at home she read thick journals from morning till night or ate frozen apples.

"Frozen apples" stand for the non-traditional symbol, the antithesis of the Eve's apple, the favorite food of a woman who is incapable of seducing. They stand for the Other woman. One may easily recognize the most unflattering portrait of a she-nihilist or *nihilistka* which left the pages of Turgenev's or Pisemsky's novel. Rita is the late prototype of Kukshina, the caricature of a woman nihilist which appeared in *Fathers and Sons* in 1861. In the story she serves this important function of reviving the old sign as another rejected option. Rita is a nihilist, which is different from a feminist. By the late nineteenth century, Russian women learned not only the distinctions between the two trends, but acquired the sense of belonging to the Other, a non-nihilist alignment. The nihilist movement was the most radical trend which soon left many women and intellectuals disillusioned.

Nihilism was popular in Russia in the fifties of the last century and by Chekhov's time it was already a forgotten movement.[48] Nihilists of both sexes were extreme individualists who were inspired by ideas of equality and social rebellion. They condemned injustice and rejected most social institutions. Females were attracted to the movement since nihilism carried illusions of better options for women. Disenchanted by the pace of Russian feminism, many Russian women became nihilists, which meant that they advocated liberation from the traditional family yoke, demanded sexual freedom and education abroad. Its extreme radicalism and individualism, deprived the movement of wide support. In addition, soon the originally popular movement was transformed into a superficial trend which manifested itself mainly in social manners, attire and choices of a mate. Sexually and otherwise liberated individuals did not become political or social reformers, and soon the very term "nihilist" became a pejorative icon. Turgenev's female nihilist portrait in *Fathers and Sons* summarized the already established societal reaction to the movement.

Women-nihilists were specially critical target because of their visible revolt, their manner of dressing. Russian nihilists inspired by French or English models discarded attire which had any signs of femininity. All muslin, lace, ribbons, feathers, flowers and the rest of the traditional feminine paraphernalia were abandoned in favor of plain black dresses. Hair was cut short. This nihilist female look was a symbolic rebellion against fashion and social custom. The *Nihilistska's* dress was the antithesis to the attire of "a muslin miss," a typical female trained to dress seductively in order to attract a desirable male. The defeminizing trend in appearance derived from the idea of equality, intended to close the gap between the sexes through changed appearance and emulation of man's behavior. Cigarettes, liqueur, short hair and masculine manners were distinctive features of a new, nihilist woman who was to approximate man in all respects. Male conduct was adopted, and frequently implied a cult of rudeness and antisocial behavior. However, society soon became very skeptical since it was hard to distinguish a true believer from a mere *poseur.* Nihilist portraits in Tolstoy, Turgenev, Pisemsky, Leskov, Dostoevsky reflect a debate around nihilism and the societal misgivings as to the usefulness of the movement. Former nihilists later joined revolutionary democrats, confused intellectuals, Marxists and monarchists.

Chekhovian Rita is a trace from the Russian intellectual past, a reminder of former infatuations among the Russian youth, but not the model for a new Russian woman in the late nineties. Sofia L'vovna does not regard Rita as a model, Rita's liberation does not go beyond cigarettes and reading thick journals. She appears lonely and unhappy in her own "nihilist" way. Rita and Ol'ga are the **signs of rejected feminine models**:

> Rita Ol'ga
> a nihilist a nun

The lives of the two female friends offer no better alternative, and Chekhov concludes the story with the *status quo.* Sofia L'vovna remains married, doomed to the idle existence of the "pink stocking," passing the time in dancing parties in restaurants, riding troikas. She, or rather Chekhov, sees no other options:[49]

198 *Semiotics of Misogyny*

> Sofia L'vovna remembered Ol'ga, and she was horrified at the thought that girls and woman of her class had no other choice, but continued riding troikas and lying or joined the monastery and killed their flesh . . .

What does Chekhov mean when he uses the word "class?" Does he attribute the woman question to the boundaries of a certain class or does he imply that a new woman is a product of a particular social group?

If his earlier women appeared to be contented, Sofia L'vovna is allowed to be unhappy in the traditional social function. None of the previous social remedies work, neither happy, comfortable marriage, nor religion. Even nihilism does not attract this new woman who seeks purpose in life. Her unoccupied mind demands some mental exercise which she cannot obtain either in a restaurant amidst the dancing Gypsies, or in a monastery. An intelligent mind locked into a young attractive female body parading as a "pink stocking" is seeking an outlet. A thinking, depressed **pink stocking** appears as the Chekhovian **semiotic precursor** of the **blue stocking**. A man is blamed for his own misfortune. His own neglect of woman's needs produced this unpleasant creature who is ready to destroy not only marriage, social order, but man himself. Volodia, the little one, who refuses to discuss science with Sofia and continues kissing her pretty hands is the symbol of the man who created a new monstrous specie--"blue stocking."

6.5 Anxiety, Tension and Sign-o-phobia

> Woman's sexual needs have less of a mental character because, generally speaking, her mental life is less developed.
> Emile Durkheim, *Suicide: A Study in Sociology.*

Relying on Lévi-Strauss, Umberto Eco defines a woman as a sign in the light of the institution of marriage.[50] According to the contemporary Italian semiotician, a woman becomes a sign "the moment she marries." Her role as a wife brings her a new symbolic value and raises her social status. Chekhov, the amateur anthropologist and intuitive semiotician of the last century, shared similar views. Much like contemporary thinkers, he acknowledged the established system of cultural norms and paid tribute to traditional culture through his fictional portraits of women who represented real women as signs. Most of his fictional women dreamt of marriage, engineered it to control men and exercised their power over them through marriage. The most expressive Chekhovian sign was the "pink stocking type" which represented this archetypal female.

However, the mythical "the pink stocking" which no longer dominated the real world, and the Chekhovian "pink stocking" became a longing sign, **sign-nostalgia** and an endangered sign whose survival was no longer secured by the cultural system. It was a metaphor which was about to lose its metaphoricity and to be transformed into an **anti-sign**. The "pink stocking" signified woman's inferiority and dependance upon man. It also legitimized patriarchal supremacy. Ironically, as mentioned earlier, the Chekhovian sign was an artistic response to the already existing new sign, "blue stocking."

However, in terms of marriage "blue stocking" was not a sign, since most of these "strange" women who stood behind the sign rejected marriage and did not participate in the traditional economic exchange. Most of them independently earned their living and avoided the trappings of marriage or the roles of the traditional "signs." Their **sign-o-phobia** or the rejection of the expected societal function made them visible outsiders already in nineteenth century Russian society, a mockery target. They were the exact opposite of what "pink stockings" were, and, in this sense, they could be defined as **anti-signs**, forces at the margins of the **societal semiotic process**, signalling the "Other", the new cultural message. The "blue stockings" were the signals of semiotic rebellion against the Chekhovian feminine ideal which was measured by the aesthetic iconicity.

The Chekhovian **woman-sign** was valued for her youth and beauty which could be successfully exchanged for property and other signs, connoting higher status and prosperity. The beautiful body of a "pink stocking" was the semiotic power of the archetypal woman-sign. She was denied any intelligence and was declared inferior to man. Nonetheless, Chekhov, the positivist and natural scientist, assisted Chekhov, the artist, in recording the appearance of the other specie, a woman of intelligence whose mind was far more valuable than her body. While reporting about this "strange female animal," Chekhov had to overcome the temptations of mocking and suppress the traditional stereotype. The result of his inner conflict is the new character, antisign Polina Rassudina from the story "Three Years" (1895).

Her last name attracts attention since Chekhovian family names usually are significant semiotic signals. The device of naming as a means of characterization was known to Chekhov from Russian and Western literary traditions and he used it extensively in his work. One may recall the story *Loshadinaiia familiia* (The Horse's Name) where the family name is the central theme, predominant motif and a crucial poetic device. Polina, the new woman, is named "Rassudina" which derives from the Russian word *Rassudok*-"reason" or "mind." Thus, her name already alerts the readers about the unusual possibilities of this female character. Ten lines separate this brief introduction from the portrait of the "blue stocking:"[51]

> She was thin and unattractive, long-nosed and gaunt-faced looking tired, and one always had a feeling that she forced herself to keep her eyes open to prevent her from falling. She had pretty dark eyes with a clever, kind and sincere expression, but her movements were awkward and angular.

Consequently, the name and portrait reveal a single semiotic goal, namely they are subordinated to the message, the new woman, "blue stocking," Chekhov, using the folkloric archetype, "eyes the mirror of the soul" imparts Polina with "clever, kind and sincere" eyes. A woman with the family name "Rassudina", "Reasoning," is also unattractive, but has "clever" eyes which implies that a "blue stocking" has a better mind than body. The **semiotic goal** in this instance may be expressed as:

anti-sign
character-sign
character-type
character-feature

name-signal

The readers are provided with the semiotic material which helps them to construct the implied signal "blue stocking." First of all, she is unattractive, named "the Reasoning" and, yet, her "eyes" are "clever." Then comes the most essential part of the character-sign--she is not married, separated from her husband and earns her living tutoring:[52]

> She was already thirty years old. She used to be married to a teacher, but had not been living with him for a long time. She earned her living teaching music and participating in quartets.

The additional component which reminds the readers of the "blue stocking" is her dress. Chekhov makes Polina untidy, denies her taste. Nonetheless, he does not attribute it to her emancipation and occupation, but rather to her lack of money. A woman who supports herself giving music lessons cannot spend much on clothes; that is why the author does not criticize her appearance. He simply says:[53]

> She liked to dress up, but could not bring herself to spending money on (clothes) and dressed tastelessly and untidily.

There is some sense of pity or empathy in this description.

Polina's "Otherness" is emphasized by the presence of the "pink stocking," Julia, Laptev's wife. Polina is Laptev's former love whom he preferred to a pretty, religious and young woman. Polina has the function of denouncing Julia, the typical "pink stocking." She says angrily to Laptev:[54]

> Whom did you marry? Where were your eyes, you, crazy man? What did you find in this stupid, insignificant girl? I loved you for your intelligence, your soul, while this porcelain doll needs your money!

Chekhov introduces the **character-antisign** as the mistaken choice of a man. Much as in the story tale of the two Volodias, he blames the man for the appearance of a **dangerous sign**, "blue stocking," which now jeopardizes the traditional "pink stocking." The man himself is the cause of his own misfortune, disruption of the societal order and gender harmony. The "crazy" Laptev who prefers "a porcelain doll" to an intelligent sincere woman is to blame for Polinka's **semiotic metamorphosis**. The mistake is demonstrated in the familiar semiotic fashion:

Polina	Julia
unattractive	beautiful
sincere	phony
clever	stupid
mind	body
soul	calculating mind
love	greed
independent	parasite
industrious	idle

However, Chekhov could not transform himself into an admirer of the blue stockings. After all, he himself preferred and valued beauty first and foremost. The impulse of **semiotic experiment** could not have led Chekhov, the misogynist, to the extreme praise of the liberated woman, the exotic newly created specie. The traditional forces of archetypal thinking frequently prevail over the far more progressive artistic vision. Then Chekhov returns to the familiar territory of the shared myth and prejudice and utters what the popular reader expects the most:[55]

> She did not like to frequent restaurants because restaurant air seemed to her to be poisoned by tobacco and men's breath. She treated all men as strangers with a peculiar preconceived notion that all of them are immoral and are about to attack her any moment. In addition, the bar music annoyed her, giving her a headache.

Here, Chekhov returns to the familiar stereotypical image of a man-hater *emancipé*, the caricature of a feminist or a "blue stocking" comes back.

Later, Chekhov again attempts to provide the explanation of the origin of the exotic female species. He flirts with the concept of class and makes Polina pronounce this:[56]

> The working class to which I belong has one privilege: the awareness of its integrity and ability not to compromise with the merchants I despise. No, I cannot be bought! I am them, not Julechka!

Chekhov here makes the reader believe that a "blue stocking" is a product of the working-class independent mentality, originating from traditional oppression and finally resulting in rebellion against paper signs-money. He intuitively adopts the ideas of French socialist utopian thinkers. Unlike the

Marxists, his notion of a working class does not imply industrial workers, the proletariat, but the working intellegentsia, a music teacher Polina.

There could be some transference of the authorial self upon this character. The conflict between the father, the merchant, and the son, the doctor, could momentarily find an outlet in this unusual monologue of a woman who condemns the merchants and their way of life. The voices of the character, narrator and real author become indistinguishable and are overshadowed by echoes of the Chekhovian self, his own past and shadows of his family ancestors. Polina, the "blue stocking," carries the additional narrative task of assuming the authorial voice and becoming occasionally the reflection of the Chekhovian self. This additional meaning of the **familiar sign** is the vocal digression of the otherwise engaged *actant*.

Polina is the new woman whom society basically fears and whom men avoid. Laptev admits that Polina not only genuinely loved him, but enriched his life:[57]

> She fell in love with him strongly, absolutely altruistically, and even while living with him, continued giving lessons and working till exhaustion. His understanding and appreciation of music he owed to her, since he was indifferent to music in the past, before they met.

Nonetheless, Laptev rejects Polina's genuine love and her rich intellect, and marries Julen'ka who could offer him nothing but her young body. Polina condemns his choice and indignantly exposes the societal preferences for a "pink stocking:"[58]

> It is regrettable and unfortunate that you are as rotten as all the rest. You need neither woman's mind nor intellect, but her body, beauty and youth . . . Youth! . . . she uttered in a nasal voice, as if making fun of somebody and smiled--youth! You need purity, *reinheit! reinheit!* she giggled, leaning back on the back of the armchair.

Laptev appreciates Polina's spiritual worth, respects her efforts to survive and is grateful to her for filling his own life with music, beauty and excitement. However, the "blue stocking-o-phobia" prevails, and Polina does not become his wife. Chekhov analysis is thinking:[59]

> Why didn't he decide to build a family with this woman who loved him so much and already was his wife and companion? She was the only human being who had been attached to him, and wouldn't it be a noble worthwhile task to give happiness, home and comfort to this clever, proud and overworked being.

He was afraid of commitment to a "blue stocking" and preferred Julen'ka, a "pink stocking" who did not love him, but offered him her piety, quiet ways and simple, understandable and predictable personality. Julen'ka posed no threat with her daily prayers, little crosses, purity, health and *Rineheit*. The "reasoning" Polina calls Laptev's infatuation with Julen'ka "poison." She is the object of the familiar male desire, a weak escape into the eternal hunt for youth, beauty and quiet boredom. The man-hunter rejects the "blue stocking" and reaches for the conquest of the cold and indifferent soul of a "pink stocking."

Ironically, the sincere Polina stands for the openness and spirituality of a "blue stocking." Her world of music, beauty, thought and active involvement in life appears lucid and more transparent than the mysterious religiosity of his young silly wife. Polina Rassudina is able to see Julen'ka's emptiness under the veil of her mysteriousness and recognize a traditional primitive female. And yet it is precisely this little seductive creature who is more pleasant and more appealing to Laptev than the clever, hardworking and loving Polina. Despite the fact that he is aware of all Polina's virtues, he still is fearful of her. The "blue stocking" intimidates Laptev, and he prefers the indifference of a "pink stocking." He may hate her, despise her primitive nature, but he would feel secure next to her. If next to Polina, Laptev may loose his sense of superiority, or may have to prove his spiritual and intellectual worth; Julen'ka guarantees peace and stability.

The same juxtaposition of the signs one may find in another Chekhov story "The House with the Mezzanine" (1896) where two sisters, Lida and Zhenia (*Misius*) represent again the **sign and anti-sign**. The familiar designation woman-"blue stocking" is diametrically opposed to the less known woman "pink stocking". On the superficial semiotic level the less familiar sign "pink stocking" carries the archetypal belief shared by a large group of readers, speakers or sign producers. The sign "pink stocking" represents the most desired, traditional woman who does not participate in

sign production and, instead, is merely used in the **semiotic exchange**. She herself had been a sign which is perceived by men as a biological, economic and aesthetic given in the universe of men. Chekhovian "pink stocking" paradoxically echoes the feminist metaphor used by Mary Wollstonecraft in her famous manifesto *A Vindication of the Rights of Woman*.[60] The Victorian feminist provides the semiotic parts for the Chekhovian later *assemblage*, the parts for his sign "pink stocking" or simply explains what stands for the sign to be created: Talking about the woman's role in society, she writes:[61]

> She was created to be the toy of man, his rattle, and it must jingle in his ears whenever, dismissing reason, he chooses to be amused."

Wollstonecraft's rattle, toy, Ibsen's doll and Chekhovian "pink stocking" are identical signs, standing for something else which is the same, the stereotyped image of a socially acceptable female, the archetypal woman.

The two signs, "pink" and "blue" stockings carry two semiotic polarities, two popular beliefs whose juxtaposition in the real and fictional worlds is the return of the popular myth about female inferiority. The collective artistic consciousness produced the sign "blue stocking" which stood for obsession with detail, an unhappy disposition to pseudo-intellectualism which later was applied to the women of a new civilization, and to any feminist rebel. It is curious that an English code, the traditional metaphor "blue" for depressed, low spirits, evoked another metaphor which left the linguistic frontiers of the English language and affected the metaphoric product in Russian. The Chekhovian "pink stocking" owes its semantic and semiotic power to the original **protosign** in another code. Russian "pink" is opposite to the English "blue," and simultaneously is identical to Wollstonecrafts's "rattle" which revives the associations with a toy, child or children's bedroom. Chekhovian choice of color remarkably fits into the Victorian universe, complementing Wollstonecraft's symbolism:

toy	pink
rattle	childish
child	womanly

The two concepts of feminism and traditional order, the two stereotypical kinds of women, aggressive and passive, the two customs--old and new, are semiotically arranged and given a new life in the fictional world where "blue" also stands for destroyed societal balance.[62] The **anti-sign** "blue" captures the trend of collective human passions, the changing collective mood evoked by the uncomfortable emancipation of one group which threatens the "Other." Chekhov expects some collective depression, anticipating collective "blues" in the future when more women may stop signifying the archetypal "pink stocking" and start to compete in the **production of signs**, an activity which was traditionally left to men only. It is remarkable that Chekhovian lenses capture only "blue color," and not the ominous "black," as in Maugham's case. The shade of his misogyny is much lighter since Chekhov accepts heterosexual reality where men and women have to survive together to preserve Beauty and Harmony of being. However, both creators of **women-signs** do not leave the territory of myth, archetypal enmity and fear of the "Other". The producers of Culture have showed what has become its second nature.

NOTES
CHAPTER 1

1. Umberto Eco, *Theory of Semiotics* (Bloomington, Ind: Indiana University Press, 1979).
2. *ibid.*, p. 26.
3. *ibid., ibid..*
4. *ibid., ibid..*
5. *ibid., ibid..*
6. *ibid.*, p. 7.
7. Jonathan Culler, *In Pursuit of Signs: Semiotics, Post-Structuralism, Literature* (Ithaca: Cornell University Press, 1981).
8. Somerset Maugham, *The Complete Short Stories* (Larden City, NY: Doubleday, 1953).
9. *ibid.*, p. VI-VII.
10. *ibid.*, p. IX.
11. *ibid., ibid.*
12. *ibid.*, p. XI.
13. *ibid.*, p. XII.
14. *ibid.*, p. XIII.
15. *ibid., ibid..*
16. *ibid.*, p. XIV.
17. *ibid.*, ibid..
18. *ibid.*, p. XI.
19. Richard A. Cordell, *Somerset Maugham* (Bloomington Ind.: Indiana University Press, 1961).
20. Boris Eichenbaum, "Chekhov at Large" in Robert Louis Jackson *Chekhov* (Englewood Cliffs, NJ: Prentice Hall Inc., 1967) pp. 21-32.

21. Leonid Grossman, "Naturalism by Chekhov" in Robert Louis Jackson *Chekhov* (Englewood Cliffs, NJ: Prentice Hall Inc., 1969) pp. 32-49.
22. Dmitri Chizhevsky, "Chekhov in the Development of Russian Literature in R.J. Jackson, *Chekhov*, pp. 49-62.
23. Barbara Heldt, *Terrible Perfection* (Bloomington, Ind.: Indiana University Press, 1987).
24. Richard Heron Ward, *William Somerset Maugham* (London: Geoffrey Bles, 1937).
25. Cordell's *Somerset Maugham*, p. 81.
26. Frederic Raphael, *Somerset Maugham* (London: Thames O. Hudson, 1976).
27. Ted Morgan, *Maugham* (New York: Simon & Schuster, 1980), p. 36.
28. *ibid., ibid..*
29. *ibid.*, p. 344.
30. *ibid.*, p. 346.
31. Leopold Bellak, "Somerset Maugham, Thematic Analysis of Ten Short Stories" in Robert W. White, ed. *The Study of Lives* (New York: Atherton Press, 1963) pp. 142-60.
32. Richard Bates, *The Women's Liberation Movement in Russia* (Princeton, N.J.: Princeton University Press, 1978); Barbara Alpern Engel, *Mothers and Daughters* (Cambridge: Cambridge University Press, 1983); Cathy Porter, *Women in Revolutionary Russia* (Cambridge: Cambridge University Press, 1987).
33. Nina Selivanova, *Russia's Women* (Westport, Conn.: Hyperion Press, 1975).
34. S.S. Koteliansky, ed. *The Life and Letters of Anton Chekhov* (London: Cassell & Co. Ltd. 1925) 59.
35. *ibid., ibid..*
36. *ibid.*, p. 60.

NOTES
CHAPTER 2

1. Dean MacCannell and Juliet Flower, MacCannell *The Time of the Sign: A Semiotic Interpretation of Modern Culture* (Bloomington, Ind.: Indiana University Press, 1982) p. 105.

2. The definition of icon shared by René Thom "From the Icon to the Symbol" in Robert Innis, ed. *Semiotics* (Bloomington, Ind.: Indiana University Press, 1985) 272, and by Thomas Sebeok, *Contribution to the Doctrine of Signs* (Bloomington, Ind.: Indiana University Press, 1976) 43.

3. Irene Portis Winner, "Semiotics of Culture" in *Frontiers of Semiotics*, ed. by John Deely et al (Bloomington: Indiana University Press: 1986) pp. 181-85.

4. S. Maugham, "Rain" in his *The Complete Short Stories* 1952 ed., Vol. 1, pp. 1-39, p. 14.

5. S. Maugham, "The Pool" in his 1952ed., pp. 104-139, p. 110.

6. S. Maugham "The Door of Opportunity" in his 1952 ed., 1078-1108, p. 1037.

7. S. Maugham, "A Man With a Conscience", 1952 ed., pp. 1306-1325, p. 1316.

8. John Gassner, "The Duality of Chekhov" in Robert Louis Jackson, ed. *Chekhov* (Englewood Cliffs, N.J.: Prentice Hall, Inc. 1969) pp. 175-184.

9. Ronald Hingley, *A New Life of Anton Chekhov* (New York: Alfred A. Knopf, 1976) pp. 85, 199-200, pp. 184-5.

10. Valentin Kataev, *Proza Chekhova, problemy interpretatsii* (Moscow: Izdatel'stvo Moskovskogo Universiteta, 1929) p. 164; Virginia Llewellyn Smith, *Anton Chekhov and the Lady with the Dog* (London: Oxford University Press, 1973).

11. A. P. Chudakov, *Poetika Chekhova* (Moscow: Nauka, 1971) pp. 248, 262.

12. I.N. Sukhikh, *Problemy Poetiki Chekhova* (Leningrad Izdatel'stvo Leningradskogo Universiteta, 1987) p. 151.

13. A. Chekhov, "Strazha pod Strazhey" in vol. 4 of his *Sochineniia* (Moscow: Nauka, 1976) pp. 20-24.

14. A. Chekhov, "Bezzashchitnoe Sushchestvo", in vol. 6., 1976 ed., pp. 87-92.
15. A. Chekhov, "Kryzhovnik", 1976 ed., pp. 55-66, vol. 10, p. 60.
16. *ibid., ibid..*
17. A. Chekhov, "Moi Zhiony", vol. 4, pp. 24-31, 1976 ed., p. 24.
18. *ibid.,* p. 25.
19. *ibid.,* p. 25-26.
20. *ibid.,* p. 26.
21. *ibid.,* p. 27.
22. Eco's *Theory of Semiotics.*
23. S. Maugham, "Winter Cruise", 1952 ed., vol. III, pp. 1344-1361, p. 1347.
24. *ibid.,* p. 1347-8.
25. *ibid.,* p. 1351.
26. *ibid., ibid..*
27. *ibid.,* p. 1353.
28. *ibid.,* p. 1357.
29. *ibid., ibid..*
30. *ibid., ibid..*
31. Robert Hodge and Gunther Kress, *Social Semiotics* (Ithaca: Cornell University Press, 1988).
32. A. Chekhov, "Ariadna", in his 1976 ed., pp. 107-133, p. 117.
33. *ibid.,* p. 1108.
34. *ibid.,* p. 43.
35. A. Grishunin in *Chekhov,* vol. 9 (Moscow, Nauka, 1977) ed. *"Primechanii"* pp. 439-450; T. I. Ornatskaya, "Primechaniia" in *Chekhov,* vol. 9 (Moscow: Nauka, 1977) pp. 439-450; E. Polotskaya *Dostizhenie khudozhestvennoi mysli* (Moscow: Sovetsky pisatel', 1979).
36. C. Peirce's **sinsign** explained in his *Correspondence with Lady Wilby.*

37. A. Chekhov, "Ariadna", pp. 107-133, p. 123.
38. *ibid.*, p. 126.
39. *ibid.*, p. 128.
40. A. Chekhov, "Duel", 1976 ed., vol. 7, p. 380.
41. *ibid., ibid..*
42. *ibid., ibid..*
43. S. Maugham, "The Three Fat Women of Antibus", vol. 1, 1952 ed., pp. 184-198, p. 185.
44. *ibid.*, pp. 185-186.
45. *ibid.*, pp. 185.
46. *ibid., ibid..*
47. *ibid., ibid..*
48. *ibid.*, p. 192.
49. Encountered in John O'Neill, *Five Bodies* (Ithaca: Cornell University Press, 1985) 65, apparently borrowed from Alexander Cockburn, "Gastroporn" in *The New York Review of Books*, Dec. 8, 1977, 15-19.
50. Maugham's "The Three Fat Ladies of Antibus", p. 196.
51. *ibid.., ibid.*
52. Chekhov's, "V bane", vol. 3, 1976 ed., pp. 178-229, p. 184.
53. Chekhov's "Aptekarsha", vol. 5, 1976 ed., pp. 192-198, p. 196.
54. Wojciech Kalaga, *The Literary Sign: A Triadic Model* (Katowice: University Press, 1986).
55. George Lakoff, *Women, Fire and Dangerous Things* (Chicago: The University of Chicago Press, 1987) 79; and Carol MacCormack and Marilyn Strathern, ed. *Nature and Culture* (Cambridge: Cambridge University Press, 1980).
56. S. Maugham, "The Letter", 1952 ed., pp. 1414-1446, p. 1427.
57. *ibid.*, p. 1415.
58. *ibid.*, p. 1417.

59. *ibid.*, p. 1422.
60. *ibid.*, p. 1444.
61. *ibid.*, *ibid.*.
62. A. Chekhov, "V ovrage", vol. 10, 1976, pp. 144-181, p. 176.
63. *ibid.*, p. 178.
64. Maugham's "Rain", p. 7-8, 1952 ed., vol. 1.
65. Rene Thom's "From the Icon to the Symbol" in Robert Innis, ed. *Semiotics* (Bloomington: Indiana University Press, 1985) pp. 272-292.
66. Maugham's "Rain", p. 36.
67. *ibid.*, p. 38.
68. Maugham's "The Mother", pp. 356-379, vol. 1, 1952 ed., p. 357.
69. *ibid.*, p. 357.
70. *ibid.*, *ibid.*.
71. *ibid.*, *ibid.*.
72. *ibid.*, p. 364.
73. *ibid.*, *ibid.*.
74. *ibid.*, p. 365.
75. *ibid.*, p. 367.
76. *ibid.*, p. 368.

NOTES
CHAPTER 3

1. A. Chekhov, "Nenuznaiia pobeda", 1974-1976 ed., vol. 1, pp. 273-358; p. 311.

2. A. Greimas, *Semantique Structurale* (Paris: Larousse, 1966); lectures at the Summer Institute of Semiotic Studies, June 1990.

3. A. Chekhov, ("Useless Victory"), 1974-1976 ed., pp. 273-358, vol. 1, p. 312.

4. *ibid.*, p. 319.

5. *ibid.*, p. 345.

6. A. Chekhov, "Brak no paschetu", 1974-1976 ed., vol. 3, pp. 98-103; p. 101.

7. *ibid.*, p. 99.

8. S. Maugham, "The Round Dozen" vol. 1, 1953 ed., pp. 377-403; p. 390.

9. *ibid.*, *ibid.*.

10. *ibid.*, p. 394.

11. *ibid.*, *ibid.*.

12. *ibid.*, p. 395.

13. *ibid.*, *ibid.*.

14. S. Maugham, "Jane", 1952 ed., vol. 2, pp. 1025-48; p. 127.

15. *ibid.*, p. 1028.

16. *ibid.*, p. 1030.

17. *ibid.*, *ibid.*.

18. *ibid.*, p. 1034.

    Maugham convincingly exhibits his knowledge of Freud and his theory of *libido* selecting the most appropriate psychoanalytic evidence to devalue women. S. Freud *On Sexuality, Three Essays on the Theory of Sexuality* (1905); *Female Sexuality* (1931).

214 *Notes*

19. A seductive female is a prominent motif in Freudian mythological psychoanalytical universe: S. Freud *A General Introduction to Psychoanalysis* (1920); S. Freud *Civilization and Its Discontents* (1933); S. Freud. *Case Histories* (1905); S. Freud, *On Sexuality* (1905).

20. S. Maugham's story, "Jane", p. 1045.

21. *ibid., ibid..*

22. S. Maugham, "Gigolo and Gigolette", vol. 1, 1952 ed., pp. 216-233; p. 229.

23. A. Chekhov, "K svadebnomu sezonu", 1976 ed., vol 4, pp. 148-149; p. 148.

24. *ibid., ibid..*

25. *ibid., ibid..*

26. Chekhov here successfully uses the archetypal narrative device of transformations previously legitimized by fairytales. More one may see in: V. Propp, "Fairy Tale Transformations" in L. Matejka and K. Pomorska, ed. *The Readings in Russian Poetics* (Ann Arbor: Michigan Slavic Publications, 1978) 94-117; A. J. Greimas "Narrative Grammar: Units and Levels" in *Modern Language Notes*, vol. 86, 1971 pp. 793-806; Claude Bremond "The Logic of Narrative Possibilities" in *New Literary History* vol. XI, Spring 1980, N3., 387-413; C. Bremond, "Morphology of the French Folktale" in *Semiotica*, N2, 1970, 247-77.

27. Chekhov, on marriage, letter to A.S. Suvorin, dd. December 30, 1888, 136-138 in S.S. Koteliansky and P. Tomlinson's *The Life and Letters of Anton Chekhov*; to the same dd May 30, 1888; Ernest Simons *Chekhov* (Boston: Little Brown and Co., 1962) 27; 52-3; 80-81; 115; 123-4; 154; 176; 233; 244; 449-638; Ronald Hingley *Anton Chekhov* (NY: Alfred A. Knopf, 1976: XI-XII 36-7; 85-6; 199-200; Sophie Lafitte *Chekhov* (London: Angus and Robertson, 1971) 206.

28. A. Chekhov, "Brak cherez 10-15 let", vol. 4, 1976 ed., pp. 222-225, p. 222.

29. *ibid.*, p. 223.

30. *ibid..*, *ibid.*

31. Chekhov, Correspondence with brother Alexander in S.S. Koteliansky and Philip Tomlinson, ed. *The Life and Letters of Anton Tchekhov*, 1928.

32. *ibid.*, p. 224.

33. S. Maugham, "The Romantic Young Lady", vol. 1, 1952 ed., pp. 328-337, p. 336.

34. *ibid., ibid..*

35. *ibid.,* p. 331.

36. A. Chekhov, ("Anna on the Neck") vol. 9, 1976 ed., pp. 161-174.

37. Surface plot is the concept inspired by the Russian Formalists and best developed by J. Lotman, who defines 3 textual layers in his *The Structure of the Artistic Text* trans. by Gail Lennoff, Ronald Vroon, (Ann Arbor: University of Michigan, 1979) pp. 138-144.

38. A. Chekhov, (Anna on the neck) p. 161.

39. *ibid.,* p. 162.

40. Chekhov is the master of onomastic parody, his names are always signs but not mere "rigid designators" in Kripke's sense, Saul Kripke, *Naming and Necessity* (Cambridge, Mass.: Harvard University Press; 1980).

    The Order of Saint Anna was established in the honour of Anna Petrovna, the favourite daughter of Peter the Great in 1736. The Order of Vladimir in 1782. Both were bestowed for high civic loyalty and honourable service to the Empire. Chekhov plays with the names, i.e. the Order and Woman's name.

41. A. Chekhov's "Anna on the Neck", p. 163.

42. The character metamorphosis is similar to that of the fantastic world of fairytales where animals and humans may assume each other's images; the only difference is that a human being is represented by an object of Culture--a medal. V. Propp's "Fairy Tale Transformations," C. Bremond's, "Morphology of French Fairy Tale".

43. A. Chekhov's, "Anna on the Neck", p. 162.

44. *ibid.,* p. 166.

45. *ibid., ibid..*

46. *ibid.,* p. 165.

47. *ibid.,* p. 169.

48. *ibid.,* p. 170.

49. *ibid., ibid..*

50. S. Maugham, "The Fall of Edward Barnard", 1952 ed., vol. 1, pp. 39-69; p. 39.

51. The myth of American dream plays a significant role in both stories, having become a cultural universal. "Cultural universals", the notion is best formulated by A. J. Greimas, "Narrative Grammar: Units and Levels" in *Modern Language Notes*, vol. 86, 1971, p. 793-806; Paul Bouissac, *Circus and Culture* (Bloomington, Ind.: University of Indiana Press, 1976).

52. S. Maugham, "The Fall of Edward Barnard", p. 41.

53. *ibid., ibid..*

54. *ibid., ibid..*

55. *ibid.,* p. 68.

56. *ibid., ibid..*

57. "Body Politic" one encounters in G. Vico's *New Science* (1725) and later on in Western discourse; Vico, Giambattista, *The New Science of Giambattista Vico* trans.. by Max Harold Fisch (Ithaca: Cornell University Press, 1968).

58. Jane Goddale "Gender, Sexuality and Marriage in Carol MacCormack and Marilyn Stratheon, ed. *Nature, Culture and Gender* (Cambridge: Cambridge University Press, 1980) 119-143.

59. S. Maugham, "Episode", vol. 3, 1952 ed., pp. 1217-1236; p. 1227.

60. *ibid.,* p. 1228.

61. *ibid.,* p. 1234.

62. *ibid.,* p. 1235.

63. *ibid., ibid..*

64. Jane Goddale's, "Gender, Sexuality & Marriage".

65. S. Maugham, "Mabel", 1952 ed., vol. 3, pp. 1361-65; p. 1362.

66. Maugham's modern reinterpretation of the primitive mythical message--woman is dangerous; Gilian Gillison reports that this archetypal concept may be verified in observations of Gimi culture, G. Gillison "Images of Nature in Gimi Thought," in C. MacCormack and Marilyn Stratheon, ed. *Nature and Culture*, pp. 143-174.

67. S. Maugham, "Mabel", p. 1362.

68. *ibid.*, p. 1364.
69. *ibid., ibid.*.
70. *ibid., ibid.*.

NOTES

CHAPTER 4

1. D. MacCannell and J. F. MacCannell's *The Time of the Sign: A Semiotic interpretation of Modern Culture.* (Bloomington, Ind.: Indiana University Press, 1982), p. 8.

2. *ibid.*, p. 8.

3. Jurij Lotman "The Poetics of Everyday Behaviour" in the 18th Century" in A. D. Nakhimovsky, ed. *The Semiotics of Russian Culture* (Ithaca, NY: Cornell University Press, 1985) 67-95; J. Lotman Binary Models in the Dynamics of Russian Culture" 30-67.

4. S. Maugham, "Appearance and Reality", 1952 ed., vol. 1, pp. 170-184, p. 171.

5. *ibid., ibid..*

6. S. Maugham, "A Man with a Conscience" 1952 ed., vol. 3, pp. 1306-1325; p. 1321.

7. *ibid.*, p. 1322.

8. *ibid.*, p. 1323.

9. *ibid., ibid..*

10. Charles Peirce, *Principles of Psychology* vol 1, p. 304, and Peirce, *Collected Papers* v. 8., p. 368 *To Lady Wilby* pp. 327-380. (Harvard: Harvard University Press, 1958).

11. A. Chekhov, ("About Women") 1976 ed., pp. 113-6; vol. 5, p. 115. "Sitting and hatching" are other Chekhovian categories which assist him in defining the female's place in the biological universe; his famous letter to his brother Alexander, dd. April, 1883, V. Romanenko, *Chekhov i nauka* (Kharkov: Krizhnoe izdatel'stvo, 1962).

12. A. Chekhov's ("About Women") p. 114.

13. *ibid.*, p. 113.

14. *ibid.*, p. 114.

15. A. Chekhov, "Linochka", vol. 6. ed. 1976, pp. 303-9; p. 304.

16. Barbara Heldt's *Terrible Perfection*, p. 55.

17. A. Chekhov, "Dushechka", 1976 ed., vol. 10, pp. 102-114; p. 11.

18. *ibid., ibid..*

19. Sherry Ortner "Is Female to Male as Nature to Culture" in C. MacCormak and M. Strathern, eds. *Nature and Culture* (Cambridge: Cambridge University Press, 1980).

20. S. Maugham, "Giulia Lazari", 1952 ed., pp. 753-87; vol. 2, p. 772.

21. *ibid.,* p. 774.

22. S. Maugham, "The Traitor", 1952 ed., vol. 2, pp. 787-820; p. 802.

23. *ibid.,* p. 805.

24. Dionysos, the female God of the Ancient past is the mythical shadow in the story. Maugham does not exploit the accepted association of Dionysos as a God of wine and agricultural patron, but rather treats him in Kerenyi's sense; Walter Olto, C. Kerenyi, *Dionysos* (Princeton: Princeton University Press, 1976).

    Anna Makolkin, "The Dance of The Dionysos in L.H. Lawrence and H. Khotkevych, *Journal of Ukrainian Studies*, Summer 1990, pp. 31-39.

25. Friedrich Nietzsche *The Birth of Tragedy and The Genealogy of Morals* trans. by Francis Golffing (New York: Doubleday and Co., 1956) p. 64.

26. *ibid.,* p. 63.

27. *ibid.,* p. 120.

28. Walter Otto, *Dionysos, Myth and Cult* (Bloomington, Ind., Indiana University Press, 1965) as well as C. Kerenyi, *Dionysos* (Princeton: Princeton University Press, 1976); Park McGinty *Interpretation and Dionysos* (The Hage: Mouton Publishers, 1978).

29. W. Otto's *Dionysos, Myth and Cult,* p. 142.

30. M. Phillips, W.W. Thomkinson, *English Women in Life and Letters* (London: Oxford University Press, 1926) 246-48; 252.

31. *ibid.,* p. 247.

32. *ibid.,* p. 252.

33. Richard Stites *The Women's Liberation Movement in Russia* (Princeton, NJ: Princeton University Press, 1978).

220 *Notes*

34. *ibid.*, p. 294.
35. A. Chekhov, ("The Pink Stocking"), vol. 5, 1976 ed., pp. 260-264, pp. 262.
36. *ibid.*, p. 261.
37. *ibid.*, p. 262.
38. *ibid., ibid..*
39. *ibid., ibid..*
40. *ibid.*, p. 263.
41. *ibid., ibid..*
42. *ibid., ibid..*
43. *ibid., ibid..*
44. S. Maugham, "Virtue", 1952 ed., vol. 2, pp. 599-633, p. 607.
45. *ibid.*, p. 608.
46. *ibid.*, p. 609.
47. *ibid.*, p. 629.
48. *ibid.*, p. 631.
49. S. Maugham, "The Treasure", vol. 2, 1952 ed., pp. 656-671; p. 659.
50. *ibid.*, p. 639.
51. *ibid.*, p. 661.
52. *ibid.*, p. 663.
53. Jordanova's contribution to *Nature, Culture and Gender*, ed. by Carol McCormack and Marilyn Strathern, pp. 42-70.

NOTES

CHAPTER 5

1. Ronald Hingley, *A New Life of Anton Chekhov* (New York: Alfred H. Knopf, 1976), Chekhov and Jews, pp. 235-6.

2. *ibid.*, p. 23.

3. *ibid.*, p. 235-6.

4. The concept of myth being returned to its original producer was developed by Anna Makolkin(a), in her "On Poetics of Biography: Transformations in Some Biographies of Byron and Pushkin", doctoral dissertation unpublished. (University of Toronto, 1987) 46-172; also in A. Makolkin, *Name, Hero, Icon.* (Berlin: Mouton de Gruyter, 1992).

5. M. M. Bakhtin, *The Dialogic Imagination* ed. by Michael Holguist (Texas: University of Texas, 1981); 55-8; M. Bakhtin, *Rabelais and His World*, trans by Helene Isvol'sky (Cambridge: MIT Press, 1965).

6. A. Chekhov, "Tina", pp. 394-413, 1961 ed., vol. 4.

7. *ibid.*, p. 395.

8. *ibid., ibid..*

9. *ibid.*, p. 397.

10. *ibid., ibid..*

11. *ibid., ibid..*

12. *ibid., ibid..*

13. *ibid., ibid..*

14. *ibid.*, p. 397-8.

15. D. M. Segal "Problems in the Semiotic Study of Mythology" in *Soviet Semiotics* ed. by Daniel Lucid (Baltimore: Johns Hopkins University Press, 1977) 59-65; 63.

16. John Stuart Mill, *On Subjection of Women*, 1869 ed.

17. *ibid.*, p. 40.

18. A. Chekhov, "Tina", p. 397.

19. *ibid.*, p. 398.
20. Prejudice is a primitive cognitive tool and a means of controlling group behaviour as proved by the history of culture, in Ivanov's sense; V.V. Ivanov "The Role of Semiotics in the Cybernetic Study of Man and Collective" 25-39 in *Soviet Semiotics*, ed. by D. Lucid.
21. "Tina", p. 399.
22. *ibid., ibid..*
23. *ibid., ibid..*
24. *ibid.*, p. 400.
25. *ibid., ibid..*
26. *ibid.*, p. 401.
27. *ibid., ibid..*
28. S. Maugham, "Mr. Harrington's Washing", 1952 ed., vol. 2, pp. 850-886; p. 864.
29. *ibid.*, p. 865.
30. *ibid.*, p. 871.
31. *ibid.*, p. 872.
32. *ibid.*, p. 873.
33. *ibid., ibid..*
34. *ibid., ibid..*
35. "It is necessary to conceal desire in order to gain possession of the object,"--says René Girard in his *Deceit, Desire and The Novel* (Baltimore, The Johns Hopkins University Press, 1961) p. 153.
36. A. Chekhov's "Tina", p. 402.
37. *ibid.*, p. 404.
38. V. Llewellyn Smith, *Anton Chekhov and the Lady with the Dog* (1973).
39. A. Chekhov's "Tina", p. 406.
40. *ibid.*, p. 407.
41. *ibid., ibid..*

42. *ibid.*, p. 408.
43. *ibid.*, p. 412.
44. *ibid.*, *ibid.*.
45. E. Simmons, *Chekhov* (Boston: Little, Brown and Co., 1962), p. 81.
46. *ibid.*, *ibid.*.
47. S. S. Koteliansky ed., *Life and Letters of Anton Chekhov*, pp. 82-85, p. 84.
48. *ibid.*, p. 84, *ibid.*.

NOTES

CHAPTER 6

1. Chekhovian concept of civilization in his letter to brother Alexander, dd. April, 1883, p. 60, Koteliansky's ed.
2. A. Chekhov, "Pecheneg", 1962 ed., vol. 8, pp. 230-240, p. 237.
3. *ibid., ibid..*
4. *ibid.*, p. 238-9.
5. A. Chekhov, "Aniuta", vol. 3, 1961 ed., pp. 477-482, p. 478-9.
6. *ibid.*, p. 479.
7. *ibid.*, p. 478.
8. *ibid.*, p. 480.
9. U. Eco, A *Theory of Semiotics*, p. 7; V. N. Voloshinov, *Marxism and The Philosophy of Language* (The Hague: Mouton, 1972).
10. A. Chekhov, "Aniuta", p. 480.
11. Charles Sanders Peirce *Collected Papers* (Cambridge: Harvard University Press, 1931) 8 vols., vol. 1, pp. 540-9.
12. S. Maugham, "The Creative Impulse", vol. 2, 1952 ed., pp. 566-599; p. 579.
13. *ibid., ibid..*
14. *ibid., ibid..*
15. *ibid.*, p. 580.
16. *ibid.*, p. 567.
17. *ibid.*, p. 568.
18. *ibid.*, p. 569.
19. *ibid.*, p. 567.
20. *ibid.*, p. 566.

21. Character-icon termed inspired by Thomas Sebeok's icon theory, T. Sebeok, *Contributions to the Doctrine of Signs* (Bloomington, Ind.: Indiana University Press, 1976) 43.

22. S. Maugham, "The Creative Impulse", p. 592.

23. *ibid., ibid..*

24. S. Freud, "Castration Complex and Penis Envy" in *Three Essays on the Theory of Sexuality* (1905) vol. 7, (Penguin ed., 1983) p. 113.

25. S. Maugham, "The Colonel's Lady", vol. 2, 1952 ed., pp. 671-88; p. 673.

26. *ibid., ibid..*

27. *ibid., ibid..*

28. *ibid.*, p. 673-674.

29. *ibid.*, p. 674.

30. *ibid.*, p. 687.

31. A. Chekhov, "Moi Zhiony" (My Wives), vol. 3, 1961 ed., pp. 125-33, p. 130.

32. *ibid., ibid..*

33. *ibid., ibid..*

34. This new perception of women was suggested by D. H. Lawrence in his novel *The Rainbow* (1915) which offers a new vision of the female psyche and anticipates his later work on psychoanalysis, *Psychoanalysis and the Unconscious* (1921). D. H. Lawrence's Anna, echoes Chekhov's heroine when" she almost against herself clung to the worship of human knowledge. Man must die in the body, but in his knowledge he is immortal. She believed in the omnipotence of the human mind (162)."

35. A. Chekhov's ("My Wives"), p. 131.

36. *ibid., ibid..*

37. *ibid., ibid..*

38. A. Chekhov's famous Letter ed. April 1883, p. 60 in S. Koteliansky's *Life and Letters.*

39. Abram Derman, *Tvorcheskii Portret Chekhova* (Moscow: Mir, 1929), p. 310.

40. A. Chekhov's ("Volodia, the Grown up and Volodia, the Little One"), vol. 8, 1977 ed., pp. 214-26; p. 215.
41. *ibid.*, p. 217.
42. *ibid.*, p. 223.
43. *ibid., ibid..*
44. *ibid., ibid..*
45. *ibid., ibid..*
46. *ibid., ibid..*
47. *ibid.*, p. 216.
48. Richard Bates, *The Women's Liberation Movement in Russia* (Princeton: Princeton University Press, 1978).
49. A. Chekhov's ("Volodia, The Grown-up and Volodia, the Little One"), p. 225.
50. Umberto Eco's *A Theory of Semiotics*, p. 27.
51. A. Chekhov's ("Three Years"), pp. 7-92; vol. 9, 1977 ed., p. 40.
52. *ibid., ibid..*
53. *ibid.*, p. 41.
54. *ibid., ibid.*
55. *ibid.*, p. 42.
56. *ibid.*, p. 43.
57. *ibid.*, p. 42.
58. *ibid.*, p. 93.
59. *ibid.*, p. 45.
60. Mary Wollstonecraft, *A Vindication of the Rights of Woman*, 1798 ed.
61. *ibid.*, p. 66.
62. *ibid., ibid.*

BIBLIOGRAPHY

Bakhtin, Mikhail (1965) *Rabelais and His World*. Trans. Helene Isvolsky, Cambridge, Mass: The MIT Press.

_____. (1981) *The Dialogic Imagination*. Trans. and ed. by Michael Holguist. Austin: Texas University Press.

Barthes, Roland (1982) *Empire of Signs*. Trans. Richard Howard, New York: Hill and Wang.

Bates, Richard (1978) *The Women's Liberation Movement in Russia*. Princeton, N.J.: Princeton University Press.

Bellak, Leopold (1963) "Somerset Maugham, Thematic Analysis of Ten Short Stories" in Robert W. White, ed. *The Study of Lives*. New York: Atherton Press.

Berdnikov, Georgy (1974) *Chekhov*. Moscow: Molodaiia Gvardiia.

_____. (1984) *A. P. Chekhov: ideinye i tvorcheskie iskaniia*. Moscow: Khudozhestrennaiia literatura.

_____. (1986) *A. Chekhov: Izbrannye Raboty*, 2 vols. Moscow: Khudozhestvennaia literatura, 1986.

Berger, A. Arthur (1984) *Signs in Contemporary Culture*. New York: Longman.

Bouissac, Paul (1976) *Circus and Culture*. Bloomington, Ind.: University of Indiana Press.

Bremond, Claude (1970) "Morphology of the French Folktale" in *Semiotica*, N2, pp. 247-77.

_____. (1980) "The Logic of Narrative Possibilities" in *New Literary History*, vol. XI, N3, pp. 387-413.

Bunin, Ivan (1955) *O Chekhove*. New York: Izdatel'stvo im. Chekhova.

Calder, Robert (1989) *The Life of Somerset Maugham*. London: Mandarin.

Celli, Rose (1957) *L'art de Tchékov*, Paris: Del Duca.

Chekhov, Anton (1960-2) *Sobranie Sochineniy* (Works) 12 vols. Moscow: Gosudarstrennoe Izdatel'stvo Khudozhestrennoi literatury.

_____. (1976) *Sochineniia* (Works) 24 vols., Moscow: Nauka.

Chekhov, Maria (1960) *Vokrug Chekhova*. Moscow: Moskovsky Rabochy.

Chizhevsky, Dmitri (1967) "Chekhov in the Development of Russian Literature" in R. J. Jackson *Chekhov*. Englewood Cliffs, N.J.: Prentice Hall, pp. 49-62.

Chudakov, Alesconder (1971) *Poetika Chekhova*. Moscow: Nauka.

Chudakov, Alexander (1986) *Mir Chekhova*, Moskow: Sovetsky pisatel'.

Chukovsky, Korney (1967) *O Chekhove*. Moscow: Gobudarstvennoe Izdatel'stro Khidozhestvennoi literatury.

Clark, Gilian (1989) *Women in the Ancient World*. Oxford: Oxford University Press.

Clements, J. Robert and Gibaldi, Joseph (1977) *Anatomy of The Novella*, New York: New York University Press.

Cordell, Richard (1961) *Somerset Maugham*. Bloomington, Ind.: Indiana University Press.

Culler, Jonathan (1981) *In Pursuit of Signs: Semiotics, Post-Structuralism, Literature*. Ithaca: Cornell University Press.

Curtis, Anthony and John Whitehead, ed. (1987) *W. Somerset Maugham*. London: Routledge and Kegan Paul.

Derman, Abram (1929) *Tvocheskii portret Chekhova*. Moscow: Mir.

Doležel, Lubomir (1984) "Aristotelian Poetics as a Science of Literature" in *Semiosis*, ed. by Morris Halle et al. Michigan Slavic Contributions, N10, University of Michigan, 1984, pp. 125-39.

Eco, Umberto (1986) *Travels in Hyper Reality*. Trans. William Weaver. San Diego: Harcourt Brace Jovanovich.

_____. (1979) *A Theory of Semiotics*, Bloomington, Ind.: Indiana University Press.

Eichenbaum, Boris (1967) "Chekhov at Large" in Robert Louis Jackson *Chekhov*. Englewood Cliffs, N.J.: Prentice Hall, pp. 21-32.

Emelianov, Victor (1981) *Chekhov: The Critical Heritage.* London: Routledge and K. Paul.

Erenburg, Il'ia (1960) *Perechityvaiia Chekhova*, Moscow: Gosudarstvennoe Izdatel'stvo Khudozhestvennoy Literatury.

Freud, Sigmund (1975) *The Interpretation of Dreams*. Trans. James Strachey. London: Penguin.

_____. (1977) *Civilization and Its Discontents*. Chicago: University of Chicago Press.

_____. (1977) *Case Histories*. Trans. by Alix and James Hrachey. London: Penguin Books.

_____. (1983) [1905] "Castration Complex and Penis Envy" in *Three Essays on the Theory of Sexuality*, vol. 7. London: Penguin.

Gassner, John (1969) "The Duality of Chekhov" in Robert L. Jackson, ed. *Chekhov*. Englewood Cliffs, N.J.: Prentice Hall Inc. pp. 175-184.

Gerhardie, William (1974) *Anton Chekhov*. London: Macdonald.

Girard, René (1961) *Deceit, Desire and the Novel.* Trans. Ivonne Freccero, Baltimore MD: Johns Hopkins Unviersity Press.

Gillison, Gilian (1980) "Images of Nature in Gimi Thought" in Carol McCormack and Marilyn Strathern, eds. *Nature, Culture and Gender.* Cambridge, Mass.: Cambridge University Press, pp. 143-174.

Goodle, Jane C. (1980) "Gender, Sexuality and Marriage: a Kaulong Model of Nature and Culture" in Carol McCormack and Marilyn Strathen, eds. *Nature, Culture and Gender.* Cambridge, Mass.: Cambridge University Press, pp. 119-143.

Greimas, Algirdas J. (1971) "Narrative Grammar Units and Levels" in *Modern Language Notes*, vol. 86, pp. 793-806.

_____. (1990) Lecture series at the Toronto Summer Semiotic Institute. University of Toronto, Emmanuel College, June 1-30.

Grossman, Leonid (1969) "Naturalism by Chekhov" in R. Louis Jackson, ed. *Chekhov*. Englewood Cliffs, N.J.: Prentice Hall Inc., pp. 32-49.

Guillen, Claudio (1971) *Literature as a System*. Princeton, N.J.: Princeton University Press.

Guirod, Pierre (1975) *Semiology*. London: Routledge and Kegan Paul.

Hahn, Beverly (1977) *Chekhov*. Cambridge: Cambridge University Press.

Harn's, Olivia (1980) "The Power of Signs: Gender, Culture and the Wild in the Bolivian Andes" in Carol McCormack and Marilyn Strathern eds. *Nature, Culture and Gender*. Cambridge Mass.: Cambridge University Press, pp. 70-95.

Heldt, Barbara (1987) *Terrible Perfection*. Bloomington, Ind.: Indiana University Press.

Hernadi, Paul (1972) *Beyond Genre*. Ithaca: Cornell University Press.

Herodotus (1986) *The Histories*. London: Penguin, p. 120-121; pp. 148-49; 245.

Hill, Bridget (1989) *Women, Work and Sexual Politics in Eighteenth Century England*. Oxford: Basil Blackwell Ltd.

Hingley, Ronald (1976) *A New Life of Anton Chekhov*. New York: Alfred A. Knopf.

Hintikka, Iakko (1962) *Knowledge and Belief*. Ithaca: Cornell Unviersity Press.

Hodge, Robert and Gunther Kress (1988) *Social Semiotics*. Ithaca, N.Y.: Cornell University Press.

Innis, Robert (1985) *Semiotics*. Bloomington: Indiana University Press.

Jensen, Sven Arnold (1957) *William Somerset Maugham*. Oslo: Oslo University Press.

Jordanova, L. J., (1980) "Natural facts a Historical Perspective on Gender and Sexuality" in Carol McCormack ed. *Nature, Culture and Gender*. Cambridge, Mass.: Carmbridge University Press, pp. 42-70.

Kalaga, Wojciech (1986) *The Literary Sign: a Triadic Model*. Katowice: Slaski Universetet.

Kataev, Valentin (1979) *Proza Chekhova, problemy interpretatsii*. Moscow: MGU.

Katzer, Julus (1961) *A. P. Chekhov (1860-1960)* Moscow: Foreign Languages Publishing House, 1961.

Kayfeld, Donald (1975) *Chekhov: The Evolution of His Art.* London: Paul Elek.

Kerenyi, Carel (1976) *Dionysos.* Princeton: Princeton University Press.

Koteliansky, Samuel ed. (1925) *The Life and Letters of Anton Tcnekhov.* London: Cassell and Co. Ltd.

Kripke, Saul (1980) *Naming and Necessity.* Cambridge, Mass.: Harvard University Press.

Kuznetzova, Margarita (1968) *A. P. Chekhov,* Sverdlovsk: Sredneural'skoe knizhnoe izdatel'stvo.

Laffitte, Sophie (1974) *Chekhov.* Trans. Moura Budberg and Gordon Latta. London: Angus and Robertson.

Lakoff, George (1987) *Women, Fire and Dangerous Things.* Chicago: The University of Chicago Press.

De Laurentis, Teresa (1981) *Umberto Eco.* Firenze: Nuova Italia.

Lévi-Strauss, Claude (1969) *The Elementary Structures of Kinship.* London: Eyre and Spottiswoode. Trans. James Harle Bell and John Richard von Sturmer.

Lotman, Jury (1979) The Structure of Artistic Text. Trans. Gail Lenoff and Ronald Vroon. Ann Arbor, Mich.: University of Michigan.

———. (1985) "The Poetics of Everyday Behavior in the 18th Century" in H. D. Nakhimovsky, ed. *The Semiotics of Russian Culture.* Ithaca, N.Y.: Cornell University Press, pp. 67-95.

MacCannell, Dean and Juliet Flower MacCannell (1982) *The Time of the Sign: a Semiotic Interpretation of Modern Culture.* Bloomington, Ind.: Indiana University Press.

Mackay, Charles (1980) *Extraordinary Popular Delusions and The Madness of Crowds.* New York.: Harmony Books.

Makolkin(a), Anna (1987) "On Poetics of Biography: Transformations in Some Biographies of Byron and Pushkin. Doctoral dissertation unpublished. University of Toronto.

Makolkin(a), Anna (1990) "The Dance of Dionysos in D. H. Lawrence and H. Khotkevych" in *Journal of Ukrainian Studies,* summer issue, pp. 31-39.

Makolkin, Anna (1992) *Name, Hero, Icon.* Berlin: Mouton de Gruyter Press.

Matejka, Ladislav and Irwin R. Titunik, eds. (1977) *Semiotics of Art*. Cambridge, Mass.: The MIT Press.

Maugham, William Somerset (1952) *The Complete Short Stories*. London: Penguin.

———. (1953) The Complete Short Stories. Garden City, N.J.: Doubleday and Co. Inc., 2 vols.

McGinty, Park (1978) *Interpretation and Dionysos*. The Hague: Mouton Publishers.

Mertz, Elizabeth ed. (1985) *Semiotic Mediation*. Orlando, Fla.: Academic Press, Inc.

Morgan, Ted (1980) *Maugham*. New York: Simon and Schuster.

Mukařovsky, Jan (1977) "Art as Semiotic Fact" in Ladislav Matejka and Irwin R., Titunik eds. *Semiotics of Art*, Cambridge, Mass.: The MIT Press, pp. 3-11.

———. (1977) "The Essence of Visual Arts" in Ladislav Matejka and Irwin R. Titunik eds. *Semiotics of Art*. Cambridge, Mass.: The MIT Press.

Nietzsche, Friedrich (1956) *The Birth of Tragedy and the Genealogy of Morals*. Trans. by Francis Golffing. New York: Doubleday and Co.

O'Neill, John (1985) *Five Bodies*. Ithaca: Cornell University Press.

Otto, Walter (1965) *Dionysos, Myth and Cult*. Bloomington, Ind.: Indiana University Press.

Perron, Paul and Frank Collins, eds. (1989) *Paris School of Semiotics*. Amsterdam: John Benjamins Publihsing Co.

Peirce, Charles Saunders (1931) *Collected Papers* 8 vols. Cambridge: Harvard University Press.

———. (1977) Semiotic and Significs, *The Correspondence Between Charles S. Peirce and Victoria Lady Wilby*. Bloomington, Ind.: Indiana University Press.

———. (1986) *Writings of Charles Peirce*. Bloomington, Ind.: Indiana University Press.

Polotskaiia, E. (1979) *Dvizhenie khudozhestvennoi mysli*. Moscow: Sovetsky pisatel'.

Pritchett, V.S. (1988) *Chekhov*. New York: Random House.

Propp, Vladimir (1978) "Fairy Tale Transformations" in Ladislav Matejka ed. *The Readings in Russian Poetics*. Ann Arbor, Mich.: Michigan Slavic Publications, pp. 94-117.

Raphael, Frederic (1976) *W. Somerset Maugham and His World*. London: Thames and Hudson.

Rossi, Alice S. (1973) *The Feminist Papers from Adams to de Beauvoir*. New York: Columbia University Press.

Sebeok, Thomas A. (1976) *Contributions to the Doctrine of Signs*. Bloomington, Ind.: Indiana University Press.

_____. (1990) *Essays in Zoo-Semiotics*, Toronto: Monograph Series of the Toronto Semiotic Circle.

Segal, Dmitry (1977) "Problems in the Semiotic Study of Morphology" in *Soviet Semiotics*, ed. by Daniel Lucid. Baltimore, M.D.: Johns Hopkins University Press, pp. 59-65.

Seltzer, Thomas (1925) *Best Russian Short Stories*. New York: Modern Library Inc.

Shestov, Leon (1966) *Chekhov and Other Essays*. Ann Arbor, Mich.: University of Michigan Press.

Simmons, Ernest J. (1958) *Chekhov*. Toronto: Little, Brown and Co.

Smirnov, Ivan (1984) "Logiko-semanticheskie osobennosti korotkikh narrativov" in *Russian Short Story*, ed. by Rainer Gribol. Amsterdam: Rodopi Series, *Studies in Slavic Literature and Poetics*, vol. 4, pp. 47-65.

Smith-Llewellyn, Virginia (1973) *Anton Chekhov and the Lady with the Dog*. London: Oxford University Press.

Soep-Maegd de, Carolina (1987) *Chekhov and Women: Women in the Life and Work of Chekhov*. Columbus, Ohio: Slavica.

Stites, Richard (1978) *The Women's Liberation in Russia*. Princeton, N.J.: Princeton University Press.

Sukhikh, Igor (1987) *Problemy poetiki Chekhova*. Leningrad: Izdatel'stvo Leningradskogo universiteta.

Thom, René (1985) "From the Icon to the Symbol" in Robert Innis, ed. *Semiotics*, Bloomington, Ind.: Indiana University Press, pp. 272-292.

Troyat, Henri (1984) *Chekhov*, Trans. Michael Henry Heim. New York: E. P. Dutton.

Vatsuro, V. E. ed. (1986) *A. P. Chekhov*. Moscow: Khudozhestrennaiia Literatura.

Vico, Giambattista (1968) *The New Science of Giambattista Vico*. Trans. Max Harold Fish. Ithaca: Cornell University Press.

Voloshinov, V. N. (1972) *Marxism and the Philosophy of Language*. The Hague: Mounton.

Ward, Richard Heron (1957) *William Somerset Maugham*. London: Georffrey Bles.

Winner Portis, Irene (1986) "Semiotics of Culture" in John Deely ed. *Frontiers of Semiotics*. Bloomington, Ind.: Indiana University Press, pp. 181-85.

Worrall, Nick (1986) *File on Chekhov*. London: Methuen.

Wollestonecraft, Mary (1798) *A Vindication of the Rights of Women*. London: St. Paul's Church Yard.

Zaitsev, Boris (1954) *Chekhov*. N.Y.: Izdatel'stvo imeni Chekhova.

Zalygin, Sergei (1971) *Moy poet*. Moscow: Sovetskaiia Rossiia.

SUBJECT INDEX

A

Actant, 148, 203
aesthetic, i, 76, 125, 128, 146, 177, 199, 205
aggression, 15, 100, 107, 126, 182, 206
allusion, 24, 106
American, 94, 152, 181, 182, 185
anatomy, 172, 173, 176
animal, 22, 24, 27, 43, 45, 48, 49, 53, 60, 71, 110, 113, 156, 157, 199
Anna, 88, 89, 92, 93, 94
anti-sign, 199, 200, 201, 204, 206
anthropology, 5, 65, 112, 115, 124, 180
antithesis, 161
anxiety, ii, 9, 15, 94, 98, 124, 186
archetype, vii, 5, 13, 17, 21, 24, 48, 64, 74, 76, 77, 87, 113, 114, 117, 124, 125, 126, 130, 155, 200, 202, 204, 205
art(istic), 7, 8, 14, 110, 111, 143, 145, 148, 179, 184, 190, 202
Aryan, 115, 116
Assyrian, 112
author(ial), 84, 89, 121, 140, 142, 149, 151, 160, 164, 181, 194

B

Barbaric, 8
beauty, 10, 83, 93, 94, 128, 159, 203, 206
behavior, 35, 37, 126
Bible, 112, 147
biographic, 88, 163, 186
biological, v, 3, 41, 111, 112, 122, 180, 205
blue stocking, iv, 117, 118, 119, 120, 121, 122, 123, 124, 136, 176, 177, 178, 187, 189, 190, 198, 201, 202, 204
body, 98, 125, 172, 179, 202

C

Cannibalism, 100
caricature, 167
character, 73, 93, 138, 139, 140, 144, 146, 151, 154, 156, 157, 160, 161, 162, 164, 172, 182, 191, 200, 201, 203
child, 111, 205
Chinese, 56, 112, 116
Christian, 40, 42, 59, 60, 115, 116, 148
civilization, ii, 25, 30, 32, 40, 41, 42, 44, 45, 46, 47, 48, 55, 58, 67, 71, 109, 115, 137, 205
code, 61
collective consciousness, 86, 142, 205, 206
collective memory, 48
critic, 5, 6, 9, 11, 90
crowd, 33, 41, 48, 121, 143, 145
cultural universal, 96
culture, i, ii, iv, v, 1, 2, 3, 4, 5, 8, 9, 13, 14, 21, 23, 25, 29, 30, 33, 37, 39, 41, 42, 43, 44, 45, 46, 47, 48, 52, 58, 60, 61, 65, 66, 68, 69, 70, 72, 77, 95, 97, 98, 99, 102, 103, 104, 107, 108, 109, 112, 113, 117, 119, 121, 127, 133, 134, 137, 153, 154, 163, 167, 178, 180, 181, 187

D

Danger(ous), v, 101, 106, 113, 114, 122, 123, 152, 154, 155, 161, 180, 181, 182, 201
Darwin(ian), 10, 16, 17, 40, 47
decoding, 54, 55, 57, 66
defamiliarize, 28
desire, 156
determinism, 112, 168
discourse, 5, 11, 43, 73, 77, 106, 129, 141, 143, 155
displacement, 23, 181, 188

E

Economic exchange, 1, 32, 47, 65, 71, 74, 80, 81, 82, 83, 84, 85, 87, 88, 94, 97, 98, 128
emancipation, 119, 201, 206
emancipé, 171, 186, 202
emotion, 138, 153, 175
English, vi, 113, 152, 205
equal(ity), 46
ethnicity, iv, 137, 140, 145, 150
Europe(an), 42, 115, 159, 161, 181, 182

F

Fairytale, 76
fantastic, v, 65, 69, 95
fascist, 115
female, ii, 15, 16, 17, 23, 38, 42, 43, 44, 48, 49, 52, 54, 61, 63, 66, 68, 69, 82, 84, 85, 88, 89, 98, 100, 106, 108, 109, 110, 119, 120, 122, 125, 126, 127, 133, 134, 139, 151, 156, 158, 167, 172, 175, 177, 180, 182, 183, 184, 186, 190, 194, 204
femininity, 48, 54, 72, 82, 115, 117, 145, 146, 197
femini(sm)st, 12, 16, 17, 42, 117, 118, 119, 121, 122, 124, 145, 152, 196, 197, 198, 205, 206
fiction(al), iv, v, 10, 11, 17, 23, 25, 31, 54, 57, 60, 69, 72, 73, 74, 79, 106, 107, 108, 124, 134, 143, 185, 188
food, iii, 43, 45, 47, 48, 50, 51, 153, 196
French, 68, 77, 134, 162, 163, 172, 182, 197
Freud(ian), 4, 11, 34, 35, 39, 47, 60, 75, 77, 124, 183
fusion (myth), 140

G

Gastronomic, 51, 52, 53, 58, 123
gastro-orgasmic, 50
gastropornography, iii, 50, 123
gastropornosigns, 47, 49, 50, 51
gender, 34, 37, 71, 78, 137, 145, 188
 bias, 130
 hierarchy, 73
 role, iv, 51, 73, 105, 145, 188
 reversal, 50
German, 42, 68, 114, 115, 116
God, 116, 129, 146
Gypsy, 179, 180, 191, 198

H

Hebrew, 112
Hellenic, i, 115, 116, 117, 185
heterosexual, 206
homo-sapiens, 17, 30, 40, 41, 44
homosexual(ity), vi, 12, 13, 14, 39

I

Icon(icity), ii, 19, 20, 29, 43, 59, 97, 104, 107, 117, 118, 124, 179, 180, 182, 184, 199
icon (religious), 152
"id", 47, 52, 66, 72, 124
impressionism, 10, 88
inequality, 17
inferior(ity), ii, 10, 41, 43, 47, 69, 103, 104, 107, 108, 112, 115, 128, 143, 144, 179, 182, 184, 188, 189, 205
instinct, 40, 73, 127
intelligence (intellect), 110, 113, 118, 136, 177, 187, 192, 199, 203, 204
isotopy, 66

J

Japanese, 146, 147
Jew(ish), 133, 134, 135, 137-152, 156, 157, 158, 160, 161, 162, 163, 164
Judaic, 115, 135

K

Killing, v, 32, 54, 55, 56, 57, 63, 98, 100, 105, 106
knowledge, 59

L

Libido (see sex), iv
literature, 11, 12, 19, 20, 24, 164, 177, 192
logo-imagery, 43
logo-materials, 88
logos, 186

M

Male, 28, 30, 34, 43, 45, 46, 65, 68, 81, 98, 99, 100, 107, 108, 113, 121, 123, 127, 129, 130, 148, 167, 175, 197, 204
mammalia, 17, 25
marriage, 2, 3, 14, 57, 65, 66, 67, 68, 69, 70, 72, 75, 78, 79, 80, 81, 82, 83, 84, 85, 86, 87, 88, 91, 98, 99, 100, 101, 123, 125, 126, 130, 142, 143, 156, 161, 170, 172, 189, 191, 192, 197, 198, 199
mask, 137, 142, 143, 156
Marxism, 197
medicine, 110
metaphor, 5, 13, 15, 92, 136, 157, 164, 192, 205
misogyny, i-ix, 5, 9, 11, 12, 13, 14, 15, 23, 24, 25, 30, 31, 47, 54, 61, 63, 64, 71, 100, 106, 121, 129, 130, 134, 135, 143, 156, 172, 182
modern, 10
money, 72, 73, 74, 78, 79, 80, 81, 82, 83, 84, 87, 88, 90, 91, 94, 96, 141, 150, 175, 202
morality, 3, 14, 40, 45, 59, 138, 192, 193
mother, 62, 111
motif, ii, 25, 69

myth, i, v, 3, 26, 30, 33, 34, 45, 65, 98, 99, 100, 108, 109, 115, 116, 119, 135, 136, 139, 140, 143, 148, 149, 150, 163, 164, 202
mythical, 3, 33, 47, 48, 81, 98, 108, 116, 136, 137, 143, 148, 199

N

Name, 82, 83, 108, 136, 200
nature, ii, iii, 4, 12, 30, 32, 33, 39, 40, 42, 44, 45, 46, 52, 58, 59, 68, 70, 95, 97, 102, 109, 112, 206
narrator, 84, 146, 170, 174, 203
narrative (adj), 43, 137, 160, 161
neologism, 118
neometonymy, 117
nihilist, 196, 197

O

Other(ness), ii, iv, vii, 43, 57, 61, 102, 105, 133, 136, 148, 150, 152, 154, 156, 165, 184, 186, 196, 201, 206

P

Panegyric, 8, 43, 129
patriarchal, 95, 167, 199
patriotism, 8, 114
pink stocking, 117, 118, 119, 121, 122, 123, 124, 131, 136, 176, 188, 192, 194, 195, 198, 199, 201, 203, 204, 206
phobia, 100
plot, 6, 87, 89, 93, 107, 144
poet(ry), 12, 146, 156, 184
pornographic, ii, 51
prostitution, 67, 74, 91, 95, 157, 164
protoicon, 117
protosign, 205
psychoanalytic, 39, 42, 47, 71, 123
puritanic(al), 42

238 *Subject Index*

R

Rape, 54
reader, 145, 149, 157, 179, 180, 194, 202, 204
representamen (Peircean term), 187
rights of women, 118, 119
romantic, 41, 73, 77, 84, 85
Russian, 41, 42, 68, 82, 93, 118, 119, 134, 139, 149, 150, 152-156, 163, 164, 167, 172, 196, 197, 200

S

Sabine, 84
satire, 25
seduction, 59, 71, 73, 78, 82, 88, 95, 124, 137, 138-152, 158, 196, 204
self, 168
semantic, 16, 66, 118, 136, 151
semeophobia, 15, 199
semiosis, 1, 20, 72, 103, 105, 113, 125, 127, 155, 180
semiotic,
    alertness, 43
    antithesis, 171
    arrangement, 206
    attire, 88
    background, 108
    balance, 115
    case, 109
    code, 107
    complexity, 164
    composits, 174
    conclusion, 169
    construct, i, 175
    effect, 118
    exchange, 71, 205
    fashion, 201
    feature, 154
    function, 160
    goal, 78, 200
    imperative, iv, 104
    implication, 193
    intention, iv, 107
    loyalty, ii, 104
    macrocosm, vii
    man, 174
    matrix, 91
    maze, 147
    message, 61
    metamorphosis, 91, 176, 201
    model, 69
    neologism, 117, 124
    other, 43
    pair, 135, 136, 142, 149
    paradox, iv, 151
    pathway, 70, 90
    performance, 69
    plane, 45
    plot, 97
    power, 199
    precursor, 198
    producer, 104
    product(ion), 104, 186, 205
    shift, 189
    significance, 94
    strategy, 53, 195
    summary, 195
    system, 54
    temptation, 123
    territory, 157
    universe, 42, 66
    value, 98, 103, 112, 171
    world, 67
semiotic, 1, 2, 4, 5, 10, 19, 21, 27, 30, 32, 37, 38, 43, 67
semiotics, iii, 1
semiovalence, 20, 21, 86, 101, 113
semitic, 115
sex(uality), iii, vi, 12, 13, 14, 30, 34, 36, 37, 38, 39, 42, 44, 46, 47, 50, 51, 55, 60, 65, 66, 68, 69, 72, 74, 76, 78, 81, 82, 83, 84, 91, 92, 97, 100, 101, 108, 115, 117, 124, 125, 126, 127, 130, 139, 141, 145, 155, 177, 178, 186, 188, 195, 196
sign, vii, 1, 2, 4, 5, 14, 19, 20, 21, 22, 28, 29, 39, 43, 48, 51, 52, 54, 57, 69, 76, 89, 90, 94, 95, 104, 106, 107, 114, 124, 154, 167, 175, 188

sign,
  cultural, 65, 113, 178, 181
  displacement, 181
  facial, 180
  familiar, 187, 190, 203
  firstness of, 107
  greater semiovalence of, 86
  maker, 96
  money, 82
  natural, 58
  nostalgia, 199
  ominous, 61, 175
  omnipotent, 101
  pleasurable, 127
  predator, 59
  production, 96, 98, 113, 133, 182
  pseudo-man, 160
  singular, 34, 43
  soothing, 121
  subversive, 183
  supersign, iii, 23, 25, 53, 54, 57
  universal, 23, 150
  unsympathetic, 127
  value of, 133
signal, 45, 909, 93, 101, 106, 123, 136, 178, 200
signify, 22
slave(ry), 130, 168, 169, 174
Slavophile, 162
space, 160
Spanish, 113
Soviet, 90
stateme, 56
stereotype, iii, 4, 13, 23, 30, 42, 61, 104, 107, 110, 119, 135, 136, 139, 143, 145, 147, 148, 149, 150, 151, 156, 157, 161, 162, 164, 165, 180, 186, 188, 195, 200, 205
subconscious(ness), 8, 47, 107
subtext, 165
superior(ity), 17, 58, 84, 114, 157, 178, 190
symbol(ic), 2, 4, 8, 21, 27, 39, 48, 59, 63, 65, 76, 84, 98, 100, 110, 117, 120, 131, 136, 150, 155, 176, 183, 198, 205

T

Thirdness (Peircean), 177

U

universals, ii, 112
universal signs, 23, 150

V

Victorian, 13, 14, 77, 205
violence, 63
virgin, 79
visual, 19, 23, 62

W

Woman-sign, iii, 39, 51, 64, 65, 69, 71, 78, 82, 125, 129, 152, 167, 171, 178, 179, 188, 199

Z

Zoomarker(s), 29
zoology(ical), 20, 25, 26, 28, 29, 32, 106
zoosemiotics, 19, 21, 33
zoosign, iii, 19-65

OHIO UNIVERSITY LIBRARY

Please return this book as soon as you have finished with it. In order to avoid a fine it must be returned by the latest date stamped below. All books are subject to recall after two weeks or immediately if needed for reserve.

DEC 0 5 2001

JUN 0 7 2002

CF